LOUISA'S LAMENT

ANNIE GRAHAM

To Jonathan

CONTENTS

Part V: The Trial

Part VI: A Beginning

FOREWORD

Louisa Ingle has been a presence in my life for over thirty years, since I came across her while researching my thesis into medical power and conflict. Although life moved on, I have always felt a sense of injustice at how she was treated; and a desire to tell her story, and that of her fellow nurses Margaret Burt, Victoria Jones and Margaret Lonsdale.

Ignored by history, these women were early pioneers who broke out of the social shackles of the 19th century to assert their independence as educated nurses at London's Guy's Hospital. As they stepped out of the shadow of Florence Nightingale to professionalise nursing in 1880, they became embroiled in a bitter dispute with the hospital's traditionalists. Their lives were crushed, and their story was buried in a footnote of the history of Guy's.

But, in large measure because of their efforts, Guy's Hospital now has one of the finest Nursing Training Institutes in the world. This is their legacy.

Part I: An Ending

ONE

The old man shut his eyes and sobbed as he gritted his teeth and gasped for air. His arm, raised in pleading, fell limp at his side as he slumped on his chaise longue trying to find a position of comfort.

"Ahh… ahh… the pain. I can't… breathe… What's happening? Help…help me…" he moaned.

"Who's the duty surgeon this evening? Oh never mind, get Mr Howse at once. Run boy, run," shouted Mr Lushington at the junior house surgeon.

Puddles of rain reflected the spill of dull yellow light from the gas lamps to relieve the gloom of a typical drizzly November night in the front quadrangle of London's Guy's Hospital. The fog, known as 'a right peculiar', had swirled up from the river a few days before. It hung motionless in the air as it held the drizzle and soot from the local factories and tenements in a fine suspension, chilling the bones and making the skin clammy to the touch. It was as if death itself lurked in that fog, looking for someone to cloak in its shroud.

"Something up, I reckon," spoke Mr Payne, the hospital's nightwatchman, to Mr Bryers as they stood at Guy's north gate on St Thomas's Street watching people, important ones at that, scurrying across the front quad pulling their hastily donned overcoats and cloaks tightly around them.

"They've been runnin' to and fro' for the last hour; backwards and forwards to the Super's 'ouse; might be old Dr Steele's ill," observed Mr Payne, holding his oil lamp to the gate and squinting as he turned the key to lock up for the night. He had seen much of the goings on in this hospital for over thirty years, ever since he had joined the institution from his army days in India in the late 1850s, after the Uprising. Guy's was quite a repository for men, both high and low born, who had returned from serving the East India Company, and latterly the Queen, in that far-flung reach of the Empire.

Dr Steele's study had been turned into a makeshift sickroom, with his discarded clothes and shoes lying on the floor alongside the used towels and bowls of camphor water. Pillows and blankets cluttered what little space there was around the chaise longue, where Dr Steele had been resting while trying to shake off his pain.

"How long has he been like this?" inquired Mr Howse, one of Guy's senior surgeons. His patient writhed in pain as the surgeon prodded his exposed throbbing belly and flank.

"Several hours, Sir, ever since evening prayers I think," came the reply from Mr Howse's nervous junior houseman.

"Shall I bring some morphia, Sir, and more fresh water to bathe his face?"

"No; we will need to open him as soon as possible," came the reply. "Get the theatre ready and make sure there's enough chloroform and ether for a big gut operation. And get any of the other senior surgeons out of bed to assist me. Try Mr Davies-Colley first, or if he's not about, Mr Golding-Bird. I fear infection. Get the antiseptic equipment ready and make sure my scalpels are sharp and soaked. We must work quickly.

"Steele! Steele! John, can you hear me?" yelled Mr Howse as he tried to call his patient's attention away from the excruciating pain of a twisted or blocked bowel. It could already be perforated and gangrenous, Mr Howse thought, as he sized up the risks of the operation.

"We need to operate now, it can't wait… John, do you understand? You know how serious it is, but it'll be alright, we'll cover the pain; time is short, we must operate now," pleaded the surgeon, as Dr Steele drifted in and out of consciousness.

Dr John Steele was Guy's Resident Medical Superintendent. He had lived in the Superintendent's House in the northeast corner of Guy's front quad since his appointment nearly forty years ago. Now, at seventy-one, he was slower than his younger medical colleagues, but still fulfilled his duties with a deft touch. He loved Guy's and he had dedicated his life to the hospital and south London's poor, and he had done much to develop its fine Medical School. Some said he represented the very best of Guy's.

"Miss Jones, get Miss Jones, I must speak to her,"

begged a breathless and tearful Dr Steele, struck with the terror of a man who knows his life is slipping away. He had felt unwell since his recent return from a long-wished-for holiday to his native Scotland, where he had met up with some of his old colleagues from Glasgow Royal Infirmary. It was as if he knew that his time was coming. Now, in his agony, his thoughts turned to the woman who had been so wronged by Guy's over a dozen years before. A memory so painful it displaced his present agony momentarily.

"I'm here, Dr Steele," whispered Miss Jones, the matron, willing him on to survive.

With an almighty effort, he raised his head, his anguished face covered in sweat and creased in pain, as he fixed his tearful gaze upon her.

"Tell her... tell her..." he blurted out between the jabbing spasms of colicky pain, "she must know everything... the account, in my bureau, send it... you must send it to her... do this for me."

Exhausted, he receded back into his own world of half-consciousness, breathing hard from the exertion. Miss Jones held his hand and stared at him intently. She who had admired him from afar knew immediately what he meant her to do. She squeezed his hand as the surgeons and the dressers lifted him onto a gurney and wheeled him to the nearby theatre block.

"I beg you, Mr Howse, do everything to save him; he is precious to all of us," spoke the grim-faced Mr Lushington, Guy's treasurer and administrator. He and Dr Steele had been colleagues and friends since Mr Lushington's appointment in 1876. Together, they had seen Guy's through many crises and changes, including the terrible events of the summer of 1880, when Dr Steele's wise counsel had come to the aid of the beleaguered treasurer and his reforming matron, Miss Margaret Burt. Dr Steele had done more than anyone to attempt to prevent the catastrophe that had unfolded.

"Holy Mary, Mother of God, pray for us sinners now and at the hour of our death. Holy Mary..." whispered Miss Jones repeatedly as she fingered the rosary beads hidden in her pocket, pleading for divine intervention to save the life of this good man. Like many High Church women in nursing, even in this modern age, she kept her Anglo-Catholic devoutness hidden.

"All the lights on at this hour," observed the nightwatchman to his mate as they proceeded in the drizzle and cold to the east gate.

"If it is 'im, better say some prayers," suggested Mr Payne to his companion.

Dr Steele bore the operation and the antiseptic procedure well enough to live a few more hours. With his breathing shallowed by the morphia for his pain, he was conscious enough to hold Miss Jones's hand, softly squeezing it as she sat next to him reciting prayers from her beloved Sisterhood's book of meditation. She gazed on his pale waxy face, wiping away the cold sweat on his forehead with the light caring touch of one who loved. All the while, she whispered her prayers for this good man.

He died in peace that night, November 6, 1892, from infection, blood loss, shock – who knows, speculated Mr Howse to himself. In the quiet of Dr Steele's room, Mr

Howse sat with his head in his hands, next to Miss Jones, as they stared at their lifeless friend in disbelief, weeping for the man they could not save; a good, kind, doctor who had served Guy's and its patients well. They were joined by the other surgeons who stood by in silent respect.

"He is gone," murmured Miss Jones to Mr Lushington as he entered the room with Reverend Flood, Guy's old chaplain of many years, now long retired. The priest and Dr Steele had been great friends and colleagues in attending to the needs of the poor and destitute in the local dives and slums around Borough and Bermondsey.

There, in the soft light of the gas lamps turned down low, and the quiet of the death room, Mr Lushington gently held Dr Steele's still warm hands as the chaplain recited prayers for the departed's soul. "Our Father who art in heaven…"

The sight of grown men weeping and Miss Jones comforting them was forlorn on this miserable November night.

"Rest in peace, dear friend." Feeling useless and lifeless, Mr Lushington withdrew to his private quarters. There is much bureaucracy that surrounds death, he reflected, but in the case of Dr Steele, there was the added burden of announcing it to the medical world. He heaved a sigh of despair as he contemplated having to talk to the editors of the medical press. Although a dozen years had since passed since their unpardonable intrusions, he felt a fresh wave of disgust.

He sat at his desk and, in the privacy of his study, wept for his friend as he sketched out some notes for the obituary.

He made a list of those to be invited to the funeral – which would be held, he decided, at Guy's in the chapel where Dr Steele had attended prayers each day. And then there was the death certificate and the letters, and of course, he would have to value and dispose of his friend's estate in the months to come.

He shed tears at the thought of closing his friend's life, and at the thought that he would never see him again, nor have earnest discussions and arguments about the hospital's medical politics, nor stroll across the Downs together on a fine weekend.

Miss Jones returned to her rooms in Matron's House on the west side of the front quad, facing Dr Steele's and Mr Lushington's quarters. Oblivious to the now heavy rain, she got soaked and her stockinged feet swished around inside her sodden boots.

The housekeeper took her things and settled Miss Jones in her sitting room by the fire with a cup of tea. There, she fell into a deep sorrow, broken only by her fretting about the time it would take her letter to get halfway around the world to the great port of Calcutta, even by the modern steamboat packets cutting through the Suez Canal. It would then have to be taken up to Ranchi by train and on to the hill station on its outskirts by donkey cart. She could not risk the news of Dr Steele's death, which would be reported in the *Times* within the week, reaching Miss Ingle without prior notice.

A telegram would be better – followed by a fuller note and Dr Steele's account. It had been a long sad day and it was not over yet. The telegraph office would be open at eight o'clock, and she wanted her telegram to be on the early morning's dispatch to India.

She forced herself to her desk. Meanwhile, her housekeeper went in search of Mr Payne to take the message to the post office ready for when it opened. After several false starts, and conscious of the costs for anything of length, she settled on the briefest of words to convey the terrible news.

> *Sad to inform that Dr Steele died after short*
> *illness, November 6.*
> *Funeral hospital chapel November 10. Last*
> *thoughts of you.*
> *Fuller note follows.*
> *VJ, Matron, GH.*

"Take this to the telegraph office at once, Mr Payne," requested Miss Jones, "and make sure it gets on the first dispatch."

Mr Payne looked at her askance.

"I know it's raining hard, and I regret that you will get soaked, but it is of the upmost importance."

Consumed with the restlessness that grief brings, Miss Jones started to compose the letter Dr Steele had requested her to write. She toyed with her pen and jotted down her first thoughts, but it was all a jumble, an incoherent cluster of words.

Staring at the dying fire, her thoughts drifted to the disastrous events of that summer in 1880 and Dr Steele's request to send his account of what had happened to Miss Ingle. Might it stir up old feelings that by now had been buried deep inside Miss Ingle's memory?

She found she could not bear the confines of her room any longer so, to her housekeeper's astonishment, Miss Jones made her way back across the courtyard to Dr Steele's quarters.

She sat in his armchair in the dark and thought about the man who had been a towering presence in her life. When Miss Burt had returned to the Midlands after three years at Guy's, Miss Jones was appointed to replace her as matron. She had been daunted by the prospect of dealing with the medical staff who had been so brutal to her predecessor. It was the kindly Dr Steele who had guided her through those early days, and she had remained in his debt ever since.

Miss Jones turned up the gas lamps to search Dr Steele's bureau for the account. Mr Lushington, alarmed by the noise, entered Dr Steele's quarters to investigate the disturbance.

"Miss Jones," he exclaimed, as he found her sifting through Dr Steele's papers, "what are you looking for that cannot wait until morning?"

"Sir, I beg your pardon. I feel I might go mad with grief. Dr Steele asked me to send his account of the dispute to Miss Ingle. He was desperate for her to know the details of his findings in the hope, I think, that she might forgive him, and us, for failing her all those years ago." It was as if Dr Steele were driving her on from the next room. In her distress, she could not rest until she had his account in her hands.

"How did such a bitter dispute arise? I was present at many of the events that summer," she recalled, "but I did not understand all the forces that were at play – potent forces, evil forces, that created such hatred between our professional colleagues."

Mr Lushington gave a heavy sigh. "I too have asked myself that question over the years. Things that were of great importance in 1880 seem less so now. It was an unsettling time. Reform was in the air – political, social, and religious. Was it the new lady-nurses that Miss Burt had introduced with their superior education and training that caused such offence to the doctors? They were a great improvement on the old drunken and uneducated nurses, so I am mystified as to why the reforms proved to be so controversial.

"Or was it the lady-nurses' over-zealous devotion as High Church women to their Sisterhood that offended them? Remember, Miss Jones, many of our doctors were devout Nonconformists who would have found your Anglo-Catholic practices far too popish."

Miss Jones blushed. "Perhaps," she conceded, "we were too enthusiastic to take over some of the doctors' traditional duties; that would have caused offence. I do readily recall one of those ladies, Miss Lonsdale. She was so confident and assertive about her position, and she caused much anger with her article and letters about the reforms. I still think of how she rowed with the doctors on their own terms in her vigorous support of Miss Burt. She was formidable."

Mr Lushington cringed at the mention of the lady's name, for she had caused him many difficulties. He had tried to dampen the raging dispute while Miss Lonsdale had sought to aggravate it with her insensitive writings and inflammatory utterances.

"The dispute had started well before Miss Burt's arrival in November 1879," Mr Lushington confided. "I travelled to Leicester's Infirmary to seek her out on behalf of Lord Cardwell, who was President of the Board of Governors, to come to London to modernise our hospital's nursing practices and introduce formal training for the nurses.

"She had achieved a great deal in this regard and her references were excellent, so we asked her to oversee our nurses' work more directly on her arrival. This caused great offence to the medical staff, who felt it a direct challenge to their authority. You see, Miss Jones, we had, and maybe still have, very traditional doctors here at Guy's."

"Sir, I was one of Miss Burt's acolytes," spoke Miss Jones in defence of her predecessor, "and I know from the outset that she had a poor opinion of the nurses she had taken charge of on her arrival. To make the case for her reforms, she complained openly that they were untrained and exhibited unbecoming behaviour. Some even drank gin on the wards."

Miss Jones paused at the awful memory. "Miss Burt and our company of lady-nurses," she whispered, "were appalled."

"Indeed," concurred Mr Lushington, "it was Dr Steele who had revealed to the Board many years earlier that some untrained nurses took money from our patients. He was also disgusted to find that they did not keep their patients clean. It was quite unacceptable."

"Oh, Dr Steele," lamented Miss Jones, looking at his desk and around his room, "he did so much for our nurses and their education." After a pause to reflect on the loss of such a good man, she mulled, "Did you know that he took the trouble to give us lectures? He was a fine teacher."

"Dr Steele," replied Mr Lushington, lost for a moment in his own reflections, "knew this area like the back of his hand. He had lived and worked here since he had arrived at Guy's forty years ago, from Glasgow.

"Like Miss Burt," he added, "he had suffered the rejection of the medical staff who had objected to his appointment even though he had held the Medical Superintendent's post at Glasgow Royal Infirmary previously. And did you know that by the time he left for London, he had suffered the personal tragedy of the death of his sister and two of his brothers?"

"I did not. I wish I had." She felt consumed with sadness at the thought of Dr Steele's loneliness.

"So you see, Miss Jones, London represented a new beginning for him," he explained, "but with his thick Scottish accent, and passion for data collection and accurate record keeping, the medical staff regarded him as a cold fish and an outsider."

"Sir, are you saying he was not regarded as a Guy's man?" she asked. Perhaps, she thought, that might explain why he was not involved in the plot.

"I am," came the reply. "Dr Steele was a worthy innovator. He had seen the benefits of Lister's antisepsis regime in Glasgow. He adopted such practices before they became fashionable. Despite the objections of some of our surgeons, he introduced Lister's ideas here at Guy's. Even if his suggestions were to the benefit of our patients, his changes were not popular."

Mr Lushington added to his homage, "But for Miss Burt, Dr Steele was a true blessing. We had far too many nurses, if you can even call them by that name, who were drunk and dirty on duty. More likely to kill our patients with their lack of hygiene than to cure them. And they could not be trusted not to rob them as they lay in their beds. Dr Steele helped to rid us of those harpies."

"What about Miss Burt's predecessor, Miss Loag? Surely she would not have tolerated such dishonesty?"

"She had tried her best to reform nursing, but age and ill health had taken their toll," came the reply, "and she disliked upsetting the medical staff, so progress was slow."

"Blessed be his soul in heaven," cried Miss Jones in heartfelt tribute, "our loss is truly great... Sir, I am in great confusion... I shall not be able to carry on without him."

Two

November's glorious in Ranchi. The seasonal rains have finished for the year, and up on the Chota Nagpur Plateau, south of the great Indo-Gangetic Plain, the days are warm and dry.

"Louisa, your camellias are lovely my dear. What are you feeding them? Do come over and work in my garden," chuckled Lydia as she turned to the group of ladies sipping their afternoon tea and nibbling pieces of shortbread and ginger cake, trying not to get their fine white cotton dresses and muslin shawls stained with annoying greasy patches from the crumbs.

"I recognise that. It's from Fortnum's, isn't it?" exclaimed Sarah as she held a distinctive tin up for all to see. "Whoever is sending you such fresh supplies from London? Have you a secret admirer you are hiding from us?"

The ladies lolled about in the generous veranda chairs, taking in the beauty of the garden in full flower.

Louisa waved for her housekeeper to bring a fresh pot of hot water. "Mary," she said, "I believe it is your turn to organise the flower committee ready for this year's Christmas festivities?"

The inquiry caused the ladies to turn expectantly to their friend, who fished out a list from her bag and put on her gold-rimmed reading glasses.

"It is," replied Mary heartily, "and I am going to be a tough sergeant major this year to get you all to do your bit. Louisa, I want camellias, roses and gardenias from you, and I'll give a list to each of you ladies shortly of my requirements, so don't pick everything before the big day."

"We await your instructions," replied Lydia. "We want our church to look beautiful, and if there are spare blooms, we can decorate the hospital and the Officers' Mess. How about that?"

The ladies sipped their refreshed teacups and adjusted their wide-brimmed hats to keep the sun off their faces. Louisa and Sarah strolled around the garden in the late afternoon sun while Mary and Lydia discussed the latest edition of *Myra's Journal of Dress and Fashion* sent from London on Louisa's subscription.

When not working, the ladies liked nothing better than to visit each other to read magazines, play cribbage, and admire their gardens' flamboyant blooms with their bright colours and delightful perfumes. It was so English, you would think you were in Surrey.

Mary readied a deck of cards for their crib game, folded the linen napkins into neat squares, and tidied the table ready for the next round of refreshments. Louisa was very particular about her linen. She loved its feel and smell when freshly pressed and kept a store of such squares not only for dining but also for her pillow to lay her head on each night. It gave her a real sense of comfort.

The ladies' pleasant afternoon was interrupted by a commotion from the house. Looking to the wide-open veranda doors, they saw Louisa's housekeeper running towards them waving an envelope.

"What is it, Ahya?" inquired Mary.

"A telegram from London for Miss Ingle," she replied. "The post boy said it was very urgent."

"Louisa, come quickly," cried Mary, calling her friend over to the house. "A telegram, there's a telegram for you from London." The ladies gathered in a huddle of concern as Louisa opened the envelope. As she read its contents, her expression changed to one of great alarm.

"No… Please no… Not true... Oh… Oh… Please… Please not Dr Steele… " Louisa crumpled to the ground, as she screwed the paper in her hand into a ball and dropped it. Her pain was palpable. Her sobbing was heartbreaking. Her world had fallen into tumult in an instant.

"Ahya, fetch Dr Macpherson at once," commanded Mary as the ladies pulled a chair around for their stricken friend. Lydia poured water onto one of the linen napkins to cool Louisa's reddened face while the others offered their comforting hands.

The servants gathered on the terrace and stared in silence, not knowing what to do. They had never seen their mistress in such a state of disarray.

"Louisa my dear, settle yourself," instructed Mary. "You

are among friends, and we will take care of you. Now, sip some lemon water."

Lydia proffered the glass of sharp liquid on Mary's matronly nod.

"Let's move her into the house and out of the sun," suggested Sarah, to which they all agreed as it was something useful to do.

As Lydia and Sarah helped Louisa into the shade, Mary picked up the screwed-up telegram and straightened it out on the tea table, pushing the cups and plates to one side. She read the message several times, trying to work out the meaning of Miss Jones's words. 'Last thoughts of you. Fuller note follows.'

Who is Miss Jones, she wondered, and who on earth was Dr Steele of Guy's Hospital?

While Dr Macpherson attended the indisposed lady, Lydia stood by ready to call Ahya if anything was needed. Mary, meanwhile, took off her glasses and whispered the contents of the telegram to the other ladies. Discreetly, they agreed amongst themselves that Louisa had never mentioned a paramour, and certainly the name Dr Steele had never come up in conversation. He was an intriguing unknown.

"Maybe he's from her days in London," speculated Lydia, who knew that Louisa had lived unhappily in Eltham in the months before travelling to India.

Ranchi sits in the beautiful hilly area south of Patna, an area blessed with many natural resources which fed its flourishing mineral and textile industries. Its commercial potential had attracted British settlers who loved the surrounding countryside with its crystal-clear waterfalls, where they liked to cool off on hot days. Lazing by the water, listening to the sound of it tumbling and rushing over the rocks; living in bungalows with verandas where punkawallas created a gentle breeze with their fans; and tending pretty gardens was a pleasant way of life. For many, it was a far cry from their original homes in Britain.

Like countless single women in their thirties and forties, Louisa and her friends had travelled to India to start a new life after some disappointment or misfortune. Invariably, there was nothing to keep them at home, and there were opportunities to work in the many schools and hospitals that served the Empire.

Louisa was helped to her bed, where Lydia and Ahya loosened her clothing and laid her head on the pillow covered with comforting linen squares. Dr Macpherson had given her some drops, so she was drowsy and free from her terrible distress, at least for now.

"I've given her some valerian," explained the doctor, drinking his tea in the garden room. "It is very strong, so on no account are you to give her any laudanum. What caused this breakdown, may I ask?"

"She received news of a death this afternoon from London by telegram," replied Mary. "We have no idea about this man or his relationship with Louisa. It is a mystery, save that we know his name and that he was associated with Guy's Hospital."

Over the years, Dr Macpherson's Scottish accent had softened to a lilt. "Guy's," he sighed, "that place of the so-called London medical elite... more like a pack of rats fighting in a sack!"

"Sir, do you know the place? Were you acquainted with this Dr Steele?" asked Lydia, trying not to appear too nosy or intrusive.

"No, my dear lady, to both questions." He looked about Louisa's comfortable room. "I studied in Glasgow and then joined the army, as many of us from north of the border do. I could have gone to London, but they look down on outsiders. It can be a struggle if you are not part of that rabble. They like to keep it all in their family firms," he explained, looking into his teacup.

"When did you arrive here?" inquired Mary, curious to know more about this new doctor who had replaced their apothecary-surgeon, Dr Gray, after his return to England.

"I'm in my sixties now so I have served in the army in Bengal for nearly thirty years. I arrived after the Uprising when the East India Company was kicked out and Her Majesty's Government took over," he said with nostalgic pride. "It was very different then. We had to set up a civil and public service and repair our broken relations. We're still sorting out the mess now."

"How interesting, do go on," urged Mary. There was a curiosity, and even a hope, amongst the ladies that they might be able to piece together at least some of Louisa's story. It was also delightful to be in the company of a gentleman – all too often in short supply in polite society.

"I arrived as a young army surgeon around the same time that Sir John Lawrence took over as the Viceroy in 1864. He had long been in India, especially in the Punjab.

With his brothers, he had worked all over the place since arriving from the East India Company's training school at Haileybury. He was a 'Hailey' man alright. Do you know they have to pass exams in several languages to come to India? He spoke Persian and Urdu like a native. Very impressive. No wonder they made him a 'Lord'." Dr Macpherson supped the beer Ahya had found for him.

The ladies smiled and nodded encouragement. They had nothing else to do that evening and Dr Macpherson's reminiscences were very interesting as their knowledge of India's history was rather hazy and one-sided.

"Old Baron Lushington wouldn't recognise us now," he said with a chuckle. "He was one of the original directors, and a Chairman, of the East India Company in the late 18th century. Looted the place like the rest of them, but his scions were better behaved, more civilised."

"Lushington, I've heard of that name," cried Lydia. "They are big in the army, are they not?"

"Indeed they are madam, and in the judiciary and the civil service. Oh yes, Baron Lushington created quite a legacy for his family in India, and at home. His son, if I recall, was the famous lawyer and judge, the Right Honourable Stephen Lushington. You are probably familiar with him as he was a vociferous Member of Parliament and one of the Queen's Privy Councillors."

Ahya brought in a tray of refreshments, prompting Mary to suggest they all stay for supper while they watched over Louisa. "You will join us, Dr Macpherson, won't you?"

It would be better than whatever was served in the Mess that evening and he was not on duty until the morning.

"Mutton – will mutton do, or fish?" asked Mary, taking charge of the household. "Ahya, can you ask cook to prepare some mutton and fish and a biryani and dhal for us and bring some fresh lemon water. Oh, and can you check on Louisa to see she's alright?"

"A connection to Guy's," mused Dr Macpherson, thinking back to their earlier conversation. "I recall Lord Lawrence retired in early 1869 and became the President of Guy's Hospital on his return to London."

Ahya moved between the ladies and Dr Macpherson with a platter of fruit to refresh their palates from all the sweet treats they had been eating during the afternoon.

"Lushington," he mulled over the name. "Lushington. Ah yes, one of the Baron's grandsons was the Viceroy's Financial Secretary. Edward Harbord Lushington. I can see him now; they used to call him 'cardboard' as he was so stiff. First-born son of Stephen Lushington if I recall and another 'Hailey' man. Probably spoke several languages too."

The ladies and their guest were joined by Jeanie Maxwell, the scholarly librarian.

"My dears, how is Louisa? I came as soon as Ahya sent news."

"She is sleeping just now," replied Mary, "but please join us for supper and you may see her when she is awake. Dr Macpherson has given her a draught to ease her upset, and he is telling us of his early days in India."

Jeanie made herself comfortable and called Ahya over to request a drink. She had been in Ranchi and the west Bengal area for as long as Dr Macpherson and had seen many come and go over the years, especially those from the governing administration. She had served all of them, meeting their requests for books and papers from London and Calcutta.

"Do you remember Edward Harbord Lushington?" asked Mary. "He has just come up in our conversation about Guy's Hospital."

"Of course I do," she said. "I can name all the senior administrators to the Viceroys. He stands out for being part of that family for a start. All those generals, adjutants, and lawyers. I recall he was one of our local magistrates and a tax collector. He served in the Bengal Civil Service for nearly thirty years before he retired."

"Really; that's interesting," spoke Lydia, "and where is he now?"

"Back in London, of course," she replied, savouring her drop of gin and its rich layer of juniper berries. "At Guy's Hospital where Lord Lawrence appointed him as the administrator. He'd clearly done such a good job for the Viceroy as Bengal's First Financial Secretary."

"I wonder if Mr Lushington knew Dr Steele," asked Sarah.

"Who is Dr Steele?" Jeanie looked quizzically at the ladies.

"That's what we're trying to work out," explained Lydia.

"Supper is served," announced Ahya.

"Next you're going to tell us that he was wounded in the Uprising," joked Dr Macpherson as he stood to escort the ladies to their supper in what was one of Louisa's best rooms.

Having spent much of her earlier adult years eating monotonous and lukewarm food in dingy cold institutional refectories, Louisa's great luxury on settling in Ranchi was to eat a variety of appetising fresh food in a comfortable bright room decorated according to the latest fashion. She had taken care over the years to buy the best glasses and tableware that she could afford, and she had sought out the finest linens with which to dress her table, even when there were no guests.

The garden's sweet fragrances wafted through the open veranda doors and clung to the soft muslin drapes, delicately perfuming the simple but stylish room. The reflected light from the evening's sun glistened as it struck the mirrors that hung from each wall, and the candles on the table added to the room's warm glow as their delicate light was refracted by the glassware. Ahya had decorated the room with bouquets as she did each evening to please Louisa, who loved cut flowers.

The ladies took their seats on either side of the head of table place, where Dr Macpherson had instinctively settled himself into the generous carver chair. Ahya took great pleasure in serving him with fresh water, slices of lemon and another beer, and then she attended to the ladies' needs as the houseboy brought in the food and laid the dishes along the centre of the table. The delicate spicy smells of the biryani and curry sauces sharpened their appetites.

Mary tapped her glass gently with a spoon so they could say grace. As she thanked the Lord for their supper, a crunching noise from Dr Macpherson's end of the table signalled that he had made a prompt start by breaking the pile of poppadoms into bite-sized pieces. Having seized a fistful of the savoury morsels for himself, he duly passed the plate to Mary, who selected her pieces before passing the dish around.

The servants piled the food onto the guests' plates and topped up the salvers of greens and chutneys as they ran low. It was all very satisfying as Dr Macpherson shovelled heaped spoonfuls of rice and meat held together with dhal into his mouth in quick succession. Being an army surgeon trains you to eat quickly, he explained as he cleared his plate well before the ladies, who were daintily trying to balance their grains of sticky white rice and sauce on the back of a fork.

"The Edinburgh blue-blooded boys used to eat their food like that," he commented with a swig of beer, trying not to look too obviously ill-mannered. "They probably would have fitted alright in London."

"Oh Dr Macpherson, your jest is intriguing to us," commented Jeanie. "Please do tell more about this rivalry between Glasgow and Edinburgh Medical Schools."

"Delighted," smiled the surgeon as he leaned back in his chair, thinking about the most scurrilous tale he could conjure for their entertainment, while Ahya brought in plates of sliced fruit, almonds and glasses of watery yoghurt.

A scream stopped the conversation in an instant. Ahya ran to Louisa's room and called for help. Dr Macpherson was by Louisa's side in a moment. The ladies crowded around him, looking over his shoulder as he comforted Louisa while taking her pulse.

"She has had a nightmare, I'm afraid," he explained. "You see this sometimes with valerian.

"Miss Ingle do not stress yourself," spoke the doctor, signalling Ahya to bring some water.

"Drink this and sit up so I can listen to your heart," he instructed as the others looked on.

"It was her again," cried Louisa, "she points her bony finger at me... she accuses me... she is shivering... her unkempt hair and bulging eyes fix me to the spot... 'You, you,' she cries... it's not true..." She fell back into a weeping delirium. It was most distressing to watch. Lydia cradled her friend.

"Dr Macpherson, please give her more drops. She needs to escape from this torment," requested an anxious Mary.

Taking the small brown bottle from his bag, this he did, and then joined the ladies in the garden room where they were contemplating what to do next to help Louisa as they sipped their tea.

"How long has she had these disturbing dreams?" asked Dr Macpherson.

"Ever since we have known her," replied Mary.

"That's right, since she joined us over ten years ago," concurred Lydia, who helped at the local hospital where Louisa worked as a nurse.

"They are too vivid and constant to be just a passing nightmare," observed Jeanie. "Perhaps there is more to this, maybe an underlying pathology, even hysteria?"

"It's getting late." Mary turned to Dr Macpherson and

asked if he would be kind enough to provide an escort as they walked down the lane with their lanterns lighting the path to their bungalows.

"Ahya, I shall return shortly to check on Miss Ingle. Miss Maxwell will watch over her until I get back. I shall not be long, and I'd like some tea ready for my patient, and me," requested Dr Macpherson as he strolled out with the gaggle of ladies.

Jeanie sat with Louisa in the fading evening light. She resolved to look up Dr Steele in the British Medical Register, which she could request from the city library in Calcutta where she knew the staff well. And Mr Lushington; she would investigate his details too, just to satisfy her curiosity.

Jeanie joined Dr Macpherson in taking some tea on his return and sat beside Louisa as he examined her again when she awoke.

"Thank you Sir, I am much recovered," whispered Louisa as she swallowed her lemon tea. "I am greatly distressed today as I have had news of the death of a friend that I held dear."

"He sounds very special for you to have given so much thought to him. When did you see him last?" inquired Dr Macpherson, trying to understand the depth of her sorrow for this man.

"We have not spoken for many years, but I think of him most days. He is precious to me. Sir, it is late, and I am exhausted. Your questions will have to wait." She was in no state to discuss anything and certainly not her feelings for Dr Steele with a stranger.

"Ahya, I have given Miss Ingle more drops. She will sleep soon. Please watch over her tonight and call me if anything changes," said the doctor as he left with Jeanie to escort her to her residence on his way back to his quarters further down the hill.

Valerian has its uses, but not for Louisa that day. She tossed and turned through the night, quietly weeping as she recalled long-buried memories.

THREE

S itting in her garden enjoying the fresh crisp air and warm sun after the church service to celebrate the third Sunday in Advent, Louisa received the package she had been expecting. As Ahya called the houseboy over to open the well-wrapped packet, Louisa sipped her tea. She recognised the neat handwriting of the opening paragraph of Miss Jones's letter.

'Louisa, my dear friend, we are all bereft and besides ourselves with grief. We had his funeral yesterday in the hospital chapel and, despite the fine eulogies, nothing eases the pain of our loss. I was with him to the end. It was peaceful after much agitation. Mr Howse, I am sure you will remember him, he is now our senior surgeon, had done his best to save him but it was to no avail. It was, I believe, time for dear Dr Steele to go to Our Lord in heaven and give an account of his actions while here on earth.'

Louisa remembered that Miss Jones was a devout Anglican, a High Church woman, an Anglo-Catholic, as she herself had once been. At least she has her faith to comfort her, Louisa thought, as she rose to inform Ahya she was going up to the waterfalls for the day.

Louisa was haunted by her past, but she took careful steps to hide any trace of it from prying eyes. Over the years, she had become adept at being invisible, taking cover in respectable ladies' groups that did good works and looked after their local churches. News of Dr Steele's death had tipped her into a deep melancholia as she remembered how despised she had been and the levels of deprivation she had endured.

Ahya had prepared a packed lunch of Louisa's favourite foods to help cheer her mistress, and placed several squares of linen in the basket.

Walking up to the waterfalls, Louisa took in the panorama of forests, green valleys and craggy escarpments. She spread her blanket on the ground in a cool spot where she could listen to the restful sound of water tumbling over the rocks and bubbling in pools. She let her shawl fall away and removed her straw hat to feel the sun's luxurious warmth on her face and shoulders. Ready now to learn of the conspiracy that had engulfed her in the summer of 1880, she stiffened her back and read on.

'It was Dr Steele's last wish that you should know about his findings and I have added to his account my own observations in the hope you might appreciate the full circumstances we found ourselves in during that spring and summer. I do not excuse the conduct of the doctors and nurses who took part in your persecution. Rather, in laying out a fuller account, I hope that it might ease your pain and that you might, with the Lord's help in prayer, find the well of forgiveness in your heart for all those who have injured you so terribly.'

Louisa felt nothing but contempt for all those who had wronged her, and it pained her to be asked to forgive them. I am not like the saintly Miss Victoria Jones, she said to herself as she laid the papers out on her blanket ready to be read in the neat sections Miss Jones had prepared.

She admired the bright blue cloudless sky and thought of its contrast to the dingy grey London skies she used to stare at from her miserable room in a boarding house in Eltham. Emigrating to India and settling in Ranchi had been a blessing. She allowed herself a faint smile of pleasure.

Ladies' dress and hairstyles were more relaxed up in the hill stations, so her chignon of dark hair was unpinned and loose, as was her unbelted summer dress. She found great comfort in these small things as she remembered just how cold and grim it could be in London in December, especially when you are a poor woman and alone. The missive continued:

'The generous revenues from Guy's many endowments and estates had kept the hospital in funds since it had admitted its first patients on January 6, the Epiphany, over a hundred and sixty years ago. Consequently, Guy's was not dependent on charitable donations, unlike many of the other hospitals in London. However, by the new decade in 1880, its annual income had fallen greatly because of the crisis in farming and the hospital's finances became increasingly precarious. To address the shortfall, Mr Lushington had been requested by the Board to make savings. This he did, as you will recall from your days here working on St Mary's Ward.'

Louisa clearly remembered the effects on the ward when this drive to save money was introduced. They had less food for the patients and the linen was changed less often, unless it was badly soiled, and the nurses' shifts were increased to twelve hours a day. She closed her eyes as she recalled how exhausted they were by the time they had to go to chapel for evening prayers.

She sighed at the memory of their daily allowance of porter being watered down. 'Nurses' Porter' they called it! The cheek of it; they took us for fools, and we were.

'In addition, as you know only too well, Mr Lushington was instructed to modernise the hospital's nursing practices and to build Guy's Training Institute for Nursing. You see, Louisa, the Governors felt it was important for Guy's to be "modern", like its rivals, and they felt that our lack of a training institution for nurses tarnished Guy's reputation. The Governors were particularly sensitive about the successes of our rival along the river, St Thomas's hospital, with its fine Nurses' Training Institute. Even our other great rival, St Bartholowmew's hospital, had one while we had nothing.'

Louisa recalled the feeling of turmoil across London that spring when the Disraeli Government fell as Gladstone had surprisingly won the general election in March. That was when she had joined Guy's as one of Miss Burt's new lady-nurses. They thought they were going to change the world with their new uniforms, crisp cuffs and collars and lacy hats, and their education.

Who would have thought that the reforming zeal of the matron was not shared by all, especially by the physicians and surgeons? And as for the nurses who objected, she felt despair and contempt for her former colleagues, especially the ward maids. Louisa got up for a stretch and to play with the cool water. It felt good to splash her face and rinse her hands in the refreshing pool. She read on.

'The dispute, Louisa, was a very public affair from the moment of the announcement of Miss Burt's appointment in November 1879. Despite her reputation, or because of it, angry letters were written to the Governors complaining about Miss Burt and her reforms by Guy's senior doctors. They were organised by Dr Samuel Osborne Habershon. I know you will remember him. He was the one who organised the medical staff's prayer meetings each morning and preached in open parks whenever he felt the need. He was a serious-minded Nonconformist and he suspected us lady-nurses of "popery" and even worse sins. He and his ilk held us in suspicion and contempt. Louisa, I weep to this day at the memory of it and the stress of the dispute has shortened my life.'

Louisa felt depressed as she read the letter and her deep loathing for Dr Habershon came to the fore. It brought back painful memories of all the sniping and whispers that had gone on in the recesses of the ward, and the open rows between some of the lady-nurses and the doctors were distressing to recall, even after all this time.

She winced as she recalled the loyalty tests applied by Miss Burt, and the sight of the crocodile of dismissed nurses with their bags lined up in protest at the hospital gates was as fresh in Louisa's mind as it was that spring day over twelve years ago.

'Louisa, it was relentless. I was, as you know, Miss Burt's deputy, and therefore privy to things that you were shielded from. They wrote to the *Times* newspaper and the medical press almost daily with their complaints full of malice against Miss Burt and her fanciful ideas about nursing accountability and making nurses' training more formal and "scientific". They even hated our new uniform. I think they feared Miss Burt was rather too inspired by the Anglican Sisterhoods of Nursing for their liking. Did you know that Dr Habershon referred to Miss Burt as the "nurse from a country hospital"? It was so sour and unworthy.'

Louisa lay back in the midday sun, breathed in the fresh forest air and took a sip of laudanum from her secreted flask. It was a lifetime ago, and time to let it all go. But she could not; the burning sense of injustice gnawed away at her very soul and there was nobody she could share her feelings with. This was the loneliness and isolation that had haunted her constantly.

'Louisa, I have enclosed the account of the dispute I promised. It is unvarnished. I have given much thought to what you are entitled to know, and I hope you will find I have judged well. The events are many and they form such a dense thicket that the matters of importance are in danger of being obscured. I have therefore focused on the course of three days where either I was present, or where Dr Steele's and my inquiries led us to discover the details of those events. They are important as they led to the terrible situation you found yourself in during that July and August.'

Once again, Louisa rose to stretch her legs. She was a bit unstable as the opiate took its effect. She was hungry too, so she unwrapped her lunch and, sitting by the waterfall, ate her favourite potato pakoras. Ahya had judged the level of spiciness required for an English lady's constitution correctly – not too hot, and accompanied by some fresh yoghurt and coriander. A flask of lemon water provided a welcome drink, and a piece of fruit cleared her palate.

'Louisa, do you remember that awful day in June when there was a riot at the hospital? We were all shocked to find the rabble consisted of our medical students. They proved themselves to be as rowdy as the dockers down on the wharves at Bermondsey. It was the start of another weary day for Miss Burt with difficult meetings all day to defend her reforms. Something changed her that day. She had had enough of the protests and her resolve to implement the changes stiffened.'

How could Louisa forget, when two hundred young men harangued the matron and the lady-nurses and yelled at them to leave the hospital at once?

She recalled how they had to carry on working their long shifts with only watered porter to quench their thirst as they did the laundry, cleaned the floors, and rushed around the ward looking after the patients. And that awful lazy ward maid, Emma. Louisa took a deep breath to calm her nerves.

'We could not know the depth of anger concerning Miss

Burt that existed in the medical staff or what this force drove them to do to get her gone. Of course, the likes of you or I would not have been privy to their deliberations but one of their number, a trusted one, did disclose to Dr Steele the details of the decisions taken on a fateful day in late June, so concerned was he to rein in the dark forces that had been released in the hospital that summer.

'Louisa, I was with Miss Burt for most of the time and I think my account explains how the conflict escalated, and I believe Dr Steele's account of the doctors' actions to be as near to the truth as we will ever get.

'It is upsetting reading, but he wished you to know the details in the hope it would help to ease your distress by showing that you were a victim of circumstance and not an intended target of their malicious actions.'

Those plotters, those hateful spineless individuals with their fancy carriages and privileged West End lives. They may have had titles and connections, but they were as bad as that guttersnipe Emma for the lying and falsehoods that they spoke.

She lolled about on her blanket, looking up at the sky for some relief from the awful place her memories had dragged her to. She racked her brains to recall the name of the senior physician who took charge of the patients on her ward. Of French extraction and a good-looking man who dressed like a true gentleman, he drove around town in a shiny new carriage that he had parked outside Guy's pathology laboratory whenever he was in the hospital. What was his name? She drifted off into an afternoon sleep trying to remember.

Louisa woke with a start. Dr Frederick Pavy, that was the name of the cad who had accused her of being cruel to his patient. She dabbed her flushed angry face and sweaty hands with a linen square dipped in the cold water.

She picked up the letter and thumbed the last two pages. What more was there to say?

'Louisa, as if all this was not enough, unbeknown to us, Dr Habershon's actions on that June day ensured there would be a conflagration. It just needed a spark and that was provided in full measure by our former colleague, Miss Lonsdale. I am sure you will remember her. She was very handsome and well-educated, a real lady, and a writer. She mixed in those circles we can only gaze at and wish for.'

Louisa remembered Miss Margaret Lonsdale in an instant, even though she had only known the lady for six weeks. She smiled to herself as she recalled how most of the junior medical staff fawned around her when she was on the wards. Her attractiveness to them was only enhanced by the lady's returned coolness as she looked down on those men who she regarded as from inferior backgrounds.

Louisa recalled the public rows Miss Lonsdale had with the senior physicians, who felt she was rather too muscular in her criticism of their care for the patients. Dr Habershon and Dr Pavy were appalled by her boldness; others were equally outraged by her, especially when she penned a very articulate article in defence of the nursing reforms. It was the spark that ignited the dispute.

Louisa remembered the last occasion she had heard from Miss Lonsdale. It was at one of the lowest points in her life when she desperately needed sympathy and help.

And what did she get from Miss Lonsdale? A book. Yes, a book. Louisa had deliberately left it in her room in Eltham when she had departed for Calcutta all those years ago.

Having lit the fire, Miss Lonsdale withdrew to her grand house in the country, to the bosom of her family who shielded her from the catastrophe she had precipitated at Guy's. Oh, to be able to just walk away from such a mess.

'Louisa, I am older and wiser now and I make these observations in the hope that it will help you to understand our place in the world and what must be endured. Although we might wish it different, we are not high-born ladies like Miss Lonsdale. The privilege of her birth gives her certain liberties that are simply not available to us.

'You see such women at our garden fetes and fundraisers. They contribute much to society; they have a voice and connections. We do not. While some wait for a suitable proposal of marriage, others do good works. They can afford to go unpaid. We cannot. Women like us must try our best to work hard in service to the Lord and the poor. We are diligent and we do not cause a stir. The Sisterhood has been our blessed gift from Him to help us to serve.'

For all our faults, Louisa thought, at least we are better than that Emma and her thieving friends who are just one step from the workhouse or the streets. But she shuddered as she remembered that she too would have come close to that pit in hell, had it not been for the kindness of Dr Steele. She wept at the thought of him now departed. She would never see him again or hear his stories about growing up in Brechin, a small place just a bit to the west of Montrose, he used to say. Louisa read the penultimate paragraph.

'I have reported the events from the last Friday in July, when I spent time with Miss Lonsdale here at Guy's. Miss Burt had recalled her to London to agree your defence and Miss Lonsdale's testimony. In the end, as you know, it was not needed but we spent part of the day in prayer for you and she was truly contrite for your situation. I hope this will be of some comfort to you and suffice to say, she too has suffered for the consequences of her actions.'

Suffered? Louisa was indignant that Miss Jones should dare suggest even a hint of equality in the two women's fates. It was all too much to bear. She went up to the rocks facing the waterfall to hear its roar and feel the rush of water in the hope that it would clear her head.

Tears filled her eyes as she remembered the feeling of being despised, and the terrible things that were said about her. Louisa's shoulders slumped at the memory of the poisonous atmosphere on the ward. She smiled as she recalled her only loyal friend that July.

Dear Charlotte, Louisa thought to herself as she toyed with the water in her bare feet, I hope she found a good life in the convent. A life in prayer or in despair, both were prisons of a sort. Still, life in the Bermondsey convent was better than the workhouse. And as for Emma, she probably ended up in jail or on the streets as the reward for her dishonesty.

Louisa had so wished for a well-connected family like Miss Lonsdale's. But for her there were no uncles and husbands of sisters, nor a father to divert the blows and offer a safe place to hide from the outrageous press and gossipers.

'Louisa, can you forgive us? Even after all the intervening years, I know you still believe that we let you down, that we abandoned you. But Louisa, we did not. Dr Steele moved heaven and earth to relieve your situation. And Miss Burt and I prayed for you every evening at service with Reverend Flood. Louisa, I am pleading on Dr Steele's behalf, and that of Guy's, for your forgiveness.'

Louisa took another sip of her comforter. She folded her shawl into a pillow and lay on the blanket to contemplate whether she should read on. It would take the rest of the day and it would be too distressing, especially as it was just before Christmas, when she always tried to be cheerful for the others. Maybe I'll read it later, she murmured to herself as she dozed off.

The fog of the opiate mixed with her memories of things past. 'You... You...' the bony finger was pointing at her, accusing her of foul deeds; Emma and Charlotte were arguing and shouting about her; the physicians and Dr Steele were hollering at each other as she looked up at them in a gallery above her head. Her heart raced as she felt herself fixed to the front of a runaway train as it hurtled out of control...

Louisa woke and sat upright feeling faint, her hair disheveled. She was out of breath; she needed to get away from her memories. The waterfall, the cooling waterfall. She could end it now in that refreshing pool. She could escape this enduring burden of memories with a leap. She looked at the sheaf of papers so carefully prepared by Miss Jones. Perhaps there is salvation of a kind here, she reflected, as she dabbed her face with a damp linen square.

PART II: THE GAUNTLET

FOUR

'Louisa, I know you have never forgiven Miss Burt for the terrible injury she caused you in July of that summer. I wept with you at her terrible decision, which was not taken lightly. She was under great pressure from the Governors to address the medical staff's concerns. Many of our nurses added to her woes, so every day became a trial for her, like the day of the riot. I have set out an account of that day in hope you might better understand.'

The great black door of Matron's House opened and there stood Miss Margaret Burt to face her accusers. It was Wednesday June 16, 1880, and Guy's was alive with malicious gossip and rumours spread by the hospital's warring factions.

After more than six months of relentless hostility, Miss Burt was exhausted. Each day was a struggle over whose ideas were in the best interests of patients, and Guy's reputation. She had to constantly address the concerns not only of the doctors but also of the many nurses and ward maids. Between them, they constantly questioned the need for change and fretted over every detail.

The acrimonious rows were at the front of her mind on rising, when at prayer each morning in the chapel, and throughout the day during her work as matron of a busy London teaching hospital. She found no peace as the escalating dispute and bad press gnawed at her confidence day after day.

June had been windy, cold, and extremely wet. Early morning fogs added to the unseasonably gloomy days, and the constant south-westerly winds brought storm after storm. Today there was a total absence of any sunshine in London. Even at half past ten in the morning, Miss Burt felt exhausted as she faced another long day explaining the benefits of her reforms. She longed for the elusive summer's warmth as she looked up at the dreary sky and contemplated the coming storm.

Matron's House looked onto a statue of the hospital's founder and benefactor, Thomas Guy. It stood on a tall plinth in the centre of the front quad. His stone eyes looked down on all who entered through the hospital's main wrought-iron gates which were hung from sturdy ornate stone pillars. The whole assembly of the gates and the adjoining railings, which ran along St Thomas's Street, reflected his great wealth and delineated the boundary between the hospital, an oasis of calm and cleanliness, and the crowded, cacophonous, and stinking world of the nearby

Borough market and the district of Southwark, with its busy roads, and raucous pubs and music halls.

Miss Burt drew a deep breath as she descended the wide Portland stone steps down to the front quad. She moved slowly and with grace despite the weight of her black formal dress uniform made of heavy drill cotton.

As she passed the founder's stony gaze, her attention was caught by angry shouting coming from the monastic colonnaded passageway to the south of the quad. It was 10.38 by her father's golden pocket watch, which was attached by a delicate chain to her belt and kept in her deep skirt pocket on the right-hand side alongside her prayer card and rosary.

Her heart sank as she drew closer to the colonnade and the indistinct shouting became clear.

"She doesn't belong at Guy's."

"Stop the reforms."

"Outrage. It's an outrage."

"Leave Guy's now."

"She's not one of us. Get rid of her."

"Patients need doctors to be in charge."

She was horrified to see the excited crowd of demonstrators were all young men, fresh-faced and well dressed. She was aghast when she realised they were all medical students at Guy's, and that they were becoming increasingly hostile at the sight of their prey, Mr Lushington. He was accompanied by Dr Steele. Both were enthusiastic supporters of Miss Burt's nursing reforms, hence the opprobrium.

As Guy's most senior officers, Mr Lushington and Dr

Steele had been requested by the Governors to attend the hospital's Court of Committees to discuss the ongoing disquiet in the hospital and the constant stream of derogatory letters that appeared in the daily and weekly press.

The young men, who were on the brink of their medical careers, were utterly confident of their position as students at one of London's finest colleges. Dressed for the weather in their worsted suits, they jostled each other for a place in the front row of the crowd as if at a fairground. By some unconscious discipline, they had formed into two lines, one on each side of the passageway, creating a gauntlet that Mr Lushington and Dr Steele had to walk through.

The colonnade, with its low ceiling and well-worn, uneven flagstones, led to the sprawl of hospital ward and outpatient blocks, and Guy's famous pathology laboratory and teaching rooms. They had been built in wealthier times on a grand scale around a well-kept lawn and garden known as the Park. With an imposing old tree at its centre, the Park offered shade on a rare sunny day, and a tranquil space to take some fresh air and a moment for quiet contemplation away from the hustle and bustle of life on the wards.

Miss Burt breathed in as deeply as her tightly buttoned-over blouse would allow as she proceeded across the front quad. Mounting the steps to the colonnade, she felt the students' seething anger as their shouts and invectives reverberated around the passageway. To quell her nerves and stay her trembling hands, she remembered the calming effect of reciting her favourite psalm in similar intimidating situations when she was a young woman not yet twenty years old.

Miss Burt's father, the Reverend John Burt, had been a church minister and prison chaplain and she had often accompanied him on his pastoral visits to Birmingham's Institute of Correction at Winson Green. On entering this gloomy prison, she had always felt fear. Her heart pounded while she waited for the prisoners to assemble for her father's Bible class and prayers. Reciting psalm 130, the *De Profundis*, always calmed her.

"Out of the depths I cried to thee oh Lord! Lord, hear my voice. Let thine ears be attentive to the voice of my pleading" … and then the familiar refrain, "I place all my trust in you my Lord, all my hope is in your spoken word…"

Miss Burt, like many of her nursing contemporaries, was a devout High Church Anglican. Prayer was a part of her day and she often sought solace from the pressures of her work in the hospital's chapel, which stood next to her quarters in Matron's House.

Whispering her comforting prayer, she checked her balance as she raised her heavy skirt to step up to the colonnade. Her well-scrubbed hands were distressingly clammy, and the starched ribbon of her white lace cap irritated her cheeks, as did its stiff bow tied under her chin.

Startled, she heard a voice of firm reassurance. "Courage Miss Burt, Courage."

It was Mr Lushington as he passed her on the steps, having walked through the gauntlet with Dr Steele. Their sphinx-like expressions had incensed the angry students. Rudely, the young men started booing and hissing.

Shocked by the ill-mannered demonstration, Miss Burt proceeded to Mary ward, which looked after emergency female medical admissions. It was located on the second floor of Hunt's House, the hospital block funded by another Guy's benefactor, William Hunt. His generous bequest gave rise to the magnificent building which stood on the east side of the Park.

The wards in Hunt's House had high ceilings giving an airy and spacious feel, along with plenty of light from their big windows which overlooked the Park. The wards were accommodated on the ground, first and second floors around a grand entrance hall which had a modish staircase at its centre. Each ward had a bathroom for its patients, a scullery with running water, and generous storage cupboards for the linen.

Walking through the gardens to the main entrance, Miss Burt reflected on what Guy's President, Viscount Cardwell, and the Governors, not to mention the press, would have to say about the morning's fracas. There would be more pressure to justify every detail of her reforms in yet more tedious meetings, and more time spent in checking the notes of the discussions for their accuracy and meaning. Mr Lushington was a stickler for record-keeping.

And there would be more plotting and letter writing by Dr Habershon and his colleagues to get her gone.

Miss Susannah Crockett, the senior nurse in charge of Mary ward for the last six years, like all the other sisters, was now called by her ward name rather than by her own name. Sister Mary ran her ward as best she could despite the ever-present tensions arising from the increasing workload and staff reductions that she had been instructed to make in the drive for savings. She had tried her best with the reforms, but they caused her relationships with the medical staff to suffer.

Having climbed four flights of stairs to reach the second floor, Miss Burt arrived on the ward in a rather breathless state. She received Sister Mary's curtsey and salutation, "Good morning, Matron." In reply to Miss Burt's inquiry about how things were progressing on the ward, Sister Mary replied without hesitation.

"Matron, I've got fifty-two beds under Dr Pavy on this ward, and we are really feeling the want of more staff. He is very demanding, and his patients are very sick. They require constant attention. Is there anything you can do to relieve us of his demands? They are unreasonable and too much to bear. I know the Night Sister feels the same."

A daughter of a poor Irishman, Mrs Margaret Keogh had married a tailor from Bermondsey about thirty years ago. He died soon after in Guy's of the common condition of phthisis (tuberculosis) and she was left destitute. Miss Loag, the former matron, had kindly offered the young widow lowly work and accommodation on one of the wards. Mrs Keogh was forever grateful and loyal to her as she worked her way up to become Guy's Night Sister.

Mrs Keogh was held in high regard by the junior medical and nursing staff as she helped them when they were alone on night duty and in a pickle. She had no formal training as a nurse, but had built up a lot of practical experience over the years and knew everybody and where everything was. She had a room on one of the wards from where she dispensed advice to all who called upon her. The senior doctors admired her too as she never argued with them, and she minded their juniors to save them attending at night.

Dr Frederick Pavy was one of Guy's senior physicians and the Medical School's lecturer in physiology. He was a leading authority on diabetes and the discoverer of the disease that bore his name where protein is found abnormally in patients' urea because of kidney problems. He visited his patients on Mary ward on most afternoons for what was called the 'ward round' where he was accompanied by his resident junior house physician, Dr Thomas Howell, and one of the ward nurses if Sister Mary was not available.

Dr Howell's job was to look after his boss's patients' daily medical needs. He kept the clinical records and ward log and made the notes of instruction for the nurses following Dr Pavy's rounds. The workload was relentless as the hospital's 'Taking-in' committee tried to meet Guy's charitable benefactors' increasing demands for it to treat more patients.

Sister Mary's staff consisted of the old-style nurses with no training and unqualified assistants, the ward maids – who scrubbed the floors and grates, and helped with the laundry and feeding. On her arrival in November 1879, Miss Burt had introduced her new training scheme for gentlewomen. She selected pious educated ladies from good families who wanted to do something worthy rather than be confined to the house awaiting a proposal of marriage. These new recruits, the probationer lady-nurses, had to have the correct altruistic motives as judged by Miss Burt.

Sister Mary implored Miss Burt, "I understand the need for Mr Lushington's search for savings, and we are working very hard, but the lady-nurses are not used to the physical work involved in stripping and making beds. And as for washing soiled cotton sheets and ironing them, they are repulsed and exhausted by these daily tasks. Life on this ward is tough.

"Our work is not helped by the ward's layout," she continued. "That corridor, where the bathroom and laundry room are, divides the ward which means the duty nurse cannot see all the patients in a single glance up and down the two rows of beds when she is seated at the nurses' table." Trying her best to work around this awkward arrangement, Sister Mary organised the most seriously ill to be in sight of the nurses, while those recovering were placed on the ward's blind side.

Miss Burt and Sister Mary walked along the ward, stopping at each bed to ask the patients how they were feeling. Sister Mary explained Dr Pavy's diagnosis, which was written on a card placed above the patient's bed, along with any of his special instructions.

"And this patient?" inquired Miss Burt as they stood at the foot of a young woman's bed. She was not yet thirty years, but looked old well before her time, and very poorly.

"This is number 2, Mrs Morgan; she has a bad case of hysteria," replied Sister Mary.

"Sister Mary, please stop referring to the patients by their bed number," Miss Burt instructed, noting the lifeless disposition of the patient. The card above Mrs Morgan's bed denoted a case of 'phthisis'. "Not hysteria?" she asked. "The treatments are very different; please check with Dr Howell and Dr Pavy and explain the discrepancy when they have clarified the diagnosis."

Hysteria was a common diagnosis for women, but it suffered from being both indistinct and not well understood. The common treatment was much bathing and walking which was very labour intensive, especially if the patients were reluctant participants in their treatment. Miss Burt disliked the use of this term as she knew from her days at other teaching hospitals that patients, particularly women, labelled as hysterics were often seriously ill from underlying conditions which were masked by this vague diagnosis.

They were distracted by a kerfuffle about whether the ward should be heated on this cold day. Mary ward had a traditional open fireplace in the centre of the ward facing the nurses' desk. Its full coal scuttles stood ready for lighting-up time but Sister Mary had decided not to put a fire in. It was June after all, and they were too busy anyway.

It didn't help that she kept the ward's high windows ajar to allow fresh air from the Park to circulate and refresh the ward's stale air.

"I think the ward has need of some heat," commented

Miss Burt. "Our patients and nurses are chilled to the bone. It would be a kindness to both if you lit the fire."

"We are trying to be frugal," came Sister Mary's bold reply.

Miss Burt observed the nursing staff as they went about their morning's work of getting the patients washed and fed, and the bed linen changed. Meanwhile, Dr Howard got in the way of the nurses constantly as he checked each patient in readiness for Dr Pavy's afternoon round.

"May I ask you to conduct your clinical round after we have finished our morning's work?" Miss Burt asked Dr Howell politely.

"Ma'am, with respect, I take my instruction from Dr Pavy, not a nurse," was his cold reply. There was the crux of the dispute, thought Sister Mary, as Miss Burt bore her humiliation without comment. To break the tension, Sister Mary led the matron to the ward office with the offer of some refreshing tea while they discussed the ward's impoverished staffing levels.

"Emma, please bring some tea for the matron," yelled Sister Mary.

Emma Costello, the ward maid, carried on with her back-breaking work as she took the piles of soiled bedding and patients' nightclothes to the laundry room in the corridor ready for the afternoon's work. She spied Nurse Ingle sitting at the desk in the other half of the ward.

"Nurse Ingle, Sister wants tea for the matron. I have to scrub the floors before dinnertime so can you see to it? I'm very busy."

Miss Ingle, and the other lady-nurses, were too high-class for her liking with all their airs and graces. And, because of Miss Burt's reforms, they changed wards every three months so none of them knew where things were and what to do. She preferred things as they had been in the old days under the former matron, Miss Loag.

Nurse Ingle, writing the morning's notes in the ward daybook, rose slowly and walked purposefully to the ward's kitchen past the freshly washed patients, who were sitting up in their beds.

Her concentration broken, she was annoyed with Emma, especially when she saw the piles of dirty linen left in the corridor. She sighed to herself that the maid would never amount to much.

A place to gather for its warmth in the winter months, the ward scullery was usually stifling in the summer, especially for the nurses in their heavy cotton dresses with long sleeves topped by a starched cotton apron. But today Nurse Ingle welcomed the warmth as she prepared the refreshments.

She put the kettle on the stove while she searched the pantry for the china teacups and saucers, and cook's lemon shortbread biscuits. She found none. Emma had obviously wolfed them down again. She checked her unkind thoughts as they were all by now hungry. It had been a long time since their breakfast of porridge and bread and butter at seven o'clock that morning.

"Nurse Distin, stop what you are doing and run to the kitchen storeroom on the ground floor for me please to get some biscuits," requested Nurse Ingle of her trainee. She thought it would be a kindness to offer Sister Mary and the matron something to eat as she knew they had an important meeting that afternoon to discuss the new Nursing Training Institute.

Nurse Ingle had joined Mary ward in early March, about twelve weeks previously. In the eyes of Emma, she was a loathsome useless newcomer, even though she had had much experience as a nurse. Even worse, Miss Charlotte Distin had joined the ward on the last day of May, so she was a novice in every sense of the word. Besides being a trainee nurse, Miss Distin was also a postulant nun from a local community of the Anglican Sisterhood. Both newcomers were the epitome of the new breed of lady-nurse.

Nurse Distin, who was folding the clean linen for storage in the floor-to-ceiling cupboards in the corridor, stopped her dreary task at once. Her metal-tipped heels clacked on the wooden floors as she hurried out of the ward and down four flights of stairs to the hospital's main kitchens on the ground floor in search of cook's tin of special treats.

"Thank you, Nurse Ingle," Sister Mary said as the tea tray was placed on her desk. "You may finish getting the ward ready for Dr Pavy's round."

"Matron," Sister Mary said, turning to Miss Burt who was sipping her tea, "may I impress upon you that although I fully understand the need for the reforms, we need more nurses.

"Mr Lushington's parsimony has taken its toll and our patients must often wait for a nurse to attend to even their private needs. We simply do not have enough. I shall of course be supportive of you at this afternoon's meeting of the sisters, but I am not alone in thinking we need to slow the changes down and make them more suitable for the doctors."

Her concerns acknowledged, Miss Burt asked if there were other problems. Without hesitation, Sister Mary piped up, "The hot water is slow again. It takes an age to run a bath. We need the works department to look at the plumbing. It is a matter of urgency."

Rising, Miss Burt replied, "Agreed. Thank you for the refreshments. I will bid you good morning, Sister Mary." It was nearly noon and Miss Burt needed to make her way to the nurses' dining hall to lead the grace. "I shall see you in the Sisters' Sitting Room for the finance and planning meeting at one o'clock sharp." With that, Miss Burt took her leave and hurried down the stairs to the ground floor, past the hospital's main kitchen, and entered the large dining hall.

This was a dingy regimented place. Long trestle tables and benches ran the length of the room. There were windows but they were high up and north facing so only let a little light in. They were especially useless on a day like today. The dining tables were covered in civilising white tablecloths which only partly deadened the noisy clatter of the plates and cutlery as they were laid for dinner.

The food was served from the central table by the maids, who then sat separately at their own table to eat. The lady-nurses and the maids did not mix.

As Miss Burt entered the hall, the clattering and noisy chatter stopped, and the nurses and maids stood to attention.

Taking her place at the lectern before the assembled women, Miss Burt led the preprandial prayer. On the finishing *amen*, she rang the hand bell to signal that all might be seated, and dinner served. It was the usual fare of grey stew of mutton and potatoes, and a hunk of bread. Hearty, nourishing food designed to sustain the women until their teatime.

FIVE

At half past midday, Miss Burt left the nurses' dining room and walked into the Park. She smiled at the tranquil scene before her of nurses, wrapped in their heavy uniform cloaks, sitting in the open air with their blanketed patients, despite the chill wind. She sensed a familiar musky fragrance of roses in full bloom as she arrived once again at the colonnade. The shouting rabble by now long gone, she was able to view the pretty gardens of the inner courtyards that flanked the passageway.

Taking care not to trip on the uneven flagstones, she made her way to the southern stairwell, then climbed to the upper corridor above the colonnade to the Sisters' Sitting Room. An airless place, it was certainly not one favourable to this afternoon's difficult discussion, so she instructed Miss Jones to open the windows.

"Good afternoon, Matron. Here are your papers for the meeting." Miss Jones curtseyed and offered Miss Burt the carefully prepared bundle.

As one o'clock approached, the sisters assembled in their sitting room. They fell broadly into two camps: those who did not support the reforms, and those who embraced them as both necessary and desirable.

The wicker chairs, with their generous padding and seat cushions, were arranged advantageously for the light by the windows. They were taken by those quick enough to bag them. The rest sat on the less comfortable balloon-back library chairs arranged in front of the glass-fronted bookcases. Blasts of fresh cold air added to the already chilled atmosphere in the room.

Miss Burt sat uncomfortably at the central table with the committee papers spread out in front of her. Miss Jones sat at the writing bureau to the matron's side with pens, ink and paper.

If only Miss Lonsdale was still here, thought Miss Burt. She was the best scribe I have had, with excellent grammar and such penmanship. The matron signalled to Miss Jones to ring the desk bell. The sisters, who were engaged in their usual social chit chat, fell silent.

"We have much to consider this afternoon and I would like to thank you for giving the time, especially Mrs Keogh." Miss Burt nodded to the Night Sister, who had risen from her bed early to attend.

"We have three items for consideration," continued the matron. "The financial position; the new nurses' training scheme; and the progress of the reforms."

The shuffling of chairs began, as if to signal a level of anxiety that disgruntlement was about to be aired. Everyone had either seen or heard the earlier commotion downstairs in the colonnade, and they all had their views about whether Miss Burt could remain in her post any longer. Miss Burt, with the accounts to March 25 before her, opened the discussion on staff costs.

"We have nineteen sisters, fifty-two nurses and nineteen probationers to pay for. We have the housekeeper and her twenty-two ward maids and assistants. In addition, we have the dormitory sister and outpatient staff, plus the linen and laundry staff, and then the kitchen and cleaning staff. We have been asked to spend less by Mr Lushington, so I ask you, where can we make the necessary savings?"

There was a sepulchral silence.

Understanding their reluctance to make any offering, Miss Burt considered the food and beverages budget.

"We could make savings in our purchases from the cheesemonger and the butcher, and what about the brewery and the baker?" Silence. Then the remonstrations began.

Sister Mary was first to speak. "Matron, we cannot find any further savings in the food and drink allowance. We have already pared back on those patients receiving the full diet allowance of meat and bread. Most patients now receive only the reduced middle or low diet allocation. Our doctors expect decent nourishment for their patients so they might recover more quickly and be sent home as soon as possible."

Mindful of not expending too much energy on this agenda item, Miss Burt decided to close the discussion.

"Thank you," she said. "I shall talk to the Chief Dispenser about his purchases, which look altogether too extravagant. And I will question the amount of sherry, port, brandy, gin and whisky, and claret and wine, that Mr Lushington has authorised in this past year, given only porter and beer are served to our patients."

The silence was broken by the shuffling of chairs as the sisters made ready for the next item.

"Now let us turn our attention to the new training curriculum and the character of Guy's Nursing Training Institute," opened Miss Burt. "The Governors desire our views. We are late in the day for our consideration, but we have the experiences of others around us to draw upon."

It was uncomfortably cold in the room as Miss Jones served the sisters their cups of tea, using the best china set, as they listened to their matron.

"There is the long-established training scheme of over thirty years offered by the Anglican Sisterhood of St John's House. It has served both King's College and Charing Cross hospitals up in the Strand very well. Then there is Miss Nightingale's Training Institute at St Thomas's hospital which has trained and graduated many nurses over the last twenty years under its Principal, Mrs Sarah Wardroper. And of course, we might look to the new Institute at St Bartholomew's under Miss Maria Machin. Sisters, I welcome your views." Miss Burt's introduction of this trickiest of issues was met with stony silence.

Shuffling and coughing broke the hush and, much to the relief of all, Mrs Keogh was first to respond.

"Miss Burt, thank you for inviting our comments. I speak as a nurse of over twenty-five years' experience here at Guy's and I have seen and heard much of these reforms during that time. I think it is well known that Miss

Nightingale's ideas for nursing were drawn from both the Catholic and Protestant traditions.

"I believe she was heavily influenced by her time in Paris with the Sisters of Charity at the Maison de la Providence, and by Pastor Theodor Fliedner at the Kaiserswerth hospital in Germany. Wasn't she a resident for nearly a year there?" she asked, playing to the crowd, already knowing the answer.

"Being a well-educated lady," she said with confidence, "Miss Nightingale was able to achieve much through her own talents and connections, and, of course, through her reputation gained at Scutari hospital in the Crimea. Doors were opened for her by her friend Sir Sidney Herbert at the War Office. She was well connected, alright."

Encouraged by the positive nods from her fellow sisters, Mrs Keogh leaned forward. She stared directly at the matron and asked, "So what is to be the foundation of our Institute, Catholicism or Protestantism?"

Her allies observed the boldness of the Night Sister's confrontation in silence, while some of her detractors gulped at Mrs Keogh's rudeness to the matron.

"I may not be a nurse formally trained to your scientific ideals but in my time on the wards, I have seen many such changes and much unhappiness amongst both doctors and nurses as a result. And we all know Dr Habershon is vexed about repeating here at Guy's the misfortunes that have occurred at King's with the Sisterhood in charge.

"I've heard that Professor Lister himself has had a dispute with them over one of his patients, a boy with an urgent case of osteomyelitis of the femur. The nurses had to check with the Mother Superior before they would proceed with the Professor's instructions.

"Dr Habershon has strong views about the involvement of the Sisterhood. He dislikes intensely these leanings to the church of Rome. I fear it could become quite toxic here if we embrace their ways."

There were gasps as the Night Sister came right out with what everyone was thinking. Miss Jones, who leant towards the traditions of Rome herself, winced.

Miss Burt stiffened her back. "I trained at King's under the Sisters of St John. This training Sisterhood was set up thirty years ago by one of King's top Professors, Dr Robert Bentley Todd. The difficulties of the Sisterhood at that institution in recent times are not because of their nursing care standards or lack of education. As one of the best and long-standing Anglican Sisterhoods of Nursing, their devotion to their work is unquestionable. I believe some of the doctors at King's, including Professor Lister, do not care for their views being challenged by nurses."

"But that is precisely what will happen here," said Sister Mary. "You just have to look at the trouble Miss Machin has had this past year at St Bartholomew's. She trained at St Thomas's and I believe she was a favourite of Miss Nightingale. Even so, she has struggled gravely since she replaced the old matron, Mrs Drake. And the sisters do not care for her new institution or reforms, even though Miss Nightingale herself supports her.

"I believe Miss Machin has been made quite ill with it all. I even heard she may be taking an extended holiday to recover from her exhaustion."

The concern in the room was palpable when Sister Mary added for good measure, "My friend who works there told me that the Chief Dispenser refers to Miss Machin as 'an ornament to Charterhouse Square'. What do you think of that?"

The sisters' upset was compounded by Mrs Keogh adding, "I know Mrs Wardroper, the excellent matron at St Thomas's, and she has had to take great care to keep the Sisterhoods at bay. And that Dr Seymour Sharkey nips at her heels constantly about nurses getting above their station. I am afraid to say that anything like the Sisterhood will have no happy future here."

Miss Burt let the dust settle, whilst Miss Jones kept her eyes focused on her paper, dabbing her pen furiously in the ink pot trying not to spill any of it.

After the painful silence, the matron, sitting bolt upright, said with determination, "Thank you for your comments. May I remind you that Mrs Elizabeth Fry, the great social reformer, set up the Quaker Nurses' Training Institute over thirty years ago and she sent her trainees here to Guy's for their ward experience. We are already a nurses' training hospital."

Cries of protest ensued from Sisters Lydia, Dorcas and Naaman, colleagues of Miss Jones from the surgical wards, as they expressed their fears that the troubles visited on King's and St Bartholomew's had already arrived at Guy's. They pointed to the fracas that very morning.

Miss Burt continued, "Dr Steele, on his arrival at Guy's, found the nurses to be indolent illiterate drunks who were up to no good, including thieving. He has demanded many changes to address the perpetual problems of drunkenness, indiscipline and insubordination among the nurses and much progress has been made. But there is more to do. There will be difficulties as we establish Guy's Nursing Training Institute, but I have my experience in doing the same at Leicester Infirmary to call upon.

"I am determined to build on Dr Steele's work and introduce a formal training scheme for our probationer lady-nurses. We will provide board and residence on site, and the nurses in training will continue to change wards every three months to gain a good spread of experience. Miss Jones and I, with your help, will nurture their learning."

Sister Mary spoke on behalf of her more reluctant colleagues. "Miss Burt, I implore you to think again. This is not suitable for our doctors, and as for Dr Habershon and his like-minded colleagues, they will have none of it, especially after the Board's Inquiry into the reforms. And then there is that unfortunate business in the spring with Miss Lonsdale..."

It was all to no avail as Miss Burt closed the discussion and moved on to hearing about their progress with the reforms. As the afternoon wore on, the gloom in the room became unbearable. The sisters were increasingly irritable as they sat there in their heavy cotton dress uniforms, starched aprons and lace caps, and stiff collar and cuffs, fretting about what further calamity might befall them when Miss Burt's plans became known.

Some rolled their eyes at the prospect of more misery and more trouble. Others thought about the effect of more resignations and sackings, while the older ones thought about the undignified newspaper stories and satirical jokes about nursing at Guy's that would follow.

Miss Jones could hardly keep up as the sisters itemised their complaints. Miss Burt listened intently, but it made no difference. Her mind was made up. Her course was set. Guy's would have its Nursing Training Institute fashioned in the mould of the Sisterhood of St John, which itself was modelled on the Kaiserswerth and its Protestant Deaconesses.

The mantel clock chimed four o'clock. That had been a laboured unhappy three hours, thought Miss Jones as she finished writing. The sisters, having been thanked, were permitted to return to their ward duties while Miss Burt and Miss Jones discussed the points of emphasis to be shown in the meeting notes.

Their deliberations were interrupted by Mr Mark Shattock, the Clerk to the Board of Governors.

"Miss Burt," he said, "following this morning's demonstration, the Governors have met with Mr Lushington and Dr Steele for an urgent discussion on the state of the reforms and the doctors' growing discontent with your conduct."

Miss Burt listened without comment as he continued, "You are requested to attend the Board of Governors to give an account of the reforms' progress. You are expected at the Court of Committees at five o'clock." With that, Mr Shattock took his leave of the matron and her assistant.

Another meeting, sighed Miss Burt. When will I have peace? She sipped her cup of tea and reflected on the sisters' concerns with Miss Jones.

"I should like you to write to the sisters on my behalf," she requested of her assistant before leaving. "Please remind the sisters of the qualifications expected of them and the nurses. They are required to be sober, honest, truthful, trustworthy, punctual, quiet and orderly, clean and neat. Also, please reiterate that Guy's recognises science as its authority in developing nursing care."

Exhausted, she left the Sitting Room and went down to the ground floor where once again she recognised that familiar sweet floral fragrance. Ah yes, she said to herself, Rosa Rugosa. Its musky perfume filled the Park and the colonnade in the late afternoon. Even though she was now forty years old, the scent brought back happy memories of her childhood spent with her grandparents in deepest Devonshire where the intensely crimson rose grows wild in the hedgerows.

Enlivened by the memory, she picked up her skirt and walked through the colonnade to the front quad to face Mr Guy's stony gaze once more.

Six

The Governors met in the grand salon known as the Court Room on the first floor of Treasurer's House. This opulent building was part of Mr Guy's legacy, and it formed the entire east wing of the front quad, facing Matron's House and the hospital's chapel.

Treasurer's House was the centre of Guy's administration. To the left of the main entrance hall was Mr Lushington's living quarters, and to its right were the offices of the Clerk to the Governors and Guy's Counting House. It was here that the hospital's accountants managed the treasury and legacy functions, including its many investments in Guy's farming estates in Lincolnshire, Herefordshire, and Essex.

Entering the elegant and spacious panelled entrance hall, Miss Burt was greeted by Mr Shattock, who bowed respectfully and asked her to wait in the hall until she was called. She watched him return to the first floor and disappear into the upper gallery.

She couldn't help but admire the stairs, which had been beautifully designed and built with hand-turned intricately patterned spindles, offset by simply decorated solid square newel posts. The wide highly planed and varnished bannisters were reminiscent of those found in London's most fashionable houses.

The airy stairwell was decorated with portraits of Guy's great men, which spoke of their important contributions to medicine and the hospital's glorious history. Looking up to the lavishly decorated stucco ceiling with its carefully notched coving, Miss Burt felt a pang of self-doubt.

Her level of anxiety increased as she thought about the President. She was painfully aware that Viscount Cardwell had been unwell, and he was greatly distressed by the ongoing dispute. It was rumoured that he had resigned. As he had been an important supporter of her reforms, she, and Mr Lushington and Dr Steele, would feel his loss.

The recent turbulent political situation would no doubt create further calls on his time. Mr Disraeli had just lost the general election and had resigned on April 18 when the Queen had invited his successor, Mr Gladstone, to form a new government, which he did on April 28. It had been seven weeks since these changes and the Board was still reeling from the instability caused.

Viscount Cardwell had been a senior minister in Gladstone's first administration. He had served as the Secretary of State at the War Office, where he had reformed the army with some success. Consequently, he knew much about effecting major change to traditional customs and practices in British institutions, and was sympathetic to the nursing reforms at Guy's.

It was rumoured that Mr Henry Hucks Gibbs, the former Governor of the Bank of England, would take over from the ailing President.

At five o'clock, Mr Shattock emerged from the Court Room and, fleet of foot, returned to the ground floor to escort Miss Burt to the salon.

"The Governors wish to receive your views on this morning's demonstration. And there is the matter of Dr Habershon's letter and his request for your resignation to consider."

A pause on the half-landing allowed Miss Burt to catch her breath while he continued, "I understand Mr Lushington would like to raise the issue of the Board's response to Dr Steele's inquiry report into the medical staff's complaints about the reforms and your conduct in them."

As they approached the Court Room, Mr Shattock stepped forward to open the heavy door. Inside the salon, the gentlemen of the Court stood to attention and bowed politely. Mr Shattock showed Miss Burt to a chair which had been placed before the Governors, who were seated on the long side of a classic large-scale Victorian dining table. Meetings of the Court were always very formal as many of the Governors were senior political, banking, and mercantile men.

While they perused their papers, which had been set out for them by Mr Shattock, Miss Burt admired the loving care and attention to detail that had been shown by the artists and specialist tradesmen who had been employed twenty years earlier to redecorate the salon. The resulting well-appointed reception room would grace any palace.

The intricately stuccoed high ceiling with its central oval Italianate painting, and gilt inlaid panels, and the Adam fireplace with marble pillars to its sides, decorated with a pair of ornate vases, gave the impression of great wealth.

The salon's large west-facing windows overlooked the front quad and brought much light when the sun was shining. But today the promised rain had arrived and it was now so dark, a thunderstorm must be coming.

Sipping the lemon water Mr Shattock had put out for her, Miss Burt waited for the questioning to start. As the tall clock in the corner struck quarter past five o'clock, she felt perilously alone as Mr Lushington, who sat to her left, made his notes, and Dr Steele, who sat to her right, read his papers.

"Good afternoon, Matron," welcomed Mr Hucks Gibbs. "I shall take the President's role for today's meeting as Viscount Cardwell is unwell." With this opening statement, Miss Burt felt a blow as she understood that the rumours about the Viscount's resignation had substance.

Miss Burt knew that the new man was a devout High Church Anglican and that he was a supporter of the Anglican Sisterhood based in Albany Street, near Regent's Park in north London. Despite these indications, she needed to hear him say that he supported her and the reforms.

"Matron Burt, we shall begin with this morning's demonstration. Our view, formed from Mr Lushington's and Dr Steele's earlier reports, is that this action cannot be allowed to pass without comment. Indeed, we have heard that two junior doctors who were present have since written to the *Times* in support of the demonstrators. I believe the letter will be published tomorrow. What is your view?"

"Sir, I am, like you, aghast at such shameful conduct. I believe we should show, as a united governing and administrative body, that such behaviour is intolerable and cannot go unpunished." She looked to Mr Lushington and Dr Steele for support, and they duly nodded in agreement.

To her relief, Mr Hucks Gibbs directed that Mr Shattock record the discussion's conclusions: that Mr Lushington would write to the offending gentleman forthwith suspending them from their duties, and that he, as President, would sign a letter to the *Times* on behalf of the Governors setting out the Board's views that this offensive behaviour would not be tolerated.

He directed that Mr Lushington and Dr Steele would see to it that the Dean of the Medical School, Dr Taylor, was fully informed of the Board's displeasure at the conduct of his students.

"Turning to the next matter," he continued, "we have it on good authority that Dr Habershon will present a letter to the Board, on behalf of Guy's medical staff, setting out their concerns once again about the reforms and their lack of confidence in you, Miss Burt. I believe they will call for your resignation once more. My understanding is," he peered at his notes, "the medical staff, having been shown the draft of Dr Steele's inquiry report into the reforms, are not happy with its conclusions. What have you to say in this matter?"

It was another heart-sinking moment for the matron.

The already unhappy atmosphere at Guy's had become poisonous in early March when Dr Habershon and the medical staff had protested vehemently to the Board about the reforms, and Miss Burt's fitness to be matron of their prestigious London teaching hospital. They were angry about her lack of consultation with them over the detail of her reforms, and felt she had usurped their authority ever since she had taken up her post.

They had called for her immediate resignation or removal by the Board. To defuse the situation, the ailing Viscount Cardwell had requested an inquiry into the facts. It was led by Lord Cottesloe on behalf of the Board. Mr Lushington, who would normally have handled the situation himself, felt he should step aside because he too had been criticised by the doctors, and was therefore an interested party.

Dr Steele had drafted the report after three long days in March when the inquiry subcommittee had heard much evidence from the aggrieved medical staff. The inquiry's view, after much deliberation, was that Miss Burt and Mr Lushington should be exonerated from the charges but, as a gesture of goodwill to appease the angry doctors, the medical staff might be offered more involvement in the affairs of the hospital. Specifically, the inquiry proposed representation on the hospital's taking-in committee which determined Guy's admission policy.

Mr Hucks Gibbs informed Miss Burt that Dr Steele had been invited to present his report to the Board on the following Wednesday, June 23, at a specially convened meeting. The medical staff, he warned, were very unlikely to be satisfied with this outcome.

Miss Burt thought carefully about her reply. She needed to counter the doctors' accusations while pointing to Dr Habershon's unreasonable position concerning her and the reforms.

This would have been quite straightforward, were it not for an embarrassing dispute concerning one of her best lady-nurses, Miss Lonsdale. Everyone had regretted what had happened over the previous ten weeks, especially as the nasty spat between Miss Lonsdale and Dr Habershon had drawn in several other senior doctors not only from Guy's, but from further afield, including the Queen's physician, Sir William Gull.

Unfortunately, their row had been conducted in the public press for all to see. It had probably contributed greatly to Viscount Cardwell's resignation.

Proceeding with care, Miss Burt apologised, as she had done previously, for Miss Lonsdale's conduct. She reassured the Board that Miss Lonsdale had now completed her three-month probationary training and had returned to her Midlands home to the care of her father, the canon at Lichfield Cathedral.

"Her fault, if one can describe her conduct so, was to express rather too forcefully, and undiplomatically, her enthusiastic support for our nursing reforms. You must bear in mind that she is a devoted follower of Miss Nightingale and her acolyte, Sister Dora.

"Sister Dora," Miss Burt explained, "was the lady-nurse who built up a great following in Walsall where she and her fellow sisters had looked after the poor with much Christian devotion. I believe Miss Lonsdale is infatuated with Sister Dora's work, judging by her recently published biography of the woman's life."

There followed an uncomfortable silence as the Governors and Mr Hucks Gibbs considered whether Miss Lonsdale's recent departure would be sufficient to calm the febrile situation. Miss Burt wondered if Mr Lushington's support was on the wane as he sat there in silence. He was the very essence of a high-born gentleman and she needed his approval.

"Sir, if I may speak," asked Mr Lushington after some time, "Miss Burt's reforms are born of necessity despite much effort over the last twenty-five years by Dr Steele.

"We have achieved much," he continued, "but there is more to do. Miss Burt was carefully selected for the task. Indeed, I visited her at her previous establishment, Leicester Infirmary, to observe her work directly and I was impressed by her achievements."

No stranger to hostility in all its forms, he would not be diverted from his course by a few rebellious doctors.

She smiled as she recalled that he had been mentioned in dispatches during the Uprising in India when on January 14, 1858, he had been wounded in an engagement with Kohli rebels near Koochrae. Little wonder Viscount Cardwell and the Governors were happy to leave the reform details to him.

"Many of our sister hospitals across London are experiencing similar tensions, so we are not alone in attracting vile criticism from doctors who either have misunderstood the reforms, or who seek to resist their progression in favour of their own interests. I believe it is the latter here at Guy's and it is unworthy.

"Gentlemen," he continued, "I believe we can achieve our aspirations of improving the quality of our nurses and the care of our patients through the establishment of a Nursing Training Institute. I implore you to continue your support for the reforms and for Miss Burt."

Relieved but still under cross-examination, Miss Burt was asked about recent damaging press reports concerning up to forty nurses who, having been sacked or having resigned because of the reforms, were now criticising nursing care standards at Guy's. The Governors were sensitive to the bad publicity and the constant stream of derogatory letters that were featured not only in the *Times* but also in the satirical magazines.

They were particularly worried as the *Times* was one of the most important daily newspapers of the period and much of its news was syndicated widely, including to the regional and international newspapers, and the many weekly and monthly publications that fed a gossip-hungry public. The medical press too was syndicated widely, with the *British Medical Journal* and the *Lancet* read across the Empire. Their editorials about Guy's nursing dispute, and the doctors' letters and feature articles, were wholly supportive of the doctors' views.

"There is no doubt that there is a wave of unhappiness running through Guy's arising from the reforms. It must be accepted if we are to achieve our goals. I can reassure you that we are past the worst of it now," declared Miss Burt.

Mr Lushington addressed the Board. "I ask you to allow me to impress upon the medical staff the consequences for them personally if they continue to write to the *Times* and the medical press about internal affairs, even to the extent that I may call for resignations." The Board agreed to his request.

"And what of the damage caused by Miss Lonsdale's unwise actions?" inquired Mr Hucks Gibbs of the Treasurer.

"Miss Lonsdale is of a class and level of education familiar to most of you who read the papers and see what is happening in our country today. There is a growing movement of such women who are increasingly confident of their position, and they can articulate ideas about their potential role and involvement in society that are simply not tolerable to most, even in these modern times."

The gentlemen of the Court nodded to each other, smiling in agreement.

"Indeed," he continued, "my own dear sisters lean to this agitation from time to time. We must try to understand this force and even learn to work with it if required. As for Miss Lonsdale, she is no longer with us, but we must deal with the consequences of her actions."

"I hope you are correct, Mr Lushington." With that, Mr Hucks Gibbs closed the meeting. It was well after half past six and the gentlemen needed to retire to prepare for their evening to be spent dining and carousing in the West End clubs of Pall Mall.

SEVEN

Miss Burt entered the hallway and leant against the cloak stand to take off her shoes, which were pinching after such a long day. The marble floor offered some relief as she pressed her swollen stockinged feet into the tiles to enjoy their soothing cooling effect.

Miss Jones smiled at the exhausted matron. "I asked cook to bring over some cold beef, bread and cheese. It's laid out in your sitting room, and I've left the draft notes from this afternoon's meeting on your desk. And I thought you might welcome a glass of porter even though it is quite chilly this evening. Please ring the bell when you are ready for me to discuss the notes, I shall be next door." Miss Jones curtseyed and left the matron to draw breath.

Her sitting room was Miss Burt's sanctuary, a private place for reflection on the day's events, and a place for contemplation on what to do next. When she had arrived the previous November, she had asked Mr Beadle, the porter, to move the desk into the bay under the large west-facing windows so she could look onto the secluded garden at the rear of the house.

Mr Beadle had counselled against this as it was a cold spot because of the ill-fitting draughty windows, even when the heavy curtains were closed. And so it was on this summer evening. Miss Jones had left the drapes open in the hope that Miss Burt's room would be brightened and warmed by the evening's meagre sunlight, but the room felt cold.

Miss Burt turned up the desk lamp as she tried to read Miss Jones's notes in the gloom, wrapping herself in the woollen shawl that Miss Jones had laid out for her.

She found it difficult to concentrate as she gazed at the vibrant plants in their fancy china pots on her windowsill. Her eyes wandered to the garden beyond, where her favourite Rosa shrubs were in full bloom. She closed her eyes as she remembered that musky perfume and thought of happier times.

"Are you ready for me, Miss Burt?" inquired Miss Jones a while later.

Her reverie broken, Miss Burt invited Miss Jones to sit beside her. "Miss Jones," the matron asked of her assistant, "you trained at Charing Cross hospital under the Sisterhood of St John's, and you were until recently a staff nurse at St Bartholomew's under Miss Machin, so you have seen at first-hand the disgruntlement that has arisen. What is it that doctors and nurses fear so greatly? What is the source of their discontent?"

Miss Jones, an experienced nurse now in early middle

age, fully understood the tensions swirling around Guy's, and the other London hospitals. She had seen it all before as the old disreputable 'nurses' were replaced with women trained in the new 'scientific' nursing practices.

"Matron, there are so many changes in our society and much discontent generally. I believe the heart of these disputes is because of the different beliefs about what nursing and its authority should be and how our dear church should guide us in these matters."

Miss Burt nodded in agreement and pressed her assistant to explain further.

"When I was just thirty years old," she confided, "I was attracted to, and joined, the Sisterhood of the Society of St Margaret's at Haggerston, up in Hackney. I wanted to be part of that community and to serve the Lord by looking after the poor in those terrible north London slums. I followed the teachings of St Margaret's devout founder, Dr John Neale."

"I recall," Miss Burt responded, "that there was terrible trouble at Haggerston at about that time, the late 1860s? Were you there?"

"I was," replied Miss Jones. "After Dr Neale died, the chaplain and mother superior, and several nuns and postulants, became so enthralled with Catholic ways that they all converted to the church of Rome. It was a great scandal that threatened to bring down the Sisterhood."

"What was your position in this fracas?" queried Miss Burt.

"I was one of those that did not want to convert to Rome. And we suffered greatly until the celebrated Mother

Kate rescued us when she became the new superior. She rebuilt the Haggerston community for the Anglican church. God bless her soul."

Although it had been important to her ten years ago, Miss Jones was now careful to distance herself from the faded Oxford Movement which sought to join the Anglican and Catholic churches. "I studied the writings of those Oxford scholars and tried to understand their doctrinal arguments, but I found it a struggle. That's when I decided to go to Charing Cross hospital in the Strand to train as a nurse under the Sisters of St John's."

Miss Burt reflected on the fault lines in the present dispute; they ran along the wider different religious affiliations. The Anglican church had fractured into many groups over the century and the different memberships were all now represented at Guy's. The High Church wing, including some suspected Oxford Movement sympathisers, existed in an uneasy working relationship with the strongly anti-Catholic Low- or Broad-Church movements, including a faction of zealous Dissenters. These Evangelicals and Nonconformists rejected the Established Church as being too 'popish'.

Miss Jones suggested that the tensions in reforming nursing across London were mainly to do with the suspicion that leanings to Rome were seeping into everyday life in hospitals through the Sisterhoods.

"Remember, some of our doctors are fervent Evangelicals and Nonconformists, and they won't tolerate any hint of Rome at Guy's. Soon after I joined the hospital in the early spring, Dr Habershon wrote to the administrator about the new lady-nurses' uniform being far too nun-like. He objected in the strongest terms, and I think he views me with suspicion."

"Thank you, Miss Jones, that is a very helpful explanation," replied Miss Burt. "It is such a boiling pot of emotions, but the work of the Sisterhoods is in our blood right from the early days of Mrs Fry's Quaker Training School and Miss Nightingale's secular copy of it at St Thomas's. Indeed, we have trained under the Sisterhoods, and they are a force for good. We will challenge their views."

Miss Burt smiled at Miss Jones and supped some porter. "There is much to ponder following today's meeting with the sisters. I need to think about Dr Habershon's letter to the Governors calling for my removal. Would you be so kind as to attend tomorrow morning when I have slept on these issues, and we can finish the notes when we are refreshed."

At the request, Miss Jones stood and curtseyed as she left the room.

Alone at last, Miss Burt tried to concentrate. The porter was bitter even though it was the nurses' watered-down variety, but it was refreshing as she gazed out on the garden and watched the Rosa shedding its petals in the blasting wind.

The mantel clock chimed eight o'clock. It was now quite dark as the storm clouds gathered, creating a deep gloom about the place. The papers on her desk begged for her attention but she was too tired, and too worried. The foundation beliefs of Guy's Nursing Training Institution bothered her.

Her training as a lady-nurse at Kings College hospital in 1871 under the Sisterhood of St John's, and her subsequent work as a nurse and matron at Charing Cross hospital under the same order, had been thorough and fulfilling, and she wanted the same for Guy's. But she was painfully aware of the irritation this would cause to some of the medical staff, especially the Nonconformists and their leader, Dr Habershon.

Miss Jones had implored her to be careful to emphasise the secular nature of training at Guy's while incorporating the best features of the Sisterhoods. She also warned about Miss Machin's mistake at St Bartholomew's where the unfortunate young matron had assumed the support of the administrator meant that the doctors and nurses supported her reforms too. They did not.

Poor Miss Machin, her inexperience had been on show for all to see. She was only twenty-four years old. No wonder she was so ill with it all.

Settling into her wingchair and resting her sore feet on the footstool, Miss Burt appreciated the warmth of her shawl around her shoulders. Drifting in and out of a porter-induced sleep, she remembered happier days in Leicester, and her arrival at Guy's the previous November. It had been cold and wet, and the thick foggy air was laden with sulphur from all the coal fires and factory furnaces, but Christmas 1879 was the last of the decade, so the celebrations were exuberant.

The wards had been decorated for the celebrations, and gifts of fruits and roasted nuts were given to the patients and their families as they listened to the choristers from St

Saviour's, the Anglican church close by on the river at London Bridge. Everyone, including the patients, had sung their hearts out on familiar carols. She recalled the delightful hospital tradition of the senior doctors carving the meat on each ward to give to the patients for their Christmas dinner. The sisters had the job of serving cook's stodgy pudding and some port to follow as a treat. It had been such a joyous time to join Guy's and Miss Burt had had high hopes for her reforming work.

Everyone was glad to see the end of the 1870s. It had been a miserable time with constant bad weather, failed harvests and food shortages. She remembered the midnight New Year's Eve party in the front quad to welcome in the new decade.

Many of the same boisterous medical students she had seen earlier in the day were there for the celebrations. Oblivious to the cold, they ran around the courtyard yelling and whooping with their flaming torches held high, shedding welcome light on the party as they pretended to be link-lighters. These students were no street urchins like the real link-lighters, but scholars from well-to-do families who were bright and connected enough to study at Guy's.

They clambered around and jostled each other, as they did at this morning's demonstration, while some climbed the founder's statue and, fuelled by the occasion and drink, placed a dunce's cap on Mr Guy's head in the manner of the local schools when they punish naughty children.

Yes, there had been great hopes for the new decade and Miss Burt, like most people, had assumed that Mr Disraeli would carry on with his reforms for the country and the

Empire. The shock of the size of his defeat in March's general election, and his resignation in April, were still the talk of the town, even now in mid-June.

But Mr Gladstone had much on his plate, including dealing with the perennial question of what to do about Ireland. The agitation for home rule and the violence that accompanied it was becoming more intense. This, and the re-establishment of the Catholic Church's hierarchy in 1850, created an enduring anti-Catholic feeling which was as strong as ever as the new decade dawned.

Miss Burt was alive to this sensitivity, and knew she had to tread with care when presenting her reforms. Although they were to be modelled on the Sisterhoods, the changes could not bear any whiff of Rome. They had to be secular. Miss Nightingale had achieved this at St Thomas's, and Miss Burt was determined she would do likewise at Guy's.

Thinking about what Miss Jones had said about the nurses' new uniform, Miss Burt concluded that it could not resemble a nun's habit. And, following a sensational church trial of Sister Priscillla Sellon in Devonport for wearing a rosary and a crucifix, no such adornment could be permitted at Guy's.

Miss Burt's thoughts were interrupted by the clanging of an urgently rung bell coming from the front quad.

"Lock. Lock. Lock."

It was the night watchmen, Mr Bryers and Mr Payne, warning all who could hear that the hospital gates would be locked in half an hour at nine o'clock. This evening ritual was preceded by the men lighting the quad's gas lamps to give an eerie dull yellow glow in the miserable gloom of this summer evening.

Was it that time already? She liked to accompany the watchmen on their lock-up rounds, so she gulped down the last of her supper and stepped into her shoes to get her tired feet ready for the last walk of the day. She searched for her thick serge matron's cloak to cover her shawl and out she went into the front quad once more.

EIGHT

Miss Burt hurried to join the night watchmen at the north gate on St Thomas's Street. A clashing and scraping as metal slammed on metal reverberated across the front quad.

"Good evening, Matron," smiled Mr Payne, peering at her through the dim yellow haze of the gaslights now shedding faint pools of light across the front quad. Miss Burt pulled her cloak around her shoulders to shield her from the cold wind and irritating fine drizzle.

"It's going to get a lot worse tonight," said Mr Payne. "I reckon we're in for a right tipping. The roses are going to love it. What do you say, Mr Bryers?"

"They'll get a good soaking alright," replied his fellow watchman. "There'll be a nasty stink off those streets in a minute when the rain soaks in. At least the dust and filth will be dampened down for a few hours."

With the men's chatter and mirth in the background, Miss Burt peered through the railings to the old St Thomas's hospital across the road and then over to the Borough and its market to the west. She caught the stench of the street that filled the night air. The smell got everywhere, including into her quarters in Matron's House which stood alongside St Thomas's Street.

And the noise! Just when the cacophony of the market traders calling for customers and yelling instructions at their delivery men, and the constant hubbub of the traffic trying to cross London Bridge was dying down, Southwark's nightlife started up and it continued into the small hours.

The constant storms in the 1870s had ruined many farmers, who then laid off their farmhands, leaving destitute families with no choice but to try for better luck elsewhere. They migrated to the towns to find work and these displaced people swelled the numbers in the cities rapidly. Miss Burt had seen the effects in Leicester, but nothing had prepared her for the sheer scale and tumult of this mass migration to London and the destitution it exacerbated.

Southwark was one of London's poorest neighbourhoods. People crowded into its cheap tenements and slum housing and eked out a meagre living in the local markets, chop houses and pubs if they were lucky. Overcrowding and poverty were rife on her doorstep.

Thieving and prostitution were daily necessities for many living in the 'stews', a disreputable area to the west of Guy's. A place of bawdy entertainment for hundreds of years, there were dog-fighting pits, theatres and music halls, but for most it was an evening of drinking and drunkenness in the many local pubs and fetid side streets.

The Borough was the main north—south turnpike where

travellers and traders from across the south coast met the local traffic as they all tried to get into the City across London Bridge. It was a busy and fraught bottleneck as coaches and their teams of horses mixed with the constant flow of heaving delivery wagons, all pushing and shoving to get across the bridge. London's population had swelled so rapidly that by the late 1870s there were simply not enough river crossings.

Instead there were constant queues as the northbound struggled across the bridge, where they met the southbound. Individuals with their bags and traders with their wares fought against each other and the carriages and horses to make progress through the crowds. The sheer number of people milling about on the streets and spilling into the roads was a constant hazard. And when the steamboat passengers disembarked at St Saviour's church, it was a particularly dangerous crush. The injured ended up in Guy's emergency wards where the surgeons were kept busy day and night.

People walked through rubbish-filled streets, dodging open sewers. They risked contagion in this tightly packed urban area and the sulphurous smoke belching out from the local printworks and factories created a thick fog which made people cough and wheeze. They too ended up in Guy's, where the physicians' work was never-ending.

And then there were the many tanneries and their stink of rotted animals in Bermondsey to the east which added to the depressing lot of those who lived and worked in the district of Southwark. By the end of the day, the smell, mixed with the sickly whiff of hops from the local breweries and the acrid stench of animal and human waste, formed a disgusting reek. Miss Burt had struggled to get used to this smelly fug, which made her eyes water.

"Ready for the Maze Pond, Matron?" asked Mr Payne as he and Mr Bryers had finished their work at the north gate and were ready to move on to lock the east gate. "I bet the smoke filth will be out tonight. What do you think, Mr Bryers?"

"No doubt about it," his chuckling companion replied. "They seem to patrol hereabouts a lot more these days. Obviously nothing better to do."

Miss Burt smiled at the thought of the Inspector of Nuisances and his officers being referred to as the 'smoke filth'. The Inspectorate had been set up in the 1850s to limit the pollution in the overcrowded city. They had had some success as the burning of cheap sea coal picked from the north east's beaches had been banned in favour of the less smoky, but more expensive, mined coal. But it all meant nothing to the locals, who carried on burning the cheap stuff.

Snuffling, Mr Bryers led the way with his lantern to the east gate. They crossed the familiar front quad, past Mr Guy's stony gaze, and walked through the colonnade to Hunt's House and the Park. The rain was steady now as they made the short walk to the old cattle drovers' road known as Great Maze Pond. In years gone by, the herdsmen from the farms to the south of London in Kent and Surrey rested and watered their cattle at the local ponds before taking them over the bridge to Smithfield meat market on the north bank near St Bartholomew's.

As the men started to close the east gate, Miss Burt looked on the old burying ground of the former St Thomas's hospital and its adjoining fields where dissenters met to rail against the corruption of the Established Church. The small chapel on the corner of the Great Maze Pond had fallen into decay. It was part of the estate which had been leased to the church, but the Governors and the Medical School now had plans for the plot once the lease expired.

The existing cramped Medical School lecture theatre and laboratories stood in the Park by the south gate. Separated both physically and in spirit from the hospital, London University held sway here. Indeed, many of Guy's senior doctors also held prestigious teaching and research appointments at the Medical School. Such appointments were important in conferring an enhanced status on doctors as they established their lucrative private practices.

While the School paid rent from its teaching income to the hospital, it held on to its independence with a firm grip. The design of a new residential college with a large dining hall, reading rooms and accommodation for the medical students, all set around an inner courtyard, was well underway. The job now was to raise the necessary funds. Miss Burt wondered if such dedicated effort would be afforded to her plans for Guy's Nursing Training Institute.

On her arrival the previous November, Miss Burt had undertaken a fact-finding tour of Southwark and Bermondsey to get the measure of what was required to improve the lot of the poor. Being situated in the Thames basin, she learnt that fog was the big problem, especially in the winter months. The 'London Ivy', as the fog was known, was so dense and long-lasting in November and December that a week would often pass before the sun was visible, even at noontime.

Link-lighters rushed about the gloomy streets offering to light the way with their flaming torches for anyone who would pay a few pennies. Of course, some of these street urchins were in cahoots with the local thieving gangs, so patrons were understandably nervous when they were out and about, and some carried heavy walking sticks to defend themselves.

Mr Lushington, conscious of the lawless Wild West out in Southwark, ensured a carriage was always available for Miss Burt's needs. And at his suggestion, Dr Steele or Mr Beadle accompanied her, whether on foot or by carriage. Together, Miss Burt and Dr Steele had visited the Saturday night markets along the Thames' south bank right up to Waterloo train station.

After pay time on Saturday night or early on Sunday morning, the working classes crowded into these places so they were almost impassable. There were hundreds of stalls lit with grease lamps, tar sticks and tallow candles, and even gas lamps and open fires. Everything imaginable was on sale.

To keep some civility, thieves, drunks, and prostitutes were constantly rounded up by the police and carted off to the local prisons in Clink Street and Marshalsea Road nearby, but the offenders went back as soon as they had done their time in the 'clink'. It was a never-ending cycle, much to the despair of local churchmen and social reformers.

Drink was a perennial problem. It had blighted the lives of many since the gin craze in the 18th century and the situation was no better now. Miss Burt had seen ample evidence of its effects as she observed life in the 'stews' and across Southwark. Indeed, there were so many inns and pubs right on her doorstep, she had lost count.

The Borough, being one of London's earliest north—south trunk roads, had been crowded with hostelries since mediaeval times as travellers stopped short of London Bridge to rest for the night when the gates to the City of London were shut each evening. These establishments were busy day and night, as the coachmen fed and watered and rested teams of horses while the travellers refreshed themselves with much food and drink.

Entertainment was provided by local actors who played to the revellers as they looked down from the inns' upper-floor galleries. The street thespians had to compete for space with the stable grooms who tended to the horses in the same inner courtyards. And to add to the cacophony, enterprising hawkers yelled up to the galleries, shouting over the din from the streets and the players.

The yards of the King's Head and the White Hart pubs were a stone's throw from Miss Burt's window, just beyond her garden wall. And the grander George Inn, with its large, enclosed yard and galleried rooms, butted right up to the southern wing of Guy's House and the colonnade nearby. It was such a security problem that Mr Lushington had posted an extra porter, Mr Parsons, on the back gates to the south and west of the Park.

This did little to discourage the publicans of the Queen's

Head, the Three Tuns and the Nag's Head whose yards backed onto the Medical School's grounds. The Talbot, which had been the model for Chaucer's Tabard Inn where the pilgrims gathered for their trip to Canterbury, had been demolished a few years earlier to become a builders' yard. In constant use, it added to the noise. And all that was just on the Guy's side of the road. There were many more pubs opposite.

As a result, each night fights broke out, people fell over and hurt themselves, and folk became ill with too much drink. Many ended up on Guy's emergency wards, where the Night Sister and her staff oversaw their care.

The same was happening all over London and this led to groups of concerned citizens trying to do something to stem the degradation due to drink. Miss Burt and Dr Steele looked to the Temperance Movement and the Salvation Army as bands of good Christian people for help in controlling the nightly influx of unfortunate individuals who were done in with drink.

Although the local authority tried their best by providing emergency shelter beds in the workhouses, many of the destitute chose the streets rather than enter one of those dire institutions. They were terrible and terrifying, especially for women and children. Much better to seek out the care of Mrs Keogh and the Guy's night staff for a few hours' respite from life on the streets.

On one of their fact-finding tours, Miss Burt and Dr Steele visited Waterloo station to look at the expansion work of the London and South West Railways to improve its links to the South Eastern Railways' station at London

Bridge. The demand for such cross-district rail improvements had become more pressing as London's economy had expanded. But the need to meet tight budgets meant shortcuts were taken, resulting in terrible accidents. Casualties ended up in Guy's emergency wards alongside the vagrants and drunks.

One of Southwark's notorious slums known as the Mint, just off the Borough, was a particularly nasty rookery of densely populated, verminous housing, completely without sanitation.

Poor people, criminals and prostitutes lived in this gloomy warren of alleyways, and it was a known place of contagion. Miss Burt found it shocking that this uncivilised place was on her doorstep.

The great expansion in jobs brought increased pressure on the authorities to provide decent housing. Miss Burt had been heartened to hear about their slum clearances to allow for new charitable developments like Mr Peabody's recently opened low-cost housing complex in Stamford Street. Dr Steele had shown her around the four-storey blocks which gave families more living space with gas lighting, running water, and sanitation.

It was the same story in Bermondsey and Rotherhithe to the east of Guy's. Rookeries and doss houses, and the ubiquitous social problems of drink, criminality, and prostitution. All along the river, slum housing jostled for space with industrial plants, the docks and warehouses, while the decaying infrastructure of overcrowded housing, rotted by years of pollution and uncleared rubbish, destroyed lives. When people got sick or had accidents, they were cared for at the local workhouse's infirmary, St Olave's Hospital.

The Sisters of Mercy, an Irish Catholic order, provided care there and in the local communities across southeast London. Miss Burt, like all Sisterhood-trained nurses, knew the Order well. It had been the first of the Catholic communities to be established in England since the Reformation when, in 1838, the Sisters were invited to set up their House near Guy's.

Their Superior, Mother Moore, having provided nursing nuns to the Crimean war effort, became a close confidant and adviser to Miss Nightingale – reinforcing for some the insidious threat of Rome in modern nursing. The threat was so real for some parliamentarians that they spent their political careers trying to rid England of such Orders. At Guy's, Miss Burt felt the full force of that anti-Rome sentiment.

"Shall we get on, the weather is closing in," called out Mr Bryers, interrupting Miss Burt's thoughts of her tormentors. She hurried to join the men as they strode past Hunt's House and through the Park to the south gate.

"With all this rain, the next thing will be a big dose of 'London Ivy'," exclaimed Mr Payne. "That fog clings to you and sticks in your lungs so fast you can't cough it up. I reckon there's poison in that fog, it's all yellow. What do you say, Mr Bryers?"

"That's right, a great fog in the summer... this June weather is very peculiar," came the reply.

"You're late," shouted Mr Parsons, who had been waiting for them. "The drunks and the vagrants'll be trying to get in soon." The night watchmen fastened the bolts and checked they were secure before leaving Mr Parsons to start his patrol of the estate.

Mr Payne and Mr Bryers hurried past the Medical School's lecture theatre to lock the west gate while Miss Burt stood outside the School, reflecting on a very different fact-finding tour she had made the previous Christmas with Dr Steele. They had visited the Royal College of Physicians on Trafalgar Square. And they had driven past the gentlemen's clubs in Pall Mall on their way to the upmarket stores in Piccadilly before going to the haunts of Guy's medical staff up in the West End. With its wide boulevards, parks, and elegant buildings, it was another world.

They had travelled across London Bridge early on the second Sunday of Advent to avoid getting caught up with the first coaches travelling between London and the channel ports. At that time of morning, traffic was light enough for them to make good progress over the bridge, up Lombard Street to the Bank of England, and along Cheapside to St Paul's. The winter solstice was only days away, so the morning's darkness formed the perfect backdrop for the Christmas lights which reminded people that the last Yuletide of the decade was upon them.

Their carriage trundled around St Paul's cathedral along Ludgate Hill to Fleet Street, which was also known as the 'street of ink' because of the many printworks that had grown up in the area over the past decade. It was a hive of activity at this early hour as the delivery waggons collected the newspapers for distribution across London, blocking the roads as they did so.

Printmen, setters, and labourers, having been up all night, roamed the coffeehouses and queued for the muffin men and street hawkers. Street urchins from the warren of slum houses around Fleet Street added to the hubbub as they too looked for something to eat. With their progress slowed, Miss Burt, sitting in the carriage getting colder by the minute, glimpsed the place of print that added to her daily torment.

In the meagre light, Miss Burt and Dr Steele approached Trafalgar Square which was always teeming with people day and night. It had become a place where vagrants, prostitutes, and drunks gathered for a night's communal rest. The police were always trying to keep order, especially as the Square was also the meeting place of anti-establishment dissenters and potential revolutionaries seeking to overthrow the corrupt Tories or Liberals, whoever was in power.

Traffic ground to a halt as people spilled into the roads around the Square. Dr Steele, being a member of the Royal College of Physicians, had arranged for refreshments to be served for him and Miss Burt. He instructed the driver to find a way around the congestion while he and Miss Burt walked through the crowds to the College, which stood on the Square's northwest corner at the eastern end of Pall Mall.

Its elegant Greek columns and its hackney carriage rank facing the Square seemed out of place in the seething mass, but it was close to many of its sister institutions, the gentlemen's clubs. With their classical architecture, many had opened in the early to mid-1800s as London had become the centre for banking, commerce, politics, and the arts.

Dr Henry Pitman, the Registrar of the Royal College of Physicians, met them at the door and showed the guests to the reading room. Permission for Guy's Medical Superintendent and its matron to visit the College had been granted by the President, Dr James Risdon Bennett, who sought to impress upon Miss Burt the stature of the College. Miss Burt simply welcomed the opportunity to sit by the fire to warm up.

She understood both the President and the Registrar were familiar with the parlous situation at Guy's, as it involved several physicians who were members of the College. Indeed, some, including Dr Pavy, were also officers of the College. Dr Bennett's views of the dispute had been informed by his staff and the medical press, particularly the *British Medical Journal* and the *Lancet*. On Dr Steele's advice, Miss Burt had chosen not to discuss the dispute with him.

Instead, Dr Steele and Miss Burt made unfailingly polite conversation with Dr Pitman as they enjoyed their refreshments, before making their way along Pall Mall past the gentlemen's clubs.

The Mall was impressive, with its bright streetlights and magnificent buildings where wide steps led up to large front doors. It signified great wealth to its patrons, and useful connections for some, especially those in the military and politics and those with interests in the Empire and the Far East.

Miss Burt was impressed by the East India Club in St

James's Square where the Company's former employees and servants, and military who had served in India, held sway. Members of Mr Lushington's family maintained a strong presence as officers of the club. Dr Steele had informed her that despite this connection, it had had to compete for patrons with the more fashionable Oriental Club in Hanover Square where gentleman who had resided in the East were admitted as members.

Riding north to Piccadilly, they enjoyed the sights of luxurious Christmas decorations in the store windows, especially at Fortnum and Mason. This upmarket department store supplied groceries and tea to society's best, and the British army. Dr Steele was partial to their famous scotch eggs and game pies, while Miss Burt liked their rich buttery shortbread.

Their carriage crossed Piccadilly to Brook Street and Grosvenor Square, the main object of Dr Steele's itinerary. They passed the Savile Club in Savile Row on the way. A more modern establishment, as it was only formed in 1868, this Club was the place for London's writers and artists. Robert Louis Stevenson, Thomas Hardy and Rudyard Kipling were all members. Finally, their carriage arrived in Brook Street where they rested at Claridge's hotel to enjoy its fine Christmas decorations.

Royal patronage had made Claridge's a very fashionable place to dine and to be seen and Miss Burt, the nurse from the country, had very much enjoyed watching London's rich at leisure. She had learnt from Dr Steele that several of Guy's senior medical staff lived in Brook Street, and Grosvenor and Wimpole Streets close by. Residents of such handsome West End terraced houses had access to private parks and railed-off communal gardens as well as stables for their carriages and horses. Quite the contrast to south London.

From Claridge's, Miss Burt and Dr Steele had strolled over to Grosvenor Square to hear the local preacher's open-air Sunday sermon.

She shuddered as she recalled that this was the first time she had come across her future tormentor. The zealous Dr Habershon had stood before her demanding passers-by to stop and listen to his message. Eyes bulging, he yelled his fire-and-brimstone speech denouncing the Church of England and imploring his audience to follow in the Lord's footsteps with his Nonconformist Baptists. The bitter cold had not deterred him as he punched the air with his Bible, knuckles white and frozen, shouting dire warnings at those who would not listen. Miss Burt had felt chilled to the bone on that December day, for she knew that this was a man who would never listen to reason, and could never open his mind to new ideas.

Dr Steele had seen her crestfallen face and had felt the cold in all senses too, so to round off their tour he had suggested they visit the newly refurbished Langham's hotel in Portland Place. Very fashionable, it was sumptuous inside, even richer than Claridge's, and it had electric lights in its forecourt.

Taking afternoon tea at such hotels was an acceptable reason for decent women to meet as they could not enter the Clubs, or the pubs, hostelries and chop houses on high streets. At Langham's, they could enjoy tea from all over the Empire and eat fancy cakes and biscuits served on delicate china plates. They could use silver cutlery laid out on white linen tablecloths surrounded by a similar class of people enjoying the pleasures of Sunday afternoon tea.

At four o'clock it had started to get cold and dark, so Dr Steele had summoned their carriage for the journey back to Guy's. She remembered the twinkling stores along Regent Street as they had travelled back through Piccadilly and Trafalgar Square to the Strand.

As they had crossed from west to east, one sparkling rich fabulous world had given way to the grime, noise, and filth of another. Riding eastwards along the Strand, they had passed her old alma mater, King's College hospital, to the north and to the south, was King's College and its Medical School, where the great antisepsis man, Professor Lister, held sway.

Back they had travelled through the City, past the Bank of England, along Lombard Street to arrive at London Bridge and Guy's, now in the dark. Miss Burt's eyes filled with tears as she remembered those Christmas sights and delights of the West End and her contrasting circumstances in the poverty of Southwark.

Mr Jeffries, the gardener, startled her. The night watchmen had already moved on.

"Matron, you'll catch your death in all this rain. We could almost be back in last December. All we need now is some snow to cap it all," he said cheerily.

With the storm rising, Mr Jeffries explained he was out in the garden at this late hour to tie in the roses and batten down as much as he could. He accompanied Miss Burt through the colonnade to her quarters and bade her goodnight.

"You need to get indoors, Matron; the rains are coming. Trust me, there's a big storm coming tonight and it's going to make a lot of mess."

She smiled. "It will be good for the roses."

It was well past nine o'clock in the evening as Miss Burt entered Guy's chapel, next to her quarters, for the day's final prayers. Along with the lockup, this was part of her day's closing routine. The lady-nurses and the night staff had already finished their evening service and were either going to bed or about to start work on the night shift.

"Good evening Matron, I trust you have had a good day," whispered Guy's chaplain, Reverend James Flood. He smiled and bowed as she took her place in the front pew where she watched him collect the prayer books from the earlier evening service.

Miss Booth, Guy's Bible Woman, had decorated the plain square chapel with Miss Burt's favourite Rosa Rugosa Rubra from the Park. At this time of year, it was in great abundance and its familiar perfume filled the chapel and took Miss Burt back to her childhood. Although she was born in the summer of 1839 in Southall Green in the village of Middlesex, she had spent most of her early life with her grandparents in a village near Yelverton, on the western edge of Dartmoor.

She was the eldest of fourteen children so, in common with many families at that time, to relieve the pressure on the young curate's household, her father had sent her and some of his other children to be raised in the country by their grandparents. They lived in Ward House, which stood in its own estate near one of the rivers that flow into the Tamar. The children could follow its path all the way to the sea at Plymouth on their walks.

Miss Burt breathed in the wide-open spaces and country lanes filled with deep pink roses and campions. They had certainly had a better life there than one being raised in the smoke and crush of London.

Miss Burt finished her prayers and slipped quietly away to her private quarters.

Meanwhile, a summer storm was rising, just as Mr Jefferies had predicted. But Miss Burt's worry was not for this storm, but for the other brewing up in Fleet Street.

What would the *Times* print about the morning's fracas? What was going to appear at breakfast tables across London? And what was Dr Habershon going to do next? As the thunder clapped, and the rain poured down, another more terrible storm was about to break.

PART III: THE PLOT

NINE

'Louisa, we still regret the conduct of Dr Pavy and his condemnation of you that summer. The terrible consequences of his actions, and those of Dr Habershon and his colleagues, were unimaginable at the time. As nurses, we can never be party to the private deliberations of the medical staff, so we were naïve concerning their connivances. Dr Steele's discreet inquiries with one of their number revealed the scale of their conspiracy to get Miss Burt gone. His account of crucial decisions taken on that day in late June will, I hope, help you to see that your role was to be the victim through which their plans could be accomplished.'

Ada Habershon breezed into the dining room, twirling and smiling as she greeted her mother. "It is such a beautiful morning, Mama. Where's Papa? We must enjoy a turn in the Square before the sun gets too strong." It was nine o'clock on Monday June 28, 1880, and it was the start of a fine summer's day already tipping 70 degrees Fahrenheit.

"Your father is walking there with Sir William as we speak. I believe they have matters of great importance to discuss regarding a calamitous situation at the hospital," replied Ada's mother, Mrs Grace Habershon, as she invited her youngest daughter to join her at the breakfast table.

The Habershons lived at number 70 Brook Street in Mayfair. Several of Dr Habershon's medical colleagues and friends lived close by, including Sir William Gull, the Queen's Physician and former Medical Superintendent at Guy's, who lived at number 74. Dr Pavy, who was an old friend of Dr Habershon's from their training days, lived around the corner at 35 Lower Grosvenor Street, and their colleague, Dr Samuel Wilks, another senior physician at Guy's, lived further along at number 77.

The doctors often met at each other's homes to discuss medical and hospital matters, and, on fine days, they walked together in Grosvenor Square nearby. This large public garden, set in the fashionable district of Mayfair, was one of the first of its kind when it was opened in the early 1700s. With its classical landscaping and many trees, it offered a pleasant walk and fresh air as the physicians discussed their worries.

Number 70 was a devoutly Christian household where prayer and service in the name of the Lord were strictly observed in the plain tradition of the Nonconformists. Although they were Protestants, Nonconformists did not accept the doctrines or practices of the Established Church. By the 1880s, many middle-class households, disillusioned by the corruption they believed evident in the Church and its closer links with Rome, became members of the various branches of the Nonconformists.

Ada, at nineteen years old, was well-educated and loved to spend her time milling about at home with her two older sisters, Gracie and Ellen, where studying the Bible, reading, and embroidering occupied much of their time in self-improvement. Ada was also a gifted hymnist for her beloved church, where Gracie played the organ. Her older brother Samuel Herbert, at twenty-two, had nearly finished his training at St Bartholomew's hospital, where he hoped to be appointed to the staff on qualifying.

Number 70's matriarch, Mrs Habershon, now aged sixty, had had her children in quick succession in midlife and, as would be expected for a woman of her beliefs and standing, had devoted her life to supporting her husband and their home and family. In this comfortable middle-class Victorian home, their successes were her successes.

"Jessie, serve the tea please," requested Mrs Habershon of her housemaid, who was standing ready with the glinting silver teapot which caught the morning sun.

"And I think you had better lay out the breakfast as it is getting late. Dr Habershon will join us presently." The maid curtseyed and sent her young assistant to the kitchen downstairs to bring the breakfast trays up.

Mrs Habershon added, "And can you ask Leach to hurry my darling son along as he will need to leave for the hospital soon."

Samuel Leach was the Habershons' butler and head of the household staff. At forty-two years old, he had done well to end up in a Mayfair household given his humble origins in Bethnal Green, one of London's most impoverished East End communities.

Leach laid out the clothes of the Habershon gentlemen each morning and helped them to get ready. They wore the standard formal attire for professional men, no matter what the weather.

Having readied the younger Habershon, Leach held the dining room door open as he rushed in to greet his mother and sisters, who were already seated at the breakfast table.

"I do apologise for being late, Mama." He leaned over to gently kiss the top of his mother's head.

"My darling boy," she smiled up at him, "would you be so kind to go and bring your father from the Square where he is walking with Sir William."

"Of course, Mama."

He turned and bolted out of the main door, held open for him by Leach, then hurried westwards along Brook Street to Grosvenor Square where the bright sunshine made him squint. Conscious of the rising heat of the summer morning, he tried to relieve the tightness of his stiff collar and black silk cravat by pulling on them, which added to his discomfort.

How he wished he could wear less formal, lighter clothes at this time of year, but it was not possible for a young doctor in training at St Bartholomew's, one of London's oldest hospitals dating from medieval times. It had a good reputation as a teaching hospital, and it was just over a mile north of his father's hospital, so they often travelled to work together in a shared hansom cab.

. . .

"Is it something to do with the notes that arrived last evening?" inquired Ada, looking anxiously at her mother and out of the window in turn. "I noticed the messengers coming and going after father had returned from giving his sermon in the Square yesterday. Is everything alright? Is father alright? Mama, what's happening?"

"Ada, your father has a busy day in front of him so please keep your concerns to yourself," chided Mrs Habershon.

Leach and Jessie laid out the buffet of smoked fish, hams and delicately cooked eggs on the chiffonier and arranged the baskets of bread and cakes along the centre of the dining table. Meanwhile, Ada, trying to be useful, placed the *Times* newspaper next to her father's placemat ready for his perusal. Breakfast in this household was always a large meal as it had to sustain the men until the evening when they would dine more formally.

Along with its sturdy oak and mahogany furniture, the Habershon's dining room was fashionable in its dark green wallpaper and heavy red velvet drapes, and its cream-cushioned dining chairs. The shaft of morning light revealed a comfortable room that was cluttered with the ornaments, glassware and accumulated bits and pieces of a successful doctor's household and his middle-class family life.

Ada and her sisters fussed over the cutlery and china plates, and the curls of butter and bowls of sweet confections, to make sure their father had everything he might desire for his breakfast.

Mrs Habershon and her daughters waited for the men to join them before starting, even though they were very hungry by this late hour.

"Father, there you are!" exclaimed young Samuel. He had spotted his father and Sir William in deep conversation in the middle of the Square. "Mama has requested that you join us for breakfast."

"Good day, Sir William," said the young Habershon as he bowed and greeted Dr Gull. Nodding and bidding both farewell, Sir William strolled off to his house at 74 Brook Street.

Looking at his father's face, Samuel inquired, "My word Sir, you look ashen. Are you well? Is there something I can do to help? What ails you so? Is there more trouble at the hospital?"

"I fear we face a woeful situation. My work of the last six months to get Miss Burt gone seems to have been in vain. It appears that Dr Steele's inquiry report into the nursing reforms supports that woman, and it is going to be accepted by the Governors. I am so distressed and, to make things worse, Sir William tells me that the dreadful Miss Lonsdale has issued a public rebuttal to my carefully worded response to her accusations about the poor state of nursing at Guy's.

"How could a respectable journal like *Nineteenth Century* stoop to print her censorious rubbish?" cried Dr Habershon, as he left the Square with his son for the short walk home.

"Sir, I think we are in a state about these nursing reforms across London, are we not?" commented Samuel, trying to be of some comfort to his father.

"Yes, we are," sighed Dr Habershon. "I fear a madness has taken over the Governors, egged on by the naïve Mr Lushington and Dr Steele."

"If it is of any comfort, Sir, we are having the same trouble at St Bartholomew's with our matron, Miss Machin. I am cheered though, as the staff are going to see her off even though the administrator and Miss Nightingale support her. It is a terrible but necessary business, I admit."

"Well, that's reassuring," replied his father, "and at least you don't have the likes of Miss Burt and Miss Lonsdale to annoy you as you go about your business."

"Rumour has it that our awful matron will be off to Australia after her current leave of absence and that will be the back of her and her silly reforms. Then we can get back to life as before," chuckled Samuel.

Dr Habershon thanked his son for his reassuring words as he opened their front door.

"Grace, my dearest, please forgive me for being so late." Dr Habershon took his seat at the head of the table. "I have much of great importance to deal with today."

After a thankful prayer to the Lord for the fine spread before them, Jessie poured the tea on Mrs Habershon's instruction, and Ada and her sisters made their choices of breads and cakes. Samuel, meanwhile, was up on his feet at the buffet helping himself to his favourite savoury foods while his mother placed the choicest cuts on her husband's plate.

"Would you like to hear a verse I have composed for the Tabernacle?" Ada asked, desperate to add some cheer to the downcast atmosphere.

"Not now, Ada," intervened her mother as Dr Habershon tried to concentrate on the front page of the *Times*. The silence was broken only by the clatter of knives and forks on the china breakfast plates.

Their hunger satisfied, the young ladies, accompanied by their brother, were ushered out so that Mrs Habershon could sit in silent vigil with her husband.

Is today my resignation day? he pondered. Have all my efforts to keep the malign influence of Miss Burt and the Sisterhood out of Guy's been for nothing? He sighed at these depressing thoughts. As a multi-medalled award-winning physician who had written several textbooks and learned papers on diseases of the stomach, it would be an unbearable end to such an illustrious career: too painful to contemplate.

Medicine was Dr Habershon's life. He was now fifty-five, and he had spent his whole medical career at Guy's since training there from the age of seventeen. Born in Yorkshire, he was educated at the church school in Brampton in Wath-upon-Dearne, just north of the industrial town of Rotherham where his family owned the local iron foundry, J.J.Habershons.

He completed his senior school education in Ongar, in Essex, where, being a bright scholar, he became an apprentice to one of London's top physicians, Dr Ebenezer Pye-Smith, at the age of fifteen. Dr Pye-Smith's father, the Reverend John Pye-Smith, was an authority on

Nonconformist theology and his writings still held sway in the Habershons' house.

Dr Pye-Smith had been one of Guy's best-known practitioners in the mid-1800s, and his private practice in the City had been so successful that he took in several apprentices at his north London clinic in Clapton, where his patients were more tolerant of students. Under his master's guidance, Dr Habershon distinguished himself in his medical studies, gaining numerous prizes, scholarships, and gold medals from the University of London, where he graduated with an M.D. in 1851. He joined the staff at Guy's in 1854.

Seated at the breakfast table, Dr Habershon looked back fondly on those happy days. It was in being part of Dr Pye-Smith's training group, known as a 'firm', that Dr Habershon had made some of his lasting friendships with his fellow pupils who were now colleagues at Guy's, including Dr Pavy.

They were joined in 1871 by their master's son, Dr Philip Henry Pye-Smith, who was himself a distinguished classical scholar as well as a multilingual physician who had studied in Paris, Berlin, and Vienna. Loyalty to each other and their master was the glue that held the 'firms' together and made them a potent force to be reckoned with.

In a class-conscious society, these 'firms' also acted as 'social elevators' helping promising young doctors, especially those from modest backgrounds, to become one of society's gentlemen.

Dr Habershon so enjoyed his life as a senior doctor both at Guy's and at his private Mayfair practice, where he had built his reputation as being a painstaking physician. He was also a proud member of Guy's Medical School faculty, where he taught and published many research papers and textbooks. His clinical practice papers for the house journal, *Guy's Hospital Reports*, were regarded as compulsory reading by the medical students.

"Grace, please forgive me, I am distracted this morning. I shall have to call another meeting of the medical staff here tonight, to discuss the intolerable situation we find ourselves in following the publication of Dr Steele's inquiry report into the hospital's nursing reforms."

He paused, closed his eyes, and winced. "He is going to support that Sisterhood woman and her ilk. And Sir William thinks the Board will back Steele's recommendations. I am in despair."

After another pause, he looked around the room and then at her and added, "My dear, I may even have to resign."

Aghast at the thought of her husband's downfall, Mrs Habershon replied, "Of course, my dear husband. I shall let Leach and cook know about the meeting and I will keep the girls out of the way for the evening."

She had hosted over twenty such evening meetings of Guy's physicians and surgeons in her home since the previous November, so Mrs Habershon fully understood what was required. She sensed the importance of this evening's gathering. Things were clearly coming to a head.

"Thank you, my dear," replied Dr Habershon. "I shall send a note later of the likely numbers."

Mrs Habershon reminded her husband that the family

had been invited to the Holland sisters' soirée that evening, next door at number 72. The sisters were the daughters of Sir Henry Holland, a prominent society physician who had trained with his childhood friend, Guy's famous Dr Richard Bright.

To assuage his wife's concerns about missing such an important opportunity for their son, Dr Habershon promised he would be home in time for the party and that he would slip away discreetly for his meeting after a suitable period in attendance.

They were interrupted by Leach, who brought a note in for Dr Habershon on a silver tray.

"Thank you, Leach," he said, opening the envelope. It was Dr Pavy's seal and handwriting.

"Is there a reply, Sir?" inquired the butler.

"Yes, yes, there is," replied the physician as he scribbled "Delighted" on the note, which Leach then returned to the waiting messenger.

Finishing his breakfast, Dr Habershon waited for his colleague in his study across the hall. This strictly private quarter also served as Dr Habershon's consulting room where he saw his fee-paying patients. Alone, Dr Habershon reflected on the gross sense of injustice that he felt at his predicament.

He had clearly failed to persuade the Board, and Mr Lushington and Dr Steele, of the medical staff's case for rejecting Miss Burt and her nursing reforms, despite much evidence of their faults which he had submitted to the Governors' inquiry. He felt dejected that his long years of loyal service seemed to have had little influence.

Guy's reputation had been enhanced by the addition of his own good standing as a distinguished and valued member of the upper ranks of London's medical profession. Surely his views should have carried more weight than those of a nurse from the country?

His feelings of loneliness at such rejection were intense. It pained him to think about it – especially as he was a Fellow and Examiner, and a Council and Board member, of the Royal College of Physicians. And he was a member of the increasingly influential British Medical Association. Indeed, he was the President-elect of the Association's Metropolitan Counties Branch, and he was due to give his inaugural speech shortly. Did none of these achievements count?

He closed his eyes in dread at the loss of his public standing and the humiliation he would feel if his threatened resignation were accepted, or worse, was forced upon him.

He thought about his conversation with Sir William earlier. While he had been sympathetic to Dr Habershon's views, especially concerning how to respond to Miss Lonsdale's incendiary article and letters, he had a feeling that Sir William's full support, if pressed, would be lacking.

Would his medical colleagues stand by him if the dispute escalated further? After all, they all had lives and reputations to keep up, and bills to pay. The ground could be softer than he would like.

Dr Habershon was more than a physician, he looked after people's souls too. He felt his contributions to society should have received more recognition from the Board. He was a Christian of serious standing amongst the Nonconformists.

He had been one of the founders of the Christian Medical Association, which ensured medical trainees and junior doctors studied the Bible as well as anatomy. He held Bible studies for the students in his house every Sunday. Surely, he reflected, these good works should have enhanced his standing in the eyes of the President and the Governors and added weight to his opinions.

Well, what did you expect? he asked himself. They are all High Church men, and as for the new President, Mr Hucks Gibbs, he lauds the Sisterhood's work in Camden and yet has shown no recognition of all my charitable work for the Ragged School.

How hard he had worked as the School Superintendent to educate the City's destitute children. Even the social reformer Lord Shaftesbury, parliamentarian and the Ragged School Union's President, had recognised his work, so was he not worthy of the Board's favourable opinion?

Looking above his desk, he caught sight of his younger self staring back at him from the wall adorned with certificates and commendations that marked his many achievements as a lifelong scholar and physician.

That picture, he remembered, was taken when he had been appointed to the staff at Guy's. He was a slim young man then, just starting out on his medical career. He looked so elegant in his black frock coat and tightly fitted waistcoat, crisp white shirt and stiff collar wrapped at the neck with a black silk ribbon forming a neat stock. His dense thatch of black hair and his bushy beard and sideburns were quite the fashion in the mid-1800s. Although seated, his upright bearing marked him out as a professional gentleman.

Now with his youth gone, he knew in his heart that he was regarded as an older, faded man at the end of his career. What he said no longer seemed to carry the weight it once had at Guy's. The thought wounded him to the core. Sitting there, now fuller in the girth and slightly hunched, his head still crowned with thick hair, now white, he felt sad that the time was approaching when he might no longer be regarded as central to Guy's 'Golden Age' of medicine.

His melancholy was checked when his eyes landed upon a large photograph of London's great medical leaders. It had been taken a few years earlier when he and his colleagues were regarded as being part of that elite medical group. The photographer had had his work cut out in organising so many physicians and surgeons to be still on the College steps that day.

On seeing himself as part of that august body, he willed himself into action. I am not a spent force yet, he said to himself. I am going to fight for our profession's views; so many doctors cannot be wrong. Full of determination, he made a mental list of the things he wanted to discuss with Dr Pavy on their journey to Guy's.

TEN

Dr Pavy's stylish brougham, with its four red wheels drawn by a pair of handsome black horses, clattered over the cobblestones along Brook Street and pulled up outside number 70 at just after eleven in the morning. Leach, on hearing the carriage's arrival, opened the front door and stepped forward to greet Dr Pavy.

A nod to the doctor's driver, who had brought the carriage from the mews which separated Brook Street from Lower Grosvenor Street, signalled Leach's permission for him to park up outside the house while Dr Habershon was readied for his departure to the hospital. Opening the carriage door and unfolding its neat footstep, Leach bowed as the faultlessly dressed Dr Pavy descended to the pavement.

"Is your man ready?" asked the urbane physician as he looked up to the window on the upper ground floor where

Dr Habershon's study window overlooked the well-kept street.

Leach rushed forward to hold the front door open for Dr Pavy, who found Mrs Habershon waiting for him in the reception hall.

"Leach, please let Dr Habershon know that Dr Pavy has arrived," requested Mrs Habershon as she took the visitor to one side.

"Dr Pavy, I am so worried about my poor husband," she confided. "He has had the world's troubles on his shoulders and the bad business at the hospital has inflamed his stomach problems." Leaning forward, touching his arm, she whispered, "Have you any cheer for him?"

"I have indeed, Ma'am," replied the charming Dr Pavy. "Our dear friend Mr Hart, editor of the *British Medical Journal*, has come up with a stinging rebuke of our busybody lady-nurses and the reforms in his latest editorial. He supports us roundly, and I am sure it will please your husband and calm his dyspepsia."

"Thank you," she murmured as her husband joined them and greeted his old friend. Turning to his butler, Dr Habershon asked Leach to prepare for another evening meeting of his colleagues.

"We will probably want a light supper after nine o'clock; nothing elaborate, cold chops will do. And make sure the boy is ready to run messages if necessary, would you?"

"Of course, Sir," replied Leach as he held the door open for Dr Pavy and his master to depart.

Mrs Habershon bade them farewell and reminded her

husband not to be late for the Hamilton sisters' soiree as the physicians walked into the bright sunshine and got into Dr Pavy's carriage.

"Go by Berkeley Square," requested Dr Pavy. "And stop at Fortnum's."

"Very good, Sir," came the driver's reply as they set off down Brook Street to Piccadilly.

"I love Berkeley Square in the summer, all those lovely trees and their rich foliage. What do you say, Samuel?" inquired Dr Pavy of his friend who, in the privacy of the carriage, looked very glum.

"There is an injustice here, Freddie; no sense of fair play. I feel strongly that my arguments have not been given the consideration that they deserve, and I personally have not been sufficiently recognised. After all, do I not honour the Lord; am I not a hardworking physician besides a good father and loyal kind husband?" blurted out Dr Habershon.

"I cannot fathom why they will not listen to our case. You above all know how hard I have tried to put the evidence about these so-called reforms before the powers that be. That woman has bewitched the Board and they have been taken in by her fanciful ideas."

"Come, come Samuel, do not let your emotions get the better of you. We have right on our side and Hart has written a good piece in Saturday's *Journal*."

Dr Pavy leaned forward and fished out his latest *British Medical Journal* from his leather bag. It was already folded open at the correct page as he passed it to his friend.

"It's on the right-hand side," said Dr Pavy, admiring the

passing trees in full leaf while Dr Habershon concentrated on Hart's latest coruscating piece.

'We are informed that, at the annual meeting of the governors on Wednesday, Lord Cardwell, the President, dissatisfied with the state of disorganisation to which the proceedings of the Treasurer have led, tendered his resignation, and Mr H Hucks Gibbs was elected President. After a long sitting, in which the recent events were discussed, and the disastrous facts of the situation, for which Mr Lushington is responsible, were very temperately and judiciously stated by Dr Pye-Smith (who was specially requested to attend), the house-surgeons, who were last week suspended by the Treasurer, having expressed in a letter to the governors their regret for the communication made by them to the public papers and withdrawn the same, were called in and reappointed. It is fortunate for the Treasurer that this course was adopted; otherwise, yet more serious consequences must have followed, which could but have tended to bring out in stronger light the hopeless nature of the contest into which he had precipitated himself. To that contest, there can be but one end. It is impossible to maintain in office a superintendent of nursing whose removal the medical staff unanimously require. It is still open to Mr Lushington to restore concord and good order by consultation with the medical staff. In a little time, this alternative may no longer be open, and only a more disagreeable one will remain to him – that of retiring from an office which he will for the first time have brought into discredit. Personally, Mr Lushington is so amiable and well-meaning a man, that the disastrous persistency in error which he has shown in administering the duties of the office of Treasurer must be to all who know him a source of peculiar regret.'

Having read this declaration, Dr Habershon felt more relaxed by the time they had arrived at Fortnum's in Piccadilly, where they came to a stand outside the store.

Dr Pavy jumped out to buy some of their best china tea and a Dundee cake. He loved the finer things in life, including shopping at Regent Street's best stores and Jermyn Street's finest tailors and outfitters. Alas, there was no time to browse the new stock today, as he quickly signed for his goods on account and hurried back to his waiting carriage.

"Over to the Strand and stop at St Mary's church," Dr Pavy instructed his driver. "And avoid the Haymarket, would you?

"I cannot abide the crowds of ruffians and the stench from the gin houses that have taken over the place. It is all too much on a fine summer day," he grumbled to his companion as they set off down Piccadilly and turned into St James's Square. Trotting towards Trafalgar Square, they passed their familiar haunt, the Royal College of Physicians, where the carriage slowed as it trundled through the milling crowds and progressed up the Strand.

"God save us, what a noise and smell; it never used to be like this," remarked an irritated Dr Pavy, anxious to get to the British Medical Association's office before the students from King's College next door spilled into the road.

He willed the carriage on through the dense milieu of

people, cabs, omnibuses, delivery carts, and teams of horses.

"I thought we would call on Mr Hart to wish him happy birthday for last Saturday. I think it was his forty-fifth. And, of course, we need to thank him for his support."

Dr Habershon was only half listening as he studied Hart's editorial. Marvellous, he thought, as he read it repeatedly to himself, he has pulled out all the stops for us.

Dr Pavy's carriage pulled up alongside St Mary Le Strand, the fine 18th-century church which stood on its own island of calm amid the Strand's chaotic traffic. This road was one of London's main east—west trunk roads, so standing a brougham in the middle of it at this hour was a bold move. Dr Pavy left his driver to face the hostile shouting and complaints while he and Dr Habershon entered the Association's House at 161a The Strand.

The plain terraced three-storey building with its narrow glazed split door and shop-window front could easily be mistaken for a butcher's shop but for the etched glass saying, 'BRITISH MEDICAL JOURNAL'.

The House was a modest headquarters, but it represented the Association's real progress since its earlier days at Great Queen Street, near Lincoln's Inn Fields, where it rented two rooms over Thomas Richards' printworks.

Dr Pavy and Dr Habershon climbed the stairs to the upper floors, where Mr Hart had established the Association's publishing business. On their way up, they peeked into the new spacious meeting room for the expanded Committee of Council, which now had forty members. They found Mr Hart on the top floor hunched over his desk.

His small stature and slight build, with his angular pale face and large grey eyes, were familiar not only to London's physicians and surgeons, but also to its parliamentarians and members of the judiciary. Hart's energetic and fearless campaigning saw him involved in many inquiries and grievances that had resulted in improvements to the state of workhouse infirmaries, the care of poor sick people, and the use of vaccines as part of public health campaigns. In addition, he had been the chairman of the Association's all-important Parliamentary Bill Committee for nearly ten years.

"Hart, my dear fellow, you have done us a great service," greeted Dr Pavy. "I do believe it was your birthday on Saturday, so I have a small gift for you." He gave him the tea which had been packed in a finely decorated tin of Chinese design and wrapped in Fortnum's distinctive gift paper. Like many gentlemen at that time, Mr Hart loved all things from the Orient, and he was famous for his collection of ephemera from the east and his knowledge of its culture.

"Pavy, you are too kind. Thank you," replied Mr Hart as he admired the tea caddy.

"And here is some of your favourite Dundee cake to accompany your tea this afternoon," added Dr Pavy as he placed the gift on Mr Hart's desk. "We are truly grateful for your kind support, and long may it continue."

"I shall do my best," replied the editor. "I am having a birthday party at the Oriental Club tomorrow evening. Please come along with your dear wife. I do so enjoy her company and Hanover Square is but a short carriage ride from your Lower Grosvenor Street."

He turned to Dr Habershon. "You must come too and your charming wife. It would be a delight to see her again."

Addressing both, he added, "I believe Mr Chenery will be there."

Unlike Dr Pavy, Dr Habershon did not like parties and, being a temperance man, he did not drink alcohol. However, the prospect of having a few words about the dispute with Mr Thomas Chenery, editor of the *Times*, and a former Professor of Arabic Studies at Oxford University, was too good an opportunity to miss. Smiling, both accepted the invitation.

"Before we leave you," Dr Pavy said, turning to the main purpose of their visit, "there is one more thing that we would like to ask of you.

"The dispute at Guy's is getting worse and I am afraid there is likely to be more trouble. Indeed, we are on our way now to a meeting with our colleagues at the hospital to bring the matter to a conclusion."

Dr Habershon added, "I have chaired many meetings since last November, as you know, and we have drafted letters of complaint to the President, the Treasurer and the Governors, and to the press. It has all been to no avail, and, to add injury, we understand that Dr Steele is going to recommend that the nursing reforms should proceed."

Mr Hart nodded in sympathy while he made his notes. He was familiar with the entire miserable story. Only last week, he reminded the physicians, he had given nearly a whole column to the latest fracas involving the demonstrating students. He had reproduced the letter written to the *Times* on June 16 by Guy's Senior House Physician, Dr Maylard, and its Senior House Surgeon, Mr Russell, in its entirety, and he had added a caustic editorial note for good measure.

"That's entirely my distress," cried Dr Habershon. "Despite your good work, Mr Lushington has forced a public humiliating climbdown on both Maylard and Russell. Under threat of dismissal, they were asked to beg leave of the Governors to express their regret at having written the letter and have asked for it to be withdrawn.

"They were forced to state that they felt it had been improper on their part. And Dr Steele, in an act of woeful misjudgement, has sent a copy of the letter to the *Times*. We are in despair, and in a state of great annoyance." Dr Habershon stared intently at Mr Hart. "We need more such editorials and articles to show the terrible injury that these reforms are causing. We want Dr Steele's inquiry report and its recommendations thrown out."

"Sir, you shall have it," came the reply, and Mr Hart added for reassurance, "I shall try to match Mr Brudenell Carter's recent derogatory piece in the *Lancet*. Did you see it? He has surpassed himself."

"We are discussing it, and our response, at this afternoon's meeting," replied Dr Pavy. "I shall let you know what we decide to do tomorrow."

Mr Hart, drawing on his skills as a campaigner, inquired, "What about the use of satire to make your point? It is all the fashion amongst the lower middle and educated working classes who pressurise our parliamentarians for action. I should gladly send a note to the editor of *Funny Folks* on your behalf. I rather like the acid wit displayed in its cartoons, but it may be too distasteful for you physicians."

But Dr Habershon was vexed on another pressing issue. "As you know, Hart," he said, shifting the conversation, "I am the Association's President-elect of the Metropolitan Counties Branch, and I have been thinking about my inaugural speech. I'd like to voice my concerns about Miss Lonsdale and her latest rebuttal of my opinion about her defence of the nursing reforms.

"She is so persistent, and she seems to have peculiarly easy access to both the *Times* and *Nineteenth Century* for a woman with her outlandish views. Would you be so kind as to give my speech a few of your column inches? The Branch's Annual General Meeting is a week on Wednesday, on July 7, in Greenwich at the Ship Hotel."

"I should be delighted," replied Mr Hart. "Do let me have the copy when it is ready so that I might plan for its inclusion."

"Thank you," replied Dr Habershon. "I shall draft it tonight, ready for you tomorrow."

Dr Pavy remarked that it was going to be a long night what with the follow-ups required from the afternoon's meeting, the sisters' soiree, and now this speech writing.

"We are men of hard work; we have been trained in such ways; and we shall cope," retorted Mr Hart, a former ophthalmic surgeon, and past Head of St Mary's Medical School, as they bade each other farewell and the physicians returned to their waiting carriage.

"Make haste to the hospital… I fear we are rather late in leaving," instructed Dr Pavy.

"Very good, Sir," came the reply as the driver manoeuvred the carriage into the flow of traffic.

The physicians heaved a sigh of relief that they had made their exit in time to avoid the crush of gleeful students rushing out of King's College after their exams.

"We should call upon Lister as he too is involved in a dispute with the awful St John's Sisterhood," suggested Dr Habershon. "Did you know their matron countermined his instructions when treating a boy who was an emergency case? It is truly shocking what these busybody nurses are up to. I believe Miss Burt trained there, so I should like his support to spike her guns."

Dr Pavy thought the idea a good one, especially as the surgeon's antisepsis practice was gaining favour, but time was pressing. "We simply must get up through Fleet Street and Ludgate Hill, and around St Paul's and through Cannon Street within the hour."

They wanted to get on with the afternoon's important business but the crowds milling along the pavements and in the roads, staring at the shop windows while mixing with the numerous cabs and other transports, slowed their progress. To make things worse, the warm sunny day had created a dreadful stench from the streets, which were full of dung from the morning's traffic.

"What did Dr Taylor say in his note to you on Sunday night?" inquired Dr Pavy.

"He, like us," replied Dr Habershon, "is concerned

about the forced climbdown of Maylard and Russell. He is enraged over Steele sending their apology to the *Times*.

"And," he added, "having been sighted on the draft inquiry report, Dr Taylor also understands that its recommendations are likely to be accepted by the Governors. Dr Wilks, with whom he has consulted, is of the mind that we need to issue an ultimatum, possibly offer resignations."

Silence followed as both pondered the seriousness of the situation.

Dr Samuel Wilks, at fifty-six, was another of Guy's senior physicians. He had been a constant member of the medical staff's regular gatherings at Dr Habershon's residence to discuss Miss Burt's appointment and her reforms. Dr Frederick Taylor, similarly, although younger than the others at thirty-three, was the Medical School's administrator and a regular attender at the doctors' group.

"Where is Gull on this?" asked Dr Pavy, who was not a great admirer of Sir William.

"Willing to lend his support, I think. He confirmed the proposition about the recommendations being accepted by the Governors this morning when I walked with him in the Square."

"He has been rather inconsistent in his efforts," commented Dr Pavy. "True, he wrote a stinging rebuke of Miss Lonsdale's article in *Nineteenth Century*. It has demolished her. But I do not trust him. He is too close to the Treasurer for my liking, and he has let us down previously. We should not rely on him. I would look to Dr Fagge and

Dr Moxon who do have form, although they are by no means of the rank of the Queen's Physician."

While Dr Fagge had been a regular attender at Dr Habershon's meetings, Dr Moxon was often absent. He was excused because he lived well north of the City in Highgate, far from the West End, but they worried about his commitment.

"And then there are the surgeons. They have been loyal supporters of our efforts and I believe Mr Cooper Forster, as their leader, will stand with us in this debacle," continued Dr Pavy.

Mr John Cooper Forster was Guy's most senior surgeon and a very rich man from both his private practice and a sizeable inheritance. He lived in Upper Grosvenor Street, at the Park Lane end, near the Earl of Dudley's London residence. The location was regarded as the better end of Grosvenor Street compared to where Dr Pavy and Dr Wilks lived in Lower Grosvenor Street.

At fifty-seven, the surgeon was relaxed about offering his resignation over the dispute. He did not need the income and was due to retire soon anyway. He had only attended a few meetings, but had given his support wholeheartedly.

"You offer wise counsel, as ever," responded Dr Habershon, as they skirted St Paul's cathedral to the south. The noise of the city workers hurrying about looking for something to eat along Cannon Street accompanied them as they made their way up to the Monument, where the carriage slowed to make the sharp turn south to cross London Bridge.

Dr Habershon confessed that he was worried about

offering to resign. Although it was the correct course of action in principle, his son and daughters would still need his support until they were ready to set up their own households.

"My dear Samuel," replied Dr Pavy, "we shall discuss whether this will be necessary later. It is, after all, the *threat* of such action that will suffice."

Eleven

They crawled across the bridge in suffocating heat and an awful stench from the river. Finally, they were able to leave the turnpike and travel eastwards along St Thomas's Street, past the hospital's front gates, to Great Maze Pond Street. As they made their way around the east wing of the hospital, they passed the site of the promised new Medical School's residences and facilities.

Turning into King Street, the carriage pulled up at the hospital's south gate where the physicians dismounted, collected themselves and brushed down the journey's dust. They greeted the gateman sitting in his lodge as they strolled into the Park on a fine sunny afternoon. Passing the School's main teaching facilities, known as the Museum Block, on their left, they made their way into Hunt's House and proceeded to the Outpatients Department which occupied most of the ground floor.

The main door was propped open to allow the

circulation of fresh air through the entrance hall to the wards on the upper floors, and to the large waiting room on their right which was full to bursting with patients ready for the afternoon clinics. The physicians hurried through the throng staring straight ahead in their well-practiced manner, to reach the inner lobby.

With some relief, they paused for breath, taking in the strong carbolic smell, and entered the calm of Guy's Dispensary. There, tucked behind the pharmacy's shelves at the rear, was Dr Taylor's modest office.

Like the other London teaching hospitals, Guy's had made great progress over the previous twenty years in modernising its education and training practices. The traditional way of students attending an ad-hoc course of lectures given by great medical and surgical practitioners and attaching the students as apprentices to their firms, had become increasingly inadequate by the 1850s. The School now had to comply with the Medical Act 1858, which required formalised common curricula, examinations, and certification.

Guy's old apothecary, Dr Stocker, took on this duty but it was too much for him. His request for help in the appointment of a tutor to drill the pupils to pass their London University exams had been long denied. As a result, Guy's standing slipped behind its great rivals as St Thomas's, King's College and St Bartholomew's hospitals had all appointed Medical School officers to manage the necessary administration and organise the new curricula and teaching timetables.

Belatedly, Guy's had appointed Dr Frederick Taylor, one

of its award-winning assistant physicians, to the full-time post of running its Medical School.

He was the son of Dr David Taylor, a prominent London practitioner who paid for his son to be educated at Epsom College – one of the premier schools where young gentlemen were prepared for entry into London's elite Medical Schools. He was only twenty-seven when he became Dean in 1874. Despite his youth, he was regarded as being rather traditional, and a bit of a cold fish.

Now thirty-three, he had built a reputation for being a fine administrator who had re-established Guy's status. He organised fundraising for new equipment and facilities, especially the Great Maze Pond expansion, through hosting alumni dinners, seeking benefactions, and calling for public donations in press campaigns.

He worked the press in support of his colleagues and their causes, as in the May 29 edition of the *Journal* where Mr Hart had given half a column to an account of a recent Guy's Alumni dinner at which over one hundred gentlemen carried the following resolution, with acclamation, concerning the reforms:

'This meeting, consisting of former students of Guy's Hospital Medical School, desires to express its very warm sympathy with the present members of the medical and surgical staff of the School, in the extra anxiety which has been associated with their tenure of office during the past few months; and at the same time to record its conviction that, in the hands of the present staff, the past pre-eminence of the school of Guy's Hospital will be most worthily maintained.'

Of the current unhappiness, Mr Hart had added: 'The subject of the present painful contest now being carried on at Guy's was barely alluded to during the evening, but all felt its presence, like a ghost at the banquet.'

With his usual thoroughness, Dr Taylor had prepared the agenda for the afternoon on matters of importance arising from the earlier summit of the doctors' group held on the evening of Tuesday June 22. It had been chaired by Dr Habershon, as usual, at his Brook Street residence. With fifteen of Guy's twenty medical and surgical staff present, they discussed the forced public climbdown of their housemen, Dr Maylard and Mr Russell, and Dr Steele's findings and recommendations arising from the inquiry into the reforms held in March.

To a man, the Staff, as the collective of the physicians and surgeons at Guy's liked to be known, were indignant at the humiliation caused by both developments and insistent that their recently agreed draft letter of demands be sent to the President and the Governors before the meeting of the Court of Committees to be held on Wednesday June 30. Dr Taylor had undertaken to finalise the letter based on Dr Wilks's draft and Dr Fagge's additions which had been agreed at the summit on June 22.

It was a delicate moment after seven long months of deliberations during which the Staff had pored over the reforms and Miss Burt's appointment. They had discussed the shortcomings endlessly and had collected evidence to back up their accusations. They had drafted numerous letters of protest and attended many meetings at Dr

Habershon's house. It had been exhausting, disruptive, and divisive. Now they needed to bring matters to a head.

Dr Wilks, together with Dr Habershon and Dr Pavy, were the hospital's senior physicians as they had all entered the Guy's roll in the 1850s. Dr Wilks was a stalwart of the evening meetings, having been present at all twenty-two of them.

On this summer afternoon, he was already present in Dr Taylor's office where he was seated by its west-facing window overlooking the Park and the Museum Block, which housed the large Demonstrating Theatre where students took their lectures. Dr Pavy's distinctive carriage was often seen outside his physiology laboratories which occupied part of the Block's ground floor.

Dr Taylor passed the list of proposed signatories to the letter to Dr Wilks for his perusal. "There are twenty including myself," he explained, as he organised the meeting's papers on his desk.

Having studied the list, Dr Wilks commented that Sir William's name was missing. "I admit he has been somewhat detached from us," he commented, "but he is the Queen's Physician and, although he is not on the staff anymore, he is still a Consulting Physician to Guy's."

"I am not sure if his inclusion finds favour with your colleagues," explained Dr Taylor. "Do you recall in mid-May when he let us down? He promised to make representations on our behalf to Lord Cardwell and the Treasurer and failed to do so."

As Dr Wilks suggested they discuss this further with Dr

Habershon and Dr Pavy, the pair entered the office with a cheerful chorus of "Good afternoon," and smiles all round.

The small room was crowded, especially as Dr Taylor was writing a medical textbook, so his research papers and draft chapters were spread everywhere, and the shelves were stuffed with Medical School papers and administration files.

The smell of carbolic from the pharmacy next door was made more pungent by the heat of the afternoon. Dr Taylor, anxious to get the meeting started, updated his seniors on the other physicians. In order of seniority, Dr Moxon and Dr Fagge, who had joined Guy's in the 1860s; and Dr Pye-Smith and Dr Goodhart, who had joined in the 1870s, were all either on their ward rounds or in clinic but were content for the meeting to proceed.

"What about the surgeons?" asked Dr Wilks.

"Same, all engaged on other pressing clinical duties," replied Dr Taylor.

"Fine," commented Dr Wilks, "but Mr Cooper Forster and Mr Bryant, our illustrious senior surgeons, were not present at Tuesday evening's meeting and I want their good opinion."

"You have it, Sir; both have offered their support, and as they have, the junior surgeons and specialists will fall in," replied Dr Taylor.

Guy's, like other late 19th-century hospitals and institutions, respected age, and one's place in the hierarchy. This was especially so in medicine, even if some seniors were out of touch and even dangerous, as Mr Thomas Bryant increasingly was.

He and Mr Cooper Forster had entered Guy's roll in the mid-late 1850s, like the senior physicians. Unlike many, Mr Bryant had no time for the modern fashion of antisepsis put about by the likes of Professor Lister. But he was still a senior surgeon, and, after Mr Cooper Forster, held sway.

On the other hand, Mr Cooper Forster, who struck a commanding figure at over six feet tall, was continually innovative. The well-built popular surgeon, who had been the captain and trainer of Guy's rowing team, had been one of the first in London to administer anaesthetics, and had studied the management of gunshot wounds in Paris. Both added to his considerable reputation as a skilled surgeon with a good, bold, and neat hand.

"May I suggest that as Mr Cooper Forster lives in the same street as Dr Wilks and Dr Pavy, and Mr Bryant lives close to Dr Habershon in Brook Street, we consult with them this evening if necessary?" suggested Dr Taylor.

Agreeing, they considered the draft letter that had been placed in front of them.

"As you can see, the draft, which I hope is now final, incorporates Dr Fagge's changes of Tuesday evening," explained Dr Taylor.

They had all seen and reworked earlier versions, so were quite familiar with the contents and Dr Taylor's semantic nuances.

"Are you content with this final draft?" he asked, hurrying them along.

The letter, addressed to the President, was explosive.

'Sir, several of our number having been asked what we

really desire as a settlement of the present controversy, we beg to submit the following requests:

1. We desire a return to the ward system which was in force prior to the arrival of the present matron.
2. The resignation or removal of the present matron.
3. The appointment of a committee on which the Staff shall be adequately represented for the management of the nursing so far as it concerns the welfare of the patients.
4. We would further induce you to invite your Treasurer to repose that confidence in the Staff, without which no institution can prosper and with which the present disasters would never have occurred.

Letter dated today, June 28, 1880, signed by the Staff.'

Conscious of the gravity of the letter, the senior physicians looked at each other and then signalled their agreement to Dr Taylor.

"Thank you," said Dr Taylor. "I shall send it to the printers once we have agreed the signatories. My proposal is that we include all members of the Staff as listed. Sir William Gull has not been included because he is not on the staff, although of course he is a Consulting Physician to Guy's and one of great standing. He has not, according to my records, attended many of the previous twenty-two meetings of the Staff chaired by Dr Habershon. May I have your instructions?"

Dr Wilks weighed in, "Sir William's involvement with the dispute has been confined thus far to his excellent article in *Nineteenth Century* where he set out a carefully worded rebuttal of Miss Lonsdale's wild accusations about the nursing standards at Guy's. His words have a potency that is helpful to our cause. I suggest we keep him in reserve for further letters to the *Times* but sight him on this letter, so he has some familiarity with the contents to aid his discussions with the President."

"I agree," replied Dr Habershon. "He will be attending the Hamilton sisters' soiree this evening so I shall ask him if he is content with our proposal. What say you, Pavy?"

"I care less for the man than most; I agree that the signatories should be as listed."

As Guy's most senior physician, having entered in 1851, Sir William was heard to make disparaging remarks about his junior, Dr Pavy, and his research work into diabetes. Although probably made in jest, Dr Pavy never forgave the slight.

"Thank you, gentlemen," said Dr Taylor. "I shall now proceed to the printers in haste and gather the signatures so that we can deliver the letter by hand to the President and Governors tomorrow."

Conscious of the need to let the senior physicians attend to their clinics and ward rounds before making the journey home to the West End, Dr Taylor asked about their wishes concerning the press.

"I believe Mr Brudenell Carter has already approached Mr Chenery for a column in the *Times*," replied Dr Habershon. "He has suggested that time would be given for a reply from the Treasurer and then an article would follow."

"I shall write this evening to thank Mr Brudenell Carter for his efforts on our behalf."

"Excellent," replied Dr Pavy who, having read Mr Brudenell Carter's letter in the *Lancet* of Saturday June 26, had been impressed with the support shown them by the old campaigner and friend of Mr Hart.

"He can be rather vitriolic when roused," cautioned Dr Wilks.

Mr Robert Brudenell Carter had been abandoned by his father after his mother died giving birth to him in October 1828. He was taken into the care of a family friend, Robert Brudenell, sixth Earl of Cardigan, who had given the infant his name. Following an education and apprenticeship with a general practitioner, he entered the London Hospital Medical School at nineteen years of age.

Qualifying as both a surgeon and a physician, he had practised in Leytonstone. He had written about the women's condition known as 'hysteria' and diseases of the nervous system before going to the Crimean War as an army surgeon. On his return, he established himself as an ophthalmic surgeon and lecturer at St George's Hospital Medical School.

Like Mr Hart, who was his neighbour in Wimpole Street, he engaged in campaigning on medical issues through writing leading articles for the *Times* and the *Lancet*. He had recently written a trenchant criticism of Miss Burt and Miss Lonsdale in the *Lancet*. He referred to the reforms as having 'to submit to a yoke which I should regard as intolerable,' and praised the Staff for 'their magnanimity' and 'sense of duty' in putting up with them.

"Shall we reconvene at your residence, Dr Habershon, at nine o'clock this evening for one final check before I have the letter delivered by hand tomorrow?" suggested Dr Taylor.

The senior physicians, all near neighbours, agreed that this would be sensible and that they would beg their leave of the sisters at just before nine on account of urgent hospital business.

"What about the other physicians?" asked Dr Wilks.

"Dr Fagge lives in residence in St Thomas's Street; Dr Moxon lives in the wilds of north London; and Dr Goodhart lives in Blackheath. It may be too much for them to travel to Brook Street for a late evening meeting, especially given they have seen earlier drafts. Is there any value in pressing them to attend?" asked Dr Pavy.

"Dr Pye-Smith lives in Harley Street which is but a short walk from Brook Street, so he may be able to attend to represent the junior physicians," suggested Dr Taylor. "I think the President and Governors view him in a favourable light after his first-class testimony to the Inquiry in March."

After the meeting closed, climbing the stairs to Mary ward on the second floor, late for his ward round, Dr Pavy reminded Dr Habershon to send a note to his wife.

"You need to ensure a light supper is available, and some peppermint cordial for the inevitable dyspepsia," he suggested. "We shall have our fill at the sisters' soiree, but Dr Taylor will be beavering away until we meet so will have had no time to eat."

Dr Habershon had already started to make a mental list of the things he wanted to discuss. There was the matter of building and sustaining a crescendo of concern in the press and the possibility of engendering a Parliamentary Inquiry through Mr Hart's good office and his Parliamentary Bill Committee.

For now, he returned to his other worry.

"I am in a state of great irritation with Miss Lonsdale. I dismissed her from my ward as her challenges to my decisions were intolerable. I was roundly offended by her censorious article in *Nineteenth Century* and, despite my reply, along with several similar letters from our colleagues, she has had the audacity to challenge us again with a defiant open letter of rebuttal.

"That headstrong girl will be the death of me. What can we do to relieve this situation?"

As he rushed to join his houseman on the afternoon ward round, Dr Pavy replied, "Perhaps we should take up Hart's suggestion of using satire to erode her position. *Funny Folks* would be a sure vehicle. Shall we consider it further tonight?"

TWELVE

"Lovely, darling. You look lovely. I wonder if Mr Borradaile Savory will think the same." Mrs Habershon smiled benevolently at Ada, who was parading around the entrance hall in her new dress.

"Mama, from what I observe, he has eyes only for Florence Pavy."

The Habershon household was full of excitement as its ladies assembled in the hallway dressed in their best costumes. It was a warm summer's evening, so the three young sisters had been given permission to wear their favourite printed cotton dresses made from the finest of Liberty's summer collection.

In contrast, Mrs Habershon wore the more formal attire of a heavy silk gown with a wired underskirt that better suited her age and station.

As they fussed over each other's dressed hair and ribbons, and their choice of shawls, the daughters chatted about the evening's prospects. Would they prefer a glass of sherbet or lemonade, or a sip of cordial, with the feast that was being prepared for them next door?

Number 72 was a hive of activity in the basement kitchen where the Holland sisters' young cook and housemaid were in a lather rushing about the place finalising the buffet. Meanwhile, upstairs, the butler, George Mophett, and the page were busy in the first-floor drawing room arranging the chairs in two neat crescents around the grand piano, copying the French tradition.

No London soiree was complete without music and this evening the Holland sisters had invited the up-and-coming Mr Charles Hubert Parry to play his new composition, 'Fantasie Sonata in One Movement'. The perfect piece for a summer evening, it was light, lyrical and brief.

Caroline and Gertrude, the Holland sisters, were used to being out and about in society as their father had attended Caroline, Princess of Wales, the unhappy wife of King George IV. Subsequently, Dr Holland had treated the King's successors to the throne, King William IV and Queen Victoria, so the sisters knew how to host a soiree.

Leach had laid out his master's evening wear and had had the hot water readied. Flustered, the physician hurried down the stairs to join his family in the hallway.

"Where is my son?" asked Mrs Habershon of Leach, who was holding the door open in readiness for the family's short walk to the reception next door.

"He will join us as soon as he can, my dear," replied her husband. "I suspect he has been detained by an urgent case at the hospital, or he is stuck in the city's traffic trying to get home. Let us proceed without him and I shall make the required excuses on his behalf."

Swallowing her annoyance, Mrs Habershon led her daughters and husband to number 72, where they were greeted by the sisters. After the curtseying and bowing, the party was shown to the drawing room on the first floor by Mophett. The evening's summer glow was amplified by the sparkling chandeliers, mirrors and trays of glassware on the dining table.

The abundance of roses arranged in chinoiserie vases, warmed by the lowering sun, perfumed the high-ceilinged lounge as Mr Parry and his violinist tuned up at the pianoforte and checked their sheet music.

Mr William Scovell Savory, the po-faced widower from number 66, was a regular at the sisters' parties. The distinguished surgeon from St Bartholomew's hospital was already seated and eating some of the game pie that had been laid out for the guests.

Mr Savory was a celebrated lecturer at the Royal College of Surgeons, and at fifty-four years old he was a man of rank and influence when it came to appointing junior staff at his hospital. Like his colleague and neighbour, Guy's senior surgeon Mr Bryant, Mr Savory was a traditional anti-Listerism surgeon, but because of his elevated status at the College he still held sway over all things surgical in London. In attendance with him was his son, Mr Borradaile Savory, a clerk in holy orders who also lived at number 66.

The younger Mr Savory had just graduated from Cambridge where he had studied law, and was now a curate at the local church, St Georges, in nearby Hanover Square. Being the same age as the Habershon sisters, all in their early 20s, the younger Mr Savory mixed freely with them, making light conversation about the weather and the latest developments in the West End theatres. As he did so, he glanced around the room trying to catch Miss Pavy's eye.

Sir William Gull, the Holland sisters' neighbour on the other side of the Habershons, was seated and in conversation with the Dowager Countess Fortescue, who lived at number 68. Now seventy-six years old, the Dubliner had been part of Irish society and political life. Her father, Mr Piers Geale of Consilla, County Dublin, had been the Crown Solicitor for Ireland.

She had married her first husband, Sir Marcus Somerville, the Member of Parliament for County Meath, in 1825 when she was twenty-one years old. He was over thirty years her senior and had had a long political career where he promoted Catholic interests and voting reforms. After only six years of marriage, Sir Marcus died.

Widowed for ten years, Elizabeth was remarried in July 1841 to Hugh, second Earl of Fortescue. He had been the Lord Lieutenant of Ireland from 1839 to 1841, while serving in the government of Lord Melbourne. Upon its fall in 1841, and her husband's elevation to the House of Lords, the couple had moved to Brook Street where she continued to reside after her husband's death in 1861, when her two sisters, Marianne and Arabella, and her niece had joined her. They had a large household of nine servants, including two footmen for her carriage.

Sir William Gull's wife, Susan, and their son, William

Cameron, who was down from Oxford for the summer, were engaged in small talk with the Habershon girls when their brother entered.

"Pardon me, Sir, I was delayed at the hospital," he explained to his father.

"Ah, there you are my darling boy," welcomed Mrs Habershon as she settled him into her circle while she called for the butler to bring a glass of cordial. Mophett, who was circulating among the huddles of conversationalists, served more refreshments and some bouchées as the guests prepared for the music to start.

Mrs Pavy meanwhile smiled sweetly as her daughter, Florence, joined the Habershon ladies and the young gentlemen in a serious discussion about the role of theatre in society. They became more excited by talk of the successful and scandalous plays now showing in the West End, including the Adelphi's *The Shaughraun*.

The melodramatic play, written by the Irish playwright Dion Boucicault, had had a long and celebrated run in New York, home of the Irish Brotherhood, and was now enjoying the same plaudits in London. Its contorted plot praised Con, the Shaughraun – a wanderer and a poacher – and his Fenian friend, who had both escaped transportation, and defeated a local corrupt squireen.

Having directed the young ladies to take their seats, Mrs Pavy joined her husband and daughter, who were seated next to the Dowager Countess. As Sir William went to the buffet, Dr Pavy expressed an interest in the play.

"Fenians," exclaimed the Dowager Countess, "a play about Fenians challenging the state? What a disgrace! We shall not visit the Adelphi to be polluted with it. We must always tread with care in matters concerning Irish politics. The 'Irish Question' is too delicate for jest on the stage. Thank goodness its run is coming to an end on Friday. We shall have no more talk of this Fenian nonsense."

The Pavys sat in nervous silence as Mophett served more punch.

Their instruments tuned, the musicians signalled that they were ready. Mophett invited the remaining standing guests to fill the rows of chairs. When they were settled, he nodded to the elder sister, Miss Caroline Hamilton, who stepped forward to introduce Mr Charles Hubert Parry.

"My dear friends and neighbours, my sister and I welcome you here this evening to listen to Mr Parry, who is just starting his musical career."

A round of polite applause greeted the musicians as they stood to take a bow. Miss Hamilton continued, "You may know that Mr Parry and his patron, Mr Grove, are compiling a Dictionary of Music for Musicians." Another round of polite applause eased the nerves of the young pianist.

"Tonight, my dear guests," Miss Hamilton resumed, "Mr Parry will play his first work for piano forte and violin, a Fantasy Sonata." She raised her hand to stop more polite applause. "It lasts no more than fifteen minutes and then we shall adjourn for our buffet. Mr Parry, please...."

As music filled the room, the soft light and warmth of the summer evening, perfumed with the roses, took the guests away to their own private thoughts. For some, of childhood summers; for others, of dreams of new adventures to come. But neither for the senior Dr Habershon, who began to fret once again about the ghastly situation at the hospital.

Like his father, the younger Dr Habershon was also agitated, but rather at the thought of having to make conversation with Mr Savory.

Enthusiastic applause interrupted the Habershon gentlemen's reflections while smiles all round concluded the musical interlude, allowing Mr Parry and his violinist to mingle with guests at the buffet table. Lavishly set, it was full of gastronomic delights. There were cheeses and savoury pies; pickles and cold chops; and slices of fowl and meats with spicy sauces. To follow, the Hamiltons' cook had prepared fruit tarts, custards and sticky dates and almonds.

Mophett served sherbets, lemonade and cordials to the young ladies, punch to the older women, and sherry and claret to the gentlemen, who quaffed their drinks as if each were their last, except for Dr Habershon who enjoyed his peppermint cordial.

His eldest daughter, Gracie, chatted to the musicians about her musical aspirations as a church organist. Meanwhile, Ada engaged in earnest conversation with her dear friend Florence and her admirer, the young Reverend Savory, about his new role as the local vicar.

Ada spoke of her admiration for her favourite preacher, the celebrated Mr Charles Spurgeon, whose charismatic ministry attracted thousands of Nonconformist worshippers every week to his south London church, the Tabernacle. She spoke of his sermons with rapturous enthusiasm despite them being one to two hours in length, but took care not to offend the High Church curate and his beliefs in the Catholic rituals and practices of the Established Church.

The soiree progressed with much enjoyment and well-informed conversation. London was truly the centre of the country's cultural and political developments, and these Brook Street residents were part of that centre.

Mophett manoeuvred his way through the guests with a message brought by the Habershons' page.

"Grace, my dear, I shall have to leave shortly to attend to the urgent matter we spoke of," whispered Dr Habershon to his wife, who smiled and nodded discreetly.

While he and Dr Pavy bid their farewells and made their apologies to the sisters, Mrs Habershon was charming Mr Savory in light conversation with her son by her side.

Sir William, now apprised of the latest developments about the letter, indicated his support, even though he had not seen the final version. He promised he would do what he could with the President and the Governors, and Mr Lushington and Dr Steele, when the time came.

In haste, but not wishing to appear rude, Dr Habershon and Dr Pavy descended the stairs to the reception hall, where Mophett was holding the door open for them. As they rushed out into the warm, still light, evening, they found Leach anticipating their arrival at number 70. Nodding to the butler, the physicians rushed up to the first-floor drawing room where refreshments had been laid out.

The Habershons' drawing room ran the breadth of the first floor, mirroring the Hamilton sisters' salon, with its large windows shedding light on the sofas and ottomans. An oval French polished table served as a writing desk for Dr

Taylor as he laid out his papers, ink pot and pens. He opened the minute book where he had recorded the discussions and agreed actions of the Staff's meetings in this room going back to Miss Burt's appointment over seven months ago. He passed copies of the letter for everyone's perusal one more time.

As his seniors swallowed their drinks and considered the now exceptionally familiar letter, Dr Taylor settled himself at his station and, with his crisp white napkin tucked into his collar, enjoyed the salty meat and duck pastries prepared by the Habershons' cook. Leach crept around the room topping up the physicians' glasses with sherry or port as they read their papers, and prepared another peppermint cordial for his master.

"If your tummy rot is so persistent, may I suggest Mr Bell's latest carminative," suggested Dr Wilks. "I believe our pharmacist, Mr Bell, has perfected a fine recipe incorporating cardamom tincture; my patients speak well of it."

Helping himself to some of Dr Taylor's paper and a pen, Dr Wilks wrote out a script for 'Mistura Carminat' and handed it to Dr Habershon, who took it out of politeness.

"Thank you, old friend, I shall send Leach for it in the morning," replied Dr Habershon, passing the script to his butler. The mantel clock chimed half past nine as Dr Taylor gave his progress report and asked one more time if they were happy with the final galley proof of the letter.

"I think I speak for all, and we are content," exclaimed Dr Wilks as he looked at his colleagues for approval. Observing the nods, Dr Taylor turned to the roll call of signatories he had managed to secure that afternoon and evening.

"The physicians are complete except, I am afraid, for Dr Moxon, who could not be found," he reported. He was met by raised eyebrows as he continued, "We have the three seniors present in the room; Dr Fagge, Dr Pye-Smith, who cannot be with us this evening as he has a more pressing engagement; and Dr Goodhart, and myself, from the junior ranks."

There was a sense of disappointment about Dr Moxon. He had attended most of the group's meetings, but despite this and his excoriating rebuttal of Miss Lonsdale's views which had been published in May's edition of *Contemporary Review*, he seemed detached from the group.

Indeed, he was known to have been critical of unnamed physicians who resided in the West End when he had warned Dr Fagge, whom he greatly admired, not to be corrupted by what he called 'grandeur'. He thought such a disaster apt to happen when a man moved to Brook or Grosvenor Street.

"Time is very short, and Dr Moxon is a troubled soul. We shall have to proceed without him," suggested Dr Wilks.

"Agreed," they said, nodding to one another as they refreshed themselves with more drinks.

"Thank you," replied Dr Taylor. "The President and the Governors will have the letter in their hands tomorrow ready for the Court of Committee's meeting on Wednesday."

"The surgeons," he added, "are all accounted for except Mr Cooper Forster who could not be found, but we have Mr

Bryant's approval. Mr Durham from the mid-rank is agreeable, and the junior surgeons Mr Howse, Mr Davies-Colley, Mr Lucas, Mr Golding-Bird, and Mr Jacobson are all confirmed."

"Good work, Taylor," Dr Pavy cried. "What about the obstetric and ophthalmic specialists?"

"Mr Hicks and Mr Galabin have confirmed, as have Mr Higgins and Mr Bader," came the reply.

Not having Mr Cooper Forster's signature was a blow, but he was often away visiting gardens and ferneries.

"It is unfortunate, but his commitment is not in doubt. We shall have to proceed without him," concluded Dr Wilks.

With all in agreement, Dr Taylor packed his bag ready for the journey to St Thomas's Street where he lived in the hospital's residences with Dr Fagge and the junior surgeons.

"There is the final matter of the involvement of the press," Dr Taylor reminded his seniors. "It might be wise to consider the possible reactions of the President and the Governors, and Mr Lushington and Dr Steele. And what is our approach to Mr Hart and Mr Chenery?"

"Thank you, Dr Taylor," replied Dr Habershon. "I believe Mr Hucks-Gibbs is sympathetic to the nurses and to the administration's triumvirate, so I expect an adverse reaction from him and probably the same from the Governors."

"Agreed, but Mr Lushington did approve your actions barring Miss Lonsdale from working on your ward in the spring and I believe she only stayed at Guy's for a short period thereafter," Dr Taylor countered. "He is, I think, persuadable."

"True, but this does not make him a supporter," intervened Dr Pavy. "Indeed, his recent actions in humiliating the housemen and his likely support for Steele's recommendations make him a slippery character."

Dr Taylor suggested that they might compromise if Mr Lushington offered them a peace token – say, increased representation on the all-important Take-in Committee.

"I believe this to be a sensible proposition," intervened Dr Wilks. "After all, we will have to work with these people when all this is over."

Silence fell on the meeting as the physicians considered the issues until Dr Pavy spoke.

"Mr Hart and Mr Chenery, and Mr Brudenell Carter, are waiting for our instructions. We need a crescendo of public concerns, a clamour for action. I suggest we ready them and, depending on the response to our letter, take the planned course of action."

"Gentlemen, it is late," said Dr Habershon, "Let us reconvene after Wednesday's meeting of the Court to consider our position."

Before his departure, Dr Taylor removed a book from his bag and passed it to Dr Habershon. "You might like to look at this when you have a moment."

"*Sister Dora*," read Dr Habershon as he looked over the title page. "Published by Charles Kegan Paul. My word, it is by Margaret Lonsdale!" His colleagues leaned over to stare at the book.

"There is something of substance in Miss Lonsdale's

writing," said Dr Taylor. "I do not think we can dismiss her lightly. I have taken the trouble to read her account of the life of this woman, Miss Pattison, known also as Sister Dora. The woman is said to be the equivalent of Florence Nightingale for the Black Country in the Midlands. I understand Miss Lonsdale worked at Sister Dora's hospital before she arrived at Guy's earlier this year. I believe she is in her thrall."

"What is it about that irritating woman that she commands access to such publishers?" asked Dr Pavy.

"I have looked into her background," said Dr Taylor. "She is the daughter of the Reverend John Gylby Lonsdale, the Canon at Lichfield Cathedral. And there is more; her grandfather was the Bishop of Lichfield and an early Rector of King's College. She is from a High Church family of distinction." The physicians sat back, aghast at the thought of Miss Lonsdale being of a class above their own.

"I suggest you familiarise yourself with her writing and the way she has narrated the events of Miss Pattison's life," suggested Dr Taylor. "Despite the hagiography, Miss Lonsdale has shown some scholarship and indeed, some critical faculties not usually seen amongst our nurses."

"Well, there you have it," interrupted Dr Pavy. "The detested lady-nurse has written a biography of someone we have never heard of... I think we are not intimidated by Miss Lonsdale."

THIRTEEN

The main hall of number 70 was like the interchange at Clapham Junction as the party of physicians met the party of ladies returning from the soiree. The result was much chatter, bowing and curtseying as Dr Taylor tried to leave with his overstuffed bag and bundles of paper to board his awaiting carriage.

Dr Pavy and Dr Wilks joined Mrs and Miss Pavy in the throng outside the house as they boarded their carriage for the short ride home to Lower Grosvenor Street.

The young Habershon ladies swirled around the hallway, while their mother commented that she had enjoyed the music and thought Mr Parry might do well with practice. The ladies were attended by their maid who took their shawls and the bouquets of roses given to them by the sisters as they waved goodbye to Miss Pavy and her family. They were so excited at the prospect of a suitable marriage for their friend.

The younger Dr Habershon, accompanying his mother, bowed respectfully to his father.

"What ails you?" asked Mrs Habershon of her husband, who was clutching his stomach.

"My dear, it is only a bit of indigestion. I have eaten too much, and am paying the price for my greed. Gluttony is certainly a sin. Dr Wilks has suggested that I try a new formulation from Mr Bell. Leach has the script for Bell's attention in the morning. As to now, our work on the letter is done, but I have a speech to write which will not wait. I am so tired, my dear, but it must be done."

The hall clock chimed half past ten as Leach closed the house for the night and Dr Habershon settled into his study, where fresh pens and a pile of blank paper had been laid out.

Leach brought in a plate of savouries and a glass of peppermint water. Tucked under his arm was the book he had found in the drawing room buried under a cushion.

"Sir, I came across this book upstairs. It looked out of place... perhaps it was left by one of your colleagues? I thought you might need it for this evening's work," remarked the butler, placing the copy on Dr Habershon's desk.

"Thank you, Leach. I suspect it is more fiction than fact, but I will let you know in the morning," came the reply as the butler gently closed the door.

Dr Habershon settled into his wingchair to read the book under the dim gas lamp while drinking his peppermint water. The opening page startled him. There staring at him was a portrait of the eponymous Sister Dora. She looked frighteningly familiar. She looked like his adversary, Miss Burt.

Sister Dora was wearing the same get-up as the Guy's matron: an over-elaborate white bonnet with a ridiculously large lace bow tied tightly under her chin and a starched white apron pinned to the bodice of a long-sleeved high-necked all-enveloping black dress.

The frontispiece showed that the book had been published in April 1880. Dr Habershon pondered the date: just over eight weeks ago, about the time he had fallen out with Miss Lonsdale.

She had been assigned to his ward as one of Miss Burt's lady-pupils in March. He recalled that she was a striking beauty even though her hair was worn in the fashion of the Queen's, pulled back tightly into a bun from a severe central parting. Her good looks turned the heads of the young doctors and his patients.

He soon realised she was an intolerable busybody know-all who was always countermining his instructions. He had refused to work with her, and after he pleaded to the administrator for her removal she was dismissed from his ward. His stomach pains jabbed him as he thought of her.

Flicking through the pages, he formed the opinion that her writing indulged too much in hero-worship. He struggled to stay awake and concentrate on the chronology of the life of Sister Dora. He found nothing noteworthy in this undoubtedly good woman's life, which was spent in nursing the poor in Lichfield and Walsall.

The account of the smallpox epidemic in the mid-1870s sparked a fleeting interest, as did the account of the good lady's visits to Paris and London, but that was it. When she had died of breast cancer on Christmas Eve 1878, he noted that the town's officials had laid on a great funeral for her in recognition of the kindness she had shown to the Walsall miners.

Dr Habershon pondered how on earth Miss Lonsdale was able to persuade a publisher like Kegan Paul to print such rubbish. Why would a publisher want to print the minutiae of this woman's mundane life? Was it to keep the memory of Sister Dora alive? Perhaps it was to satisfy the trend for the literary genre known as 'women's books'.

As he looked at the book's last page, he thought the best part was before him where it said in capitals, 'THE END'. Thank the Lord for small mercies.

Sitting at his desk, he looked at the pile of journals calling for his attention. Some were already read and bookmarked for further work. There were past editions of the *British Medical Journal* and the *Lancet*, some prints of his beloved *Guy's Hospital Reports*, and a few copies of the monthly journals *Nineteenth Century* and *Contemporary Review*.

He would not normally have given his time to this latter type of publication, aimed at society's educated elite who wanted something contemporary to discuss to make them feel important and influential. But it was necessary on this occasion, following the publication of Miss Lonsdale's article. The *Nineteenth* had a lot to answer for.

He remembered when he had first seen the provocative piece with Miss Lonsdale's censorious accusations, entitled

'The Present Crisis at Guy's Hospital'. It was April 17, the date that Disraeli had resigned.

His stomach pained him as he recollected that Dr Taylor had been so incensed by the article's aspersions that he purchased sixty copies of the edition in a futile attempt to suppress its circulation. Each copy had cost half a crown and Dr Taylor had charged this expense to the School.

The administration had also been greatly distressed, especially as Lord Cardwell had already asked Mr Lushington and Dr Steele to conduct an inquiry into the issues raised by the reforms and the unhappiness they had caused to the staff.

Dr Habershon had read Miss Lonsdale's article many times and had made extensive notes on her arguments. His reply was published in the May edition to much praise from his colleagues both at Guy's and across London. The unrepentant Miss Lonsdale, having been sacked and now returned home to Lichfield, had had the audacity to pen yet another article in reply to his. It was published in the June edition which lay open on his desk.

Dr Habershon took off his jacket and removed his bow tie ready for the night's work. He dipped his pen into the inkwell and jotted a few notes for his forthcoming speech as the new President of the British Medical Association's Metropolitan Branch.

I shall have to focus my talk on the present nursing crisis, he thought, as he read Miss Lonsdale's latest attack on him and the medical staff. Her outlandish views could not go unchallenged.

He consulted his notes and his article of riposte. He re-

read the articles written in support of his arguments by Sir William Gull; Dr Octavius Starkey, of the Westminster Hospital; and Dr Seymour Sharkey, of St Thomas's Hospital. Even Mr Alfred Henriques of the London Hospital was moved to rebut Miss Lonsdale's accusations.

He checked the sharpest of exchanges between the elusive Dr Moxon and Miss Lonsdale. Moxon had clearly spent considerable time in his Highgate Woods study penning a long rebuttal for the May edition of the *Contemporary Review*. The crushing demolition of Miss Lonsdale's case was a forensic examination of every aspect of her complaints and recommendations, and her personality.

But still she came back with a further response in the June edition of the *Nineteenth*. Dr Habershon had to concede that she had an impressive level of confidence to maintain her position in the face of such vilification and hostility.

It was exhausting and depressing reading it all again. This was a case of too much injudicious letter writing, and it had to be stopped. *What about the speech* nagged his inner voice, urging him to get on with the task in hand so that he could get some sleep.

No, Miss Lonsdale had caused such widespread offence and it was up to him to squash her arguments once and for all. With a renewed burst of concentration, Dr Habershon checked his notes on her first article. In her criticism of the 'old' nursing system, she had discussed the ignorance of the nurses, their poor behaviour and attitudes, and their want of basic education and training. She had criticised the traditional needs of such nurses to merely understand 'particular medical men's fancies' for their patients, and to limit their scope of practice to pandering to their wishes with a view to gaining their approbation.

She was particularly brutal in her criticism of their ignorance of the first principles of nursing, and acid in her attack on the night staff, stating that sometimes they even slept while on duty, having worked elsewhere in the day. Dr Habershon could only speculate what Mrs Keogh thought about such accusations.

Miss Lonsdale had the greatest admiration for Miss Burt and her reforms, explaining them in the context of addressing the fundamental problems outlined in her criticisms. She wrote about the need for recognised standards and training by qualified tutors, with rotations across different wards. She argued that this was the correct way to increase nurses' breadth of practice.

It was an attempt to steal the dignity of medicine, and Dr Habershon was particularly vexed by her discussion on the need for nurses to be drawn from the class of educated gentlewomen like herself. She was emphatic about the need for such gentlewomen to wear a sombre uniform, like a nun's, to denote their authority. Worse, she suggested these women be accountable to the matron, and not to doctors.

His anger flashed as he reflected on this proposed challenge to medical authority and her praise for the detested Sisterhoods as agencies for improvement. He was appalled at her suggestion that the matron should be called 'Mother'. What popish nonsense! He crammed the last duck savoury into his mouth to quell his rumbling stomach.

His anger rose further as he read his notes about her offensive views on 'medical men' putting their private patients' needs over those in public institutions. He scowled as he recalled how Miss Lonsdale had rounded on the medical students as uncouth, badly behaved men lacking manners.

Miss Lonsdale had even suggested that the students had added to the low moral tone on the wards. No wonder the Staff held this woman in such contempt.

He jabbed his pen in the inkwell to load it sufficiently so that it would keep flowing while his tumbling ideas were converted into his scrawly writing. He wrote as if he was in an exam where there was too much to say for the time given. There followed much furious writing, many splodges of ink, crossings out, restarted sentences. He was manic in his attempt to keep up with his train of thought.

It was like being a medical student again, as he focussed on Miss Lonsdale's failings, without mentioning her name. It gave him great pleasure to criticise the Sisterhoods and to state that the idea of them being suitable agencies to organise and train nurses was preposterous.

As he got more excited about what he wanted to say, he became less inhibited. He corrected his work over and over as he tried to sharpen his arguments. Rejected drafts were screwed up and thrown in the bin and on the floor around his desk. His blotter was messy with ink spills and his carelessly placed pens dripped dark spots into the desk's carmine leather inlay.

Sleep called him as he struggled to find an excoriating

closing statement. He had done enough to send Mr Hart a draft in the morning.

Within minutes of tidying his papers and finishing the crumbs on his plate, he slumped onto the chaise longue by the window with the intention of taking a moment's rest. But the bolsters and soft cushions enveloped him and soon induced much-needed sleep, even though he was still wearing his party clothes.

Mrs Habershon crept in well after midnight to find him flat out on the chaise. She gently placed his jacket over him and turned down the lamps. She started to tidy up the mess around his desk. She saw a neat pile of written work beside the pile of journals, and a letter, as she removed his empty plate.

Curious to see what he had written, she looked at the top sheet marked 'Speech for the Metropolitan Branch of the British Medical Association's Annual General Meeting, July 1880.' Further down she saw 'Address given by Dr Samuel Osborne Habershon, Branch President', underlined. It was a well-earned election by his peers to mark his long medical career; public recognition, indeed. Her face creased into a smile of pride for her husband.

Turning the page, she read the usual opening tribute to the Association and its good works, mainly Mr Hart's. Past the opening paragraphs, he had written in praise of training for nurses, setting out the need for agreed principles of care to inform that training which should by necessity be delivered by doctors, underlined.

Nurses, he wrote, should be under doctors' control, and he explained the need for an auxiliary band to support nurses. She smiled with relief that he had taken her advice to be cautious, as she could not see anything that might cause offence. But her expression changed to that of alarm when she read the jarring sentence:

'Women who have borne the brunt of rougher work are more suited than those who have been brought up in the lap of luxury for the enduring fatigues of a nurse's life.'

No doubting the sentiment was correct, but the comment felt barbed. Was it aimed at someone specific?

Turning the page, she could hardly believe what she saw; had her husband written this? Surely not, she thought, as she looked over the words again. Looking at his scrawly writing, she felt a madness, perhaps from exhaustion, must have overtaken him.

The April edition of the *Nineteenth* lay open on the desk at page 683. Dr Habershon had marked paragraphs heavily with exclamation marks as if to draw attention to his anger at them.

His wife peered at the text and drew back in shock at the insinuations made by Miss Lonsdale in one of the underlined sections. My word, she said to herself, he has had a lot to contend with, as she whispered the lady-nurse's offending sentence to herself.

'But further, and quite apart from this, there can be no manner of doubt that a kind of moral restraint is exercised upon the conduct and general behaviour of the young house physicians and surgeons, as well as upon the medical students, consciously or unconsciously to themselves, by the mere presence of a higher class of women as nurses in the wards of hospitals.'

When she saw the founder of Guy's quoted by Miss Lonsdale as a justification for subordinating the Medical School to the comfort and due consideration of patients, 'Doctors are made for the sick, not the sick for doctors,' Mrs Habershon felt out of her depth. Clearly the troubles at the hospital these past six months must have been vicious. Originally offended that he had spoken disdainfully of the 'nursing species' in his speech, she became more sympathetic to his thesis.

She closed her eyes and thought of him standing in a public forum of doctors and surgeons talking about being thwarted by 'meddlesome interference of a conceited and ignorant busybody called a nurse'.

She worried about him reading out the list of offences committed by these 'conceited nurses,' who were guilty of being 'objectionable specimens'. There was more as she turned the page: 'most pretentious,' 'meddlesome and officious,' 'lethargic and obstinate,' 'worn out and intemperate,' and most cruelly, 'unsympathetic and heartless'.

She winced at what she read next. He had reserved his strongest comments and the reasons for his objection to the religious Sisterhoods for the speech's end-piece. He proffered that 'devoted nurses would be better without the bondage' of such institutions, claiming that they 'would be of more real value' because they were freer.

The depth of her husband's detestation of the Sisterhood's religious characteristics and rigid rules became apparent when she read his penultimate paragraph.

'Religious observances are placed above the duties of

the nurse, and she must conform to the requirements of the Order. It is a state where religious feeling and sentiment have sway. The dress, in all its detail, is of great moment; and badges must be worn, and the cross made into an ornament. It would seem sometimes as if the form of the nurse's cap was of especial value – it may be, extending to broad lengths of stiff starchy material. Would that it benefitted the patient to the same extent as it panders to the pride of the wearer! Unfortunately, these sisterhoods are often a bondage to those who are entrapped by them, and but few have the moral courage to break that bond. When a hospital hands over its nursing to such an institution, it does so bound hand and foot, and with eyes blinded…'

She shuddered at the thought of his audience at the Ship Hotel in nine days' time, full of drink and bravado on a warm July night by the river, egging him on to be more outrageous.

Casting around for fresh thinking, she picked up the envelope next to the pile of journals. It was addressed to a Mr William Sawyer of Pelham Place, South Kensington.

She peeked inside the folds and saw a sketch of a nun in the Order of St Vincent de Paul wearing the instantly recognisable overblown winged headdress. It was annotated with her husband's scrawly writing.

I shall have to inquire after this in the morning, she thought, as she put the note back on the desk and left her husband to rest a while longer.

PART IV: THE LETTER

FOURTEEN

'Louisa, I know you hold Miss Lonsdale in contempt. She inflamed the delicate situation that Easter with her overly critical writing, and she denounced you in that letter too readily, but I believe she meant you no harm. She was as shocked as any of us when she saw the consequences of her actions and I witnessed her distress at your fate. I have set out an account of that last Friday in July when she returned to Guy's to help Miss Burt and me prepare for the court case.'

Miss Lonsdale looked up at the sky from the dormer window of her old room in Matron's House. It had been raining all week but today, the clouds had lifted to give a bright summer's day. She readied herself to walk over to Paternoster Square in the City for a meeting with her publisher, Mr Charles Kegan Paul, of Kegan Paul and Company.

At just over a mile, walking would be preferable to taking a hackney carriage which would only get stuck in the grinding traffic on London Bridge. And she needed the air to freshen her mind in anticipation of a difficult meeting.

She had not slept well for the past month and last night had been no exception. Her worries were great, and the morning's papers had offered no relief.

"Have you all you need?" inquired Miss Jones, as she drew open the main door of the House. "A walk in the sunshine taking in some fresh air will do you good. It sounds like you will have an important discussion about the future for your book. Please be prompt for the matron this afternoon, as we will have much to do to prepare for the trial next week."

Miss Lonsdale was by now worn out with the many battles she had provoked with her notorious article in April's *Nineteenth Century*. She had managed to maintain the confidence and wit to carry the fight to her opponents, but the relentless criticisms of the past month, and now this dreadful development at the hospital, had proved too much to bear. And worse, she felt Miss Burt's reforms were in danger.

She stepped down to the front quad and hurried across to the main gate. Pulling her bonnet close to her face, she dashed along St Thomas's Street to the Borough and melted into the throng of people who jostled their way along to London Bridge. The sun was refreshing as she stopped halfway across to gaze downriver.

The cluttered dockside on her right was a familiar sight, with the masts of many tall ships poking up in a competition to reach the sky. She caught a whiff of the smoky stink from the tanneries in Bermondsey. She heard the cacophony of shouting from the wharfmen and labourers as they moved their cargoes to and from the warehouses that crowded this part of the river. She smiled at the familiarity of these everyday routines which carried on no matter what the weather.

Miss Lonsdale had travelled to London from her family home in the cathedral city of Lichfield the previous day at the invitation of Miss Jones, who had requested her attendance at an urgent meeting with Matron Burt. Taking the new fast service provided by the London North Western Railway from the Midlands, Miss Lonsdale had arrived at Euston station where she had taken a hackney carriage to Guy's. Miss Jones had arranged lodgings for her in her old room in Matron's House.

Isolated and lonely, miserable and upset, Miss Lonsdale had had no one to turn to, except for her friend, the kindly Miss Jones.

Mr Paul had also requested an urgent meeting with her to discuss the situation's potential effect on the sales of *Sister Dora*. He had had plans for its wider publication on the Continent, and possibly in America, but that was all in jeopardy now.

"Move along Miss, you're blocking the way," urged a city-type who did not care for a loiterer.

London Bridge was no place to stand and admire the river at this time of the morning. She felt jostled, pushed and shoved, and was about to give a sharp reply but thought better of it.

She was no stranger to London. Her grandfather, the Reverend John Lonsdale, had been the third Principal of King's College and had done much to develop its hospital as the fine teaching hospital in the Strand that it had become. Indeed, she had worked there as a pupil lady-nurse three years earlier, and her uncle, the Reverend James Gylby Lonsdale, had been a classics professor of some repute at King's.

She marched with the throng on to the north bank, where she paused for a moment to decide her best route to Paternoster Square. Perhaps King William Street was preferable to the busier Cannon Street, especially at this time of day, and the alternative of taking the Upper Thames Walk was unthinkable for a lady even in daylight. Its many narrow passages to the slipways and wharfs stank of the river and harboured ruffians, drunks, and prostitutes.

At least King William Street was safe at this hour and there were shops to peer into as she made her way up to the Bank of England.

Arriving at the junction with Mansion House and the Royal Exchange, she paused for a moment's rest at the Duke of Wellington's bronze equestrian statue. Its wit made her smile as it had been made from the melted down cannons captured at the battle of Waterloo.

The sun was higher, and it was warmer now, especially for a lady dressed in heavy wired skirts and a tight-fitting jacket to cover her high-necked blouse. Not to mention the bonnet.

The City's streets, alleyways and inner courtyards were bustling and its shopkeepers were out and about opening the awnings to protect the goods in their windows while offering passers-by a little shade. Miss Lonsdale drew up her skirts and dodged the carriages and carts as she crossed over to Poultry, past St Mildred's on the corner, and strode up Cheapside. She reckoned it was about a half mile to Mr Paul's office, so she would aim to arrive by quarter to ten to settle herself before the ten o'clock start.

Striding past St Mary-le-Bow and St Matthew's churches, she made good time and as she saw the dome of St Paul's, she thought about the substance of the meeting. Mr Paul wanted to discuss the series of articles in the *Nineteenth Century* which he had published for its founder Mr James Knowles. It was still a relatively new monthly journal as Mr Knowles had only started it in 1877 to rival his former journal, the *Contemporary Review.* Mr Knowles was no stranger to controversy. He liked to stimulate debate, but the current fracas involving Miss Lonsdale's article might have proved too much.

The ferocity of the doctors' responses had taken everyone aback, especially Dr Moxon's article published in the May edition of the *Contemporary.* Miss Lonsdale surmised that he must have spent many hours composing, drafting, and correcting his essay. The product of his brooding labours was nothing less than a vindictive personal attack.

What really upset her was its reception. It had found favour with many. Still, confident of her position, she had penned a response rebutting his rebuttal of her original article. She felt vindicated as she recalled that Mr Knowles had agreed to publish her letter in the June edition of the

Nineteenth where she had responded to Dr Moxon's insulting insinuations. And, for truth's sake, she corrected his factual mistakes which she had listed for the readers.

Things were different now. She felt on shaky ground as her position was becoming more fragile. Lost in her thoughts, she found herself at the five-way junction facing Sir Robert Peel's statue. The City's main post office on the wide boulevard St Martin's Le Grand was on her right and St Paul's Yard and the Cathedral were to her left. Feeling suddenly weak, she steadied herself by holding the post office's railings.

"Are you alright, Miss?" inquired a concerned passer-by.

"Thank you, Sir, I am," she replied, pulling herself up to cross over to Paternoster Row as St Paul's struck the three-quarters bell.

The thought of Dr Moxon and his comments made her angry. He had not shown her the respect an educated gentlewoman like her might reasonably expect. How dare such a man, the son of a tax collector, make annoying comments about her work?

Paternoster Row was an awkward narrow cobblestone street running south of the main east to west turnpike, Newgate Street. Crammed with publishers, booksellers, printworks and warehouses, it was the heart of London's book and journal publishing industry. As she passed the offices and shop windows, she hoped to see a copy of *Sister Dora* on display. Alas, she was disappointed.

The Row was dense with people, who fought for space with the carriages and delivery carts. The medieval road was hopelessly inadequate for the volume of traffic. She pushed her way on to Paternoster Square and the offices of Kegan Paul and Company.

As she arrived at building number 1 of the revamped Square, St Paul's great bells rang for ten o'clock. Although now open and relatively spacious for an inner courtyard, this former site of Newgate market still had its share of drunks and vagrants sleeping off the drink from the many public houses around the Square. With the White Hart on the west side and the Duke's Head and the pubs in Ivy Lane on the east, Miss Lonsdale could smell the fetid atmosphere from the night before.

Mr Paul's assistant, perched like a schoolmaster at his high desk at the office entrance, asked Miss Lonsdale to take a seat in the reception area. The glazed window etched with 'Kegan Paul and Company' let the light in but obscured her view of the crowded Square. She found some relief in just sitting and resting her feet. She took off her bonnet and tidied her hair, tucking in the wispy loose ends to restore its neatness around the harsh central parting that was the fashion.

She could hear how busy it was outside as the deliveries were offloaded and the dispatches were carted off either to Newgate Street to the north or to Ludgate Hill to the south. The usual Friday crush was made worse as it was also the end of the month when all the monthlies were sent out.

As the sun moved round, shafts of light illuminated the reception room and its shelves around her where Kegan Paul's latest and most prized publications were on display. There were leather-bound works by the Poet Laureate,

Tennyson, who Mr Paul had inherited from the poet's previous publisher, Henry King's of Cornhill, when he had taken over King's publishing business.

As she ran her fingers lightly across the book spines, Miss Lonsdale reflected on how far she had come since her teenage years when she had joined Miss Charlotte Yonge's essay-writing group for young ladies who were daughters of gentlemen of the High Church. They were known as the 'goslings,' and each girl had taken a bird's name as a pseudonym. Miss Lonsdale's had been 'magpie'.

Miss Yonge was a renowned and prolific novelist whose influence on her goslings was tremendous. The young ladies took turns to write and criticise each other's essays, and they went on writing holidays together. Miss Yonge wrote much in support of the Oxford Movement, where several of its leaders, including the Reverend John Keble, were her friends, and this sentiment pervaded her group's thinking and identity.

Scanning the shelves for *Sister Dora*, Miss Lonsdale was brought up sharp by the display of recent copies of *Nineteenth Century*. The sight of them plunged her back into her earlier agitated state.

Mr Paul would surely know about the calamity at the hospital, as it had been reported in yesterday's *Times* for all to see. Her spirits fell as she sank into a state of misery.

Only four months ago, she had been a confident High Church gentlewoman of thirty-three years with an impeccable lineage who had been assigned to the wards as a lady-nurse, and her biography of Sister Dora had just been published by Kegan Paul.

It had been a time of heightened tensions at Guy's, with the doctors' and old-style nurses' accusations reaching a crescendo. She had been so incensed by their condemnatory submissions to Lord Cardwell's inquiry, especially from Dr Habershon and Dr Pavy, that she had taken herself off to the hospital's library at every spare moment to write a defence of Miss Burt and her reforms.

How angry she had been as she penned the piece that was to become her signature article!

It was as if the protests of the medical staff and the events that they had engendered since Miss Burt's appointment had taken on a life of their own. That life had become like an unstoppable train hurtling to its inevitable crash.

Miss Lonsdale winced at the thought and felt a deep sense of upset that her own actions might have had a hand in the catastrophe.

"Miss Lonsdale, please forgive the wait." Mr Paul stood before her. "I have had much to do this morning. Tomorrow is 'Magazine Day', the last day of the month when we have to get all our dispatches ready for the booksellers and newsagents across the country, and the trains will not idle for us."

FIFTEEN

M r Paul invited Miss Lonsdale to be seated at the chair he held out for her while his assistant poured freshly brewed tea into a porcelain cup. She detected its fragrance; it was her favourite assam tea and she was grateful for the refreshment after her walk.

"I hope you are pleased with your book," inquired Mr Paul.

"I am, Sir. I am delighted with the quality of the publication."

"The sales are going well, and I am pleased with its progress. In due course, I should like to discuss its further publication with our Continental and American partners."

Miss Lonsdale felt her spirits lift.

Mr Charles Kegan Paul, now fifty-two years old, had been raised in Somersetshire, where his father had been a curate in Ilminster. Educated at Eton and Oxford, he had been ordained as a Deacon in the Church of England in the Lent of his twenty-third year. A year later, he had been welcomed into the Church as a priest with his first curacy in Oxfordshire, which was followed by a chaplaincy at Eton.

After twenty years, he found himself increasingly out of sympathy with the Church. While still a priest, he had dabbled in writing and editing but he now wanted to be part of the booming publishing industry, so he threw in his career in the Church to develop his literary career.

Circulations had been driven up in recent years by a combination of increasing literacy resulting from the many education reforms, and the relaxation of taxes on print media. Demands for more niche journals, papers, and books went through the roof to meet the many diverse tastes of a more literate population. Astute publishers like Mr Paul, who invested in new print technologies, could only benefit from such growth.

"Your father and uncle are well, I hope?" Mr Paul was familiar with Miss Lonsdale's relatives, having spent years studying their writings as fellow churchmen.

"They are in good health, thank you Sir. Both now benefit from their retirements. My father continues in Lichfield and my uncle has removed from his parish in Bath to live in Somersetshire."

Mr Paul had copies of her article and letters in front of him and a copy of yesterday's *Times* was open. Tucked underneath, Miss Lonsdale glimpsed the front cover of *Funny Folks*. She detested the satirical comic in the same vein as the penny dreadful papers. Her heart sank as she felt the weight of the past four months on her shoulders.

At eleven o'clock, a peal of bells rang out from St Paul's

and a dozen other churches in the vicinity to mark the hour. Mr Paul leaned forward.

"Miss Lonsdale, I should like a frank discussion concerning your reputation and the consequences for Kegan Paul of any injury to it."

She feared her literary career was about to be ended before it had really begun. Swallowing hard, she listened intently as he ran through all that was so familiar to her concerning her article and letters, and the responses they had generated.

He was particularly concerned about both Dr Habershon's recent article and Dr Moxon's overblown tirade against her. Neither could be ignored. And then there was the rebuttal article from the Queen's Physician, Sir William Gull, which had accused her of serious shortcomings.

"Additionally, I have it on good authority that Miss Nightingale has spoken ill of you in a letter to Mr Knowles where she expresses your want of any true understanding of nursing. She, too, is displeased by you."

Of all the criticisms she had received, this one from her idol wounded Miss Lonsdale the most grievously.

"Then there is the letter from Mr Hucks Gibbs, Guy's President, to the *Times*, where he also denounces you!"

Miss Lonsdale breathed slowly to calm herself as she listened to more of the charge sheet. Mr Paul was aghast at the level of venom directed at her in Saturday's *British Medical Journal* report of a speech given by Dr Habershon on July 7. And to make matters worse, he had to contend with the cartoon version of the speech which ridiculed the Sisterhood and Miss Burt's reforms.

"Then there is the issue of the impending trial. Counsel must consider whether your article of April and subsequent reply in June contributed in a meaningful way to the poisonous atmosphere on the wards and was therefore a contributing factor in the death of Dr Pavy's patient."

She understood if that link were to be established, Kegan Paul, as the publisher of the *Nineteenth Century*, and Mr Paul as its proprietor, would be disgraced alongside herself.

Although weeping inside herself, Miss Lonsdale stated that any connection between her article and the death of the patient was surely tenuous. There must have been an underlying pathology to the death, she asserted, and this would have to be brought out in court. She pleaded with Mr Paul to stand by her and wait for the details, despairing as to whether she would ever become part of Mr Paul's celebrated writers' circle. Gone too, she thought, would be her opportunity to publicise her book and write others. No one of repute would want to be associated with her. The gloom showed on her face.

"Miss Lonsdale, I too have been denounced so I sympathise with how you must feel," spoke Mr Paul softly. "You are not alone. Almost twenty years ago when I was a master at Eton, I wrote on the bounds of the Church of England, and I was condemned as a heretic by the Bishop of Oxford."

Miss Lonsdale looked at him in disbelief.

"Yes Miss Lonsdale, and I can tell you it was most

unpleasant to be condemned by that critic of anything modern, Samuel Wilberforce… old 'Soapy Sam' himself… and when that handwringer asked me publicly to withdraw the Tract, I refused."

Miss Lonsdale looked at him, astonished at what he had told her, and she felt buoyed by it.

"You too," she said in a whisper.

"I was in such disarray at his condemnation until I received the support of Eton's Provost. He allowed me to stay on at Eton despite the fracas. I was truly grateful for his faith in me and when I found a new position at Sturminster parish which better suited my family's growing needs, I moved with his blessing.

"And let me tell you, I have supported the modernists with vigour ever since," he added.

She felt some relief that her budding career might yet be saved. She had so wanted to be part of Mr Paul's exciting liberal-minded literary world.

He seemed well-connected to successful women writers whose unconventional lifestyles were tolerated, like Mary Anne Evans, who wrote under the pseudonym 'George Eliot'. She admired such women who were assertive about their views in a society which was altogether restrained. They seemed to be in no need of a man by which to define themselves.

She envied Mr Paul's visits to Miss Evans's Sunday Salon parties at her Regent's Park home. Miss Lonsdale dreamed about joining the author and her friends to discuss her favourite books like *The Mill on the Floss*, *Silas Marner* and *Middlemarch* which she had read as a teenager with her sisters at Eccleshall Castle in Staffordshire, her grandfather's residence. The vast house and its library, and the surrounding parklands, had hidden many reading spots.

Mr Paul's connections extended to those involved in the intense arguments about the future of the Established Church and its relations with Rome. As a young priest, he had been a Broad Church man, but he now mixed with proponents of both sides of the argument. He had been an undergraduate with the scholarly Mark Pattison and they had stayed friends ever since. Now, as the influential Rector of Oxford's Lincoln College, the Reverend Mark Pattison mixed with senior members of the Oxford Movement, whose networks were opened to Mr Paul.

When Miss Lonsdale's governess had fallen ill, she had been impressed by the nursing care given by Sister Dora from a local Anglican community. She was the Rector's sister, Miss Dorothy Pattison, and she inspired Miss Lonsdale to follow her into the High Church's nursing sisterhood. Miss Lonsdale's mentor, Miss Yonge, had held very traditional views about women's domestic duties, but she saw the Anglican Sisterhoods as an acceptable outlet for gentlewomen who yearned to do useful work, so she approved of Miss Lonsdale's choice.

After Sister Dora's death, Miss Lonsdale was commissioned by Mr Paul to write a biography of the good lady to mark her achievements and to keep her memory alive. He introduced her to the Rector for her research. Miss Lonsdale found him to be a traditionalist like Miss Yonge, but unlike her he did not approve of any gentlewoman going out to work, including his sister's work, even though it had been under the aegis of the Anglican Sisterhood.

Miss Lonsdale had been appalled at his disapproval, which extended to him refusing to attend his sister's funeral eighteen months previously because she had been a working woman.

"We will need to build a defensive wall around you and Kegan Paul," declared Mr Paul. "We need to shield you and our name from any criticisms that might arise in the trial. From what I have read of the appalling Dr Habershon and his medical colleagues, it seems to me that you embody for them the challenge of the unfamiliar. Your lucidity and confidence in writing is altogether too much for them. It is too scholarly and too lawyerly, and most unbecoming in a gentlewoman.

"I have studied their responses to your article," he continued, "and I think they may also find your class and connections quite intimidating. Just look at what Dr Habershon has said about you in both his article and his ill-advised speech in Greenwich earlier this month. He clearly thinks *Sister Dora* has no merit at all and I am concerned that his nonsense might affect our sales.

"Dr Habershon's judgement," he persisted, "is clouded by his detestation of you and the Burt Sisterhood that you represent and defend. He seems to think that the lady-nurses at Guy's are popish agents reporting the medical staff's actions to some higher authority, probably accompanied by the lighting of candles and the ringing of bells." Mr Paul paused for thought.

"The poor man is deluded, and he has clearly not read

the passages where you praise medical authority and express a willingness to accede to it on the wards. I think your reference to the young doctors' uncouthness and lack of manners may have hit a sensitive spot, probably because it is true."

"Medical students can be some of the most loutish men anywhere, even at Guy's," commented Miss Lonsdale.

"Talking of boorishness and vulgarity, I am equally if not more appalled at the rubbish written by Dr Moxon," he scorned. "I suspect he knew that we would not have printed his piece in the *Nineteenth,* so he has taken it off to the *Contemporary.* Well, Miss Lonsdale, they are welcome to him. At over twenty pages of personal attacks on you, it is the most shameful conduct I have ever seen. I question whether he is a gentleman."

Mr Paul searched the papers on his desk and pulled out the July 7 edition of *Funny Folks* with its stingingly offensive cartoon.

He mused that it seemed to follow the sentiments of Dr Habershon's speech rather too closely, suggesting that there must have been a plot instigated by Dr Habershon, and possibly others, to publicise their grievances and use the press to attack Matron Burt and her reforms, and Miss Lonsdale.

He pointed to the sketch showing the Guy's lady-nurses as wicked know-all hags dressed in the uniform of the Catholic nursing nuns of the Order of St Vincent de Paul, with their distinctive large, winged headdresses. They were shown countermining the instructions of a bespectacled old doctor, turning Guy's upside down and frightening patients.

"Sir, it is too offensive. The drawing implies our nursing reforms would usher in Catholicism and that we lady-nurses as High Church women are not to be trusted. It suggests we are too close to Rome. I am deeply offended by the slur."

"This is what we must refute with vigour," replied Mr Paul. "It is unacceptable that nursing in our hospitals might be seen to be under the malign influence of a higher authority, especially one sited in Rome."

"I, we, have been assassinated. I am in despair at the suggestion. As Miss Yonge would say, an Anglo-Catholic is not a Roman Catholic."

She felt a dark cloud of depression forming over her once again.

"And the other critics?" she asked quietly. "What of them… there are so many… can we fight them all and their collective ignorance? Some are very senior and influential."

She looked at him and thought of, but did not dare speak, Miss Nightingale's name.

"A pall of gender, class and religion, lies over the wards, Miss Lonsdale," came the reply. "Your arguments are too subtle for these unsophisticated people who have not been schooled sufficiently in the theological debate of the century. That is left to the likes of us and those close to the Church.

"The articles by Starkey, Storey and Henriques are noisy but worthless. They are all camp followers, supporting their colleagues. Ask yourself, did they train together… are they bound by their 'firm' pledges… are they linked by marriages formed at soirées in the West End where the successful make their way in due course?"

"Sir, I am out of my depth in these medical politics. I find it all quite unpleasant," replied Miss Lonsdale, reaching for her tea.

"I am worried about Sir William's opinion. His reach is great, and it could do you, and us, some harm," spoke Mr Paul after a pause.

Miss Lonsdale sensed a change in tone. She was not yet out of the woods.

"While the others rant about their obsessions concerning you, the Church and the Burt reforms, and diminish their arguments in the process, Sir William offers a pithy analysis of your views while emphasising your youth and inexperience. The result is quite damning as he questions the legitimacy of your observations."

"Sir, I understand he is a well-connected senior physician, but I never saw him at Guy's, not once, so how can he comment on Matron Burt's reforms, and my observations?

"I am the one who has had the most recent experience on the wards, and I wrote about what I saw. The legitimacy of my observations about the poor state of nursing at the hospital are indisputable... I reject his criticisms."

Mr Paul held a copy of the journal open at the physician's article and pointed to the second paragraph. "Sir William is entirely sympathetic to the need for a better class of nurses for the sick. But, as you can see, he suggests you have weakened your argument and raised up prejudice against your cause from, and I quote, 'a want of fairness or want of knowledge which have prevented a liberal recognition of the labours of those who have hitherto worked in this great field'. Miss Lonsdale, he accepts that things are not perfect but rejects your aspersions on nurses as a class."

"What is wrong with pointing out that too many of these old-style nurses spend too much time in the nearest public house and that their moral character is unsatisfactory? Perhaps," she added boldly, "he is sensitive about his own impoverished background. I believe his father was a wharfinger on one of Guy's estates in Essex."

"Miss Lonsdale," he replied, trying again, "he is not being censorious when he suggests that your opinion rests upon the most limited and superficial experience of only a few weeks as a learner of the rudiments of nursing. He is questioning the currency of your views. In this, he is echoing the views of Miss Nightingale."

Mr Paul leaned over his desk to show her where he had marked pages 885 and 890.

'I am constrained to say that this sort of writing... comes near to "evil-speaking"...

'Of course, it is not to be expected that this young writer knows much about the subject upon which she exercises her pen; therefore it would be unbecoming of me to press too hard upon the foolishness of her remarks. I would not write so strongly, but that the public may not be able to gauge the authority of the writer or the importance of the subject.'

Miss Lonsdale shuffled uncomfortably in her chair as the arrows started to find their target. Perhaps, she thought, she had been too hasty in forming her judgements and too harsh in her criticisms. She recalled with some dread her comments on the Medical School and its questionable values concerning the students' free access to the wards. Sir William's defence of his colleagues had been vigorous.

'The usefulness of our hospitals would be hopelessly impaired, if any hindrance were thrown in the way of the student in his practical studies... As to any inconvenience to the patients themselves, not only is none occasioned by the performance of the duties in question, but on the contrary it begets a feeling of confidence and satisfaction.'

"You are in danger of being seen as partial and exaggerated in your writing," said Mr Paul. "He accuses you of jealousy of the medical staff and he expresses his doubt that your article is all your own work. Who does he think had a hand in this?"

"I have no idea why Sir William made those comments other than in spite. If there is a hand other than my own, perhaps he may be referring to Mr Knowles in his editorial role. He is known to enjoy stimulating debates around controversial issues, is he not, and I believe he is acquainted with Sir William. Perhaps there is tension between them."

"You will need a softer attitude," suggested Mr Paul. "We need to reduce the excitability of the situation. Miss Lonsdale, I want no more letters from you until this all blows over. I suggest if you are not called as a witness, you stay out of sight and let the trial take its course. I am no lawyer, but it seems to me that the case is without merit, and I am confident that it will be thrown out."

Miss Lonsdale agreed to his plan despite her misgivings. Her family had friends in Wales, and they would certainly be happy to accommodate her until things were back to normal. After all, she mused, there was much reading and walking to be done, and maybe some time for nursing in a country hospital far away from the metropolis.

"What about the satirical press?" she inquired. "How will you overcome their lust for scandal and poking fun?"

"Mr William Sawyer is already in receipt of a note from me," replied Mr Paul. He had sought to divert the editor's attention to other stories in return for some future favour. "I shall approach Mr Chenery of the *Times* and Mr Hart of the *British Medical Journal* first as they have the potential to do the most damage with their editorials, which are syndicated around the country and to the international press. I will approach Mr Wakley of the *Lancet* too as they all have the power to commission articles from hotheads like the self-righteous Brudenell Carter. I have little regard for his histrionic wailing, but he exerts some influence because of his family name. I shall try to get a favourable opinion from the *Spectator*... the editor is reasonable," he continued. "But I fear that I will have little purchase on the rascals at *Punch* and the tabloids.

"We need to secure an agreement with the London papers," he added, thinking about the other important circulations. "They are going to relish this case as it is in the heart of London and involves doctors and nurses fighting. I imagine they will fill the press gallery at the Old Bailey next week. Nothing like a murder or manslaughter to get them out.

"Where are you going to now, Miss Lonsdale," he inquired. "May I call a cab for you?"

"Thank you, that won't be necessary," she replied as she stood and tied her bonnet in place ready for her walk. "I have some time before I need to return to the hospital, so I shall walk over to the Central Court to see the trial list for next week. I would like to know which judge has been assigned to hear the case."

"Let us hope it is not Judge Hawkins." Mr Paul showed her to the door. "His judgements can be mixed... they are, at times, illogical... and cruel!"

Sixteen

Crossing to the west side of the Square, Miss Lonsdale joined Ave Maria Lane at Amen Corner. She loved these old medieval narrow streets as they twisted and turned, and she smiled as she made her way into the courtyard of Stationers' Hall. It was one of London's oldest livery companies with a dignified frontage and a garden where she often rested after visiting the Hall's panelled rooms with their magnificent windows and ceilings.

"Bread rolls for sale... Want one, Miss?"

She pointed to the bun she wanted and handed over a halfpenny for it. Turning away from the seller and taking a seat in the garden, she took a generous bite and felt the desired relief as the warm bread satisfied her hunger pangs.

While eating, she kept her wits about her. The area was notorious for pickpockets, especially around the end of the month when there were more people about doing their book business, and the crowds gave ample opportunity to evade capture. Discreetly wiping the crumbs from her face and jacket, she left the garden and walked round the back of St Martin's church into Ludgate Hill.

The church with its tall steeple, designed by Sir Christopher Wren, had been rebuilt after the Great Fire. Its unfussy elegance stood in marked contrast to the grim high-walled judiciary buildings along the Old Bailey to her right. The courthouse had been built and rebuilt on the site of the old Sessions House and now had four court rooms, and fine offices and dining rooms for the judges and lawyers, and the clerks of the court and their staff. In contrast, the prisoners' holding cells in the basement were dire.

The Bailey, as the street was known, had defined the western boundary of the City of London in medieval times. Now, London's Central Criminal Court and Newgate Prison ran the length of it and Friday afternoons were some of its busiest times as judges tried to clear their cases and get the guilty locked up before the weekend. Those on remand, and the convicted who were not jailed in Newgate Prison, were carted off in horse-drawn prison vans known as Black Marias to the Houses of Correction across London.

The police parked their vans along the street and the drivers fed their horses while they waited for the prisoners. All this added to the chaos in the area as the Bailey was a main south—north throughfare which connected Ludgate Hill and Newgate Street.

If the case was of special interest or involved a famous person, the press pack added to the crowds who often gathered outside the Court for a glimpse of the prisoners as they were brought out. Pushing and shoving were the rule as people tried not to step or fall into the road, by this time of day covered in horse dung and discarded rubbish.

Miss Lonsdale pushed her way through the crowded malodorous street to the glass-cased noticeboard outside the entrance gate where the Clerk of the Court had posted the following week's timetable of trials. She fingered the glass as she worked along the lists looking for the case.

She saw it and gasped for breath.

> *Pleasance Louisa Ingle indicted for, and*
> *charged on the Coroner's Inquisition*
> *with, feloniously killing and slaying*
> *Louisa Morgan.*
> *Messrs Poland and Montagu Williams,*
> *Prosecuting.*
> *Sir John Holker Q.C. and Mr Mead,*
> *Defending.*
> *Presiding, His Honour Judge Henry*
> *Hawkins.*

"Anyone you know, Miss?" inquired a policeman, trying to shield her from the pushing and shoving at the gate. With Mr Paul's earlier warning about Judge Hawkins ringing in her ears, she looked at the officer and was momentarily dumbstruck.

"Officer, do you know anything of the judges... Judge Hawkins?" she asked.

"Best not to get in front of him, shall we say. Miss, they

will be bringing out the prisoners very soon. Better be away before this crowd becomes too boisterous. If you want to know about one of Hawkins's recent cases, have a look at the Euston cellar murder. It's most peculiar... and the press are all over it... a sensational madness over a servant girl... too big for her boots."

She followed him through the crowds and thanked him for guiding her back to Ludgate Hill where she straightened her bonnet and brushed the dirt off her jacket and skirt. She had most of the afternoon free and would have liked to have had some refreshments, but the Chapter Coffee House and Dolly's Chop House, which were both close by in the Row, were not open to unaccompanied gentlewomen like her. She thought about Lincoln's Inn, where she knew the Clerk. He might serve her some tea.

The walk to the Inn was less than a mile along Fleet Street and through the lanes around the back of the Royal Courts of Justice. She knew the area well as her old alma mater, King's College hospital, was in Portugal Street by Lincoln's Inn Fields where she used to stroll on her days off.

Fleet Street was its usual tedious self, the crush made worse by the many drunks staggering around because they could not hold themselves upright. Gin, she cursed, had a lot to answer for.

Dishevelled, she arrived at St Dunstan's church where she called in to straighten her bonnet and smarten herself. No time today to admire one of her favourite church interiors with its distinctive octagonal vestibule, as she stepped back into the melee on Fleet Street and turned up Chancery Lane to make her way to the Inn.

What relief as she entered the Inn's gate that led to its private walled garden, around which its barristers resided and worked in their chambers. In another time, might she too have gone to Oxford or Cambridge in preparation for a legal career in one of London's four Inns like the men in her family?

"Good afternoon, Miss Lonsdale, how very nice to see you again," greeted the Clerk, Mr Styles, who had been called to the gatehouse to accompany the lady into the Inn.

"It's been a few months since we've seen you. I think it was Easter time... weren't you researching for an article you were writing? Are you well, and your father?"

"I am, thank you, and my father too," she replied as they walked into Mr Styles's office where he offered her a chair facing his desk, which was piled high with briefs waiting to be allocated.

"Mr Styles, I am in town on important business, and I need to look at the latest Law List. Have you a copy of this year's edition?" she asked, smiling at the sinewy old man who had been at the Inn since his twenties.

"We have indeed, and you are welcome to view it. Anyone of interest to you, and why so if I may ask?"

"I am afraid it concerns a case of manslaughter listed for the Central Court next week. I have some knowledge of the issues and the persons involved. It is most distressing."

"I think you are referring to the case against Miss Ingle of Guy's Hospital, are you not? I have been following the developments of the nursing dispute in the *Times* for months and I read the report of the Coroner's Inquest on the deceased on Tuesday... a case of death by cruelty and neglect... how are you involved, Miss Lonsdale? Are you looking for representation?"

"No, I am not," she replied. "I am trying to help Miss Burt, Guy's matron, to build the case for Miss Ingle's defence with Sir John Holker. He has been retained by the hospitals' administration."

"Sir John?" he queried. "He was the Attorney General for Disraeli until the recent change in government... a fine prosecutor and a senior barrister... but do you think he is sufficiently experienced as a defence lawyer?"

"I do not know, which is why I'd like to look at the Law List... I'd like to check the legal teams involved so I can inform Matron Burt of any weakness," she replied.

"Well, let's get you seated in the library... you know your way around so find a spot with good light and I'll get the List for your perusal. It's Friday afternoon so there will be nobody in there to disturb you," smiled Mr Styles.

Miss Lonsdale found her favourite place in the empty library and helped herself to some newly sharpened pens and an ink pot from the stand. She had her own paper, which she fished out of her bag.

"Who is assisting Sir John?" inquired Mr Styles as he laid the volumes of the List out on the inspection table. "And who is prosecuting?"

"I believe Mr Mead is defending and Mr Poland and Mr Williams are prosecuting," she replied, recalling the details listed on the Court's Notice.

"My word, they are the same lawyers as in the Dobbs cases!"

"The Dobbs cases?"

"Hannah Dobbs was the accused in the Euston cellar murder. It's been running in the courts all year… you must have seen it in the papers… caused quite a sensation… the *Illustrated Police News* and the tabloids have had a field day with it."

"I have no knowledge of it, and I cannot bring myself to look at the gutter press," replied Miss Lonsdale with disdain.

"Dreadful, nothing but dreadful. That cunning housemaid… quite a showgirl who played the press with some skill… vilified a decent man, her landlord, who sued for defamation and then he got tried for perjury… very nasty indeed.

"The first and third cases were heard at the Central Court before His Honour Judge Hawkins no less, and the second was before the Bow Street magistrate."

"Judge Hawkins is listed for Nurse Ingle's case," interjected Miss Lonsdale. "What do you know of him?" She felt a pang of concern as she recalled the policeman's comments.

"Judge Hawkins must be the same age as your father. He trained at Middle Temple and was called to the bar when he was in his mid-twenties… took silk over twenty years ago when he was in his early forties… been very successful as a fighting advocate… worked on a few important cases… and juries liked him… had a record of winning verdicts."

Mr Styles selected the 'H' volume and thumbed the pages to find the judge's entry.

"A slender man... quite handsome." He laid the opened volume in front of Miss Lonsdale. "I think he is fond of horse-racing... may be a member of the Jockey Club too... suspect he'll get his peerage soon enough.

"He became a judge of the Queen's Bench Division nearly four years ago," he continued. "Likes to be known as Sir Henry Hawkins rather than the usual Mr Justice Hawkins." Mr Styles laid a copy of the court report of the Dobbs cases before her. "Hates cruelty and deliberate outrages against either person or property... uses the death penalty if deserved... look at the Penge case, I think.

"Known as 'Hanging Hawkins' by the tabloids but I think that's unfair. In fact, I think he moves to leniency for first offences. A decent High Church man from what I hear... known for his devoutness.

"Ring the bell if you need me," he said, leaving the room. "I'll bring some tea later."

Miss Lonsdale began to read the entries in the Law List. The question that nagged her following Mr Styles's comment was whether Sir John was good enough as a defender. The seeds of doubt had been sown. Perhaps Mr Mead as his assistant could make up for any deficiencies.

Sir John Holker, she read, was in his early fifties and had been a senior lawyer, a Queen's Counsel, for nearly fifteen years. He was also the current Member of Parliament for Preston, near Manchester, and until recently had served as the Attorney General. All well and good, but did that make him a good defence lawyer?

Looking at the notes of the first Dobbs case where he had been the prosecutor, she surmised that he had seemed to be slow in making his arguments.

Mr Mead, on the other hand, as the defence counsel was aggressive and relentless in his inquisitorial style. And he had successfully introduced an element of doubt in the minds of the jurors concerning the charge of murder against Miss Dobbs, who was found not guilty. Perhaps Sir John, she reflected, could lean on Mr Mead in Nurse Ingle's forthcoming trial.

And what of Mr Poland and Mr Williams, she asked herself as she stared at the shelves of books facing her, how effective might they be as a prosecution team? Mr Harry Bodkin Poland, who was about the same age as Sir John, had spent his life since qualifying at Inner Temple Inn practicing at the criminal bar in London, which had made him very wealthy. He was from a family of eminent lawyers and his quiet, lucid, and unimpassioned style, and his sense of fairness, were liked by juries.

Mr Poland's assistant for the Ingle case, Mr Montagu Williams, had had a more colourful career. First he had been a teacher and then an army officer, then he had tried his hand at acting followed by a stint as a playwright. He then pursued the family's legal tradition and entered Middle and Inner Temple Inns, where he was called to the bar in 1862.

Looking at his record as a defence lawyer, Miss Lonsdale noted that he had lost several of his cases with the result that his clients were hanged. He seemed to be better as a prosecutor, she thought, reading the sordid details of the defamation and perjury trials in the Dobbs case notes where Mr Poland had been the defence counsel for Hannah Dobbs's landlord.

Mr Styles came in with a cup of tea and a plate of biscuits. "Don't worry, there's no one to tell tales on us," he whispered, placing the tea tray down.

"My word, you've been industrious," he remarked as he looked at her sheaf of notes.

"Well, Mr Styles, I have identified possible weak spots in the defence lawyers, and I'm worried about how good the prosecutors might be, given their records."

"I'm afraid there isn't much you can do about it now as the pairings have been notified to the court. But from what I've read, the case is without merit and will probably be thrown out by Judge Hawkins anyway."

"I hope so," she replied, sampling her tea. "I shall express my concerns to Miss Burt and she may permit me to approach Sir John and Mr Mead this weekend as they prepare the defence case.

"Mr Styles, may I ask what will happen to Nurse Ingle if the trial proceeds and she is found guilty?"

"I'm sure it won't come to that. But in the case of manslaughter, she could be sentenced to life in prison. She would be surrendered in court and taken down to the holding cell where she would be clerked into Newgate Prison. It's a fierce place and I don't think she would serve her time there. She'd probably be transferred to one of the prisons for women and children. It would be a life of hardship, boredom and lice."

Miss Lonsdale stared at the library's high stained-glass windows with the afternoon sunlight streaming in. It illuminated the coloured glass pictures of saints enduring their martyrdom, and she wept.

"Come now, my dear lady, it won't come to that. Justice will prevail and the case will be thrown out, you mark my words."

She composed herself, dabbed her eyes and cheeks and packed her things, ready to depart.

"Forgive me for asking, Miss Lonsdale, but in your letter to the *Times* earlier this week, I believe you were critical of Miss Ingle," queried Mr Styles.

"Indeed, I was. I was so shocked at the accusation… no lady-nurse would have done such a thing. I questioned whether she was ever one of us… I have had my doubts since this revelation. My primary concern is to defend Miss Burt and the reforms."

"I wish you well and you are welcome to use the Inn's library again," he said. "Would you like me to call you a cab to take you back to Guy's? If you leave now, you will probably avoid the worst of the Friday crush."

"That would be a kindness, Mr Styles."

"How is your uncle, Sir Edmund… I hear he is the Vicar General in York?" asked the clerk, who had entered Lincoln's Inn at the same time as Sir Edmund Beckett. They had progressed together, he from being a runner to the senior clerk of the Inn and Sir Edmund from being an apprentice lawyer to one of the country's top barristers.

"Well, thank you, Mr Styles."

He showed her to the gate house and spoke to the driver who was waiting for them. "Make haste to Guy's Hospital before the streets get too busy."

As the cab slowly made its way through the traffic and the crowds, Miss Lonsdale passed the statues she had seen earlier that morning. There were none of the women who had achieved so much like Mary Wollstonecraft, Elizabeth Fry, Florence Nightingale... it was an injustice that had to be put right.

She wondered what it would take to commission one for her mentor, Sister Dora. She made a mental list of the people she would need to write to about raising the necessary funds and she thought about where the statue might stand. It would have to be in Walsall, she decided.

She had had dealings with the men of that local authority in the past and recoiled at the thought of having to deal with them again. There was always Sister Dora's brother, the Rector, though he had disapproved of his sister's work. Maybe a local fundraising event in Walsall, although the people were so impoverished they could hardly afford a loaf of bread, so were unlikely to give her enough money for a statue.

At the Monument, the driver made the sharp turn south to cross London Bridge as her thoughts turned to the meeting with Miss Burt at five o'clock. She had an hour to read the Coroner's Report that Miss Jones had promised to make available for her in the chapel. They had agreed that it would be inappropriate for Miss Lonsdale to be seen in the Medical Library given the circumstances.

As they arrived at the hospital's main gate in St Thomas's Street, Miss Lonsdale dismounted the carriage and pulled her bonnet down to make her way quickly across the front quad.

Mr Gladstone, she thought, in a flash of inspiration as she entered the hushed church. Although she knew he was not inclined to spend public money, surely he would support her cause for such a good woman. She would write to him for the funds upon her return to Lichfield.

SEVENTEEN

M iss Lonsdale caught the faint waft of extinguished candles as she closed the main door of the chapel behind her and walked around the white marble statue of the founder placed at the entrance facing the altar.

She stopped in front of it, as she had always done, to admire the fine work by John Bacon of the Royal Academy, a local Southwark man of the last century. She looked up at Mr Guy set in the formal dress of a gentleman of the late 1700s with his flowing robe tumbling behind him. The sculptor had shown him stooping tenderly to help an emaciated beggar with his left hand while pointing to the hospital steps with the other.

She liked Mr Guy's family crest of three crowned leopards and fleurs-de-lis which topped the centre of the dark green marble decorative arch that framed the sculpture. Such a deserving honour for this great benefactor! She read the crest's moto: 'DARE QUAM ACCIPERE'. Being a scholar, she knew its meaning and the biblical source. 'More blessed to give than to receive,' she thought with satisfaction, Acts 20:35.

But the sight at the bottom left of the tableau reminded her of the current difficulty. It showed two porters carrying a stretchered patient at the top of the front quad steps leading to the colonnade. The place of Miss Burt's humiliation, when the students had rioted and had formed the gauntlet of hate. Had that really been only six weeks ago?

She took a seat in the back-row pew, arranging her voluminous skirt neatly around her. She had the place to herself and took off her bonnet to feel the afternoon sun's warmth as the light streamed in. Relaxing, she loosened her boots to relieve her swollen feet. She clasped her hands in prayer and begged for divine intercession as Mr Styles's words came back to her, 'hardship, boredom and lice'.

The prayer books were piled up on the other back pew ready to be laid out for the evening's service. She picked one up and thumbed through the pages looking out for her favourite hymns. She had spent much of her time in this place when not on duty on the wards. With her fellow nurses, she had attended morning and evening prayers led by Miss Burt as part of their daily routine.

"Miss Lonsdale, what a delight to see you again," spoke the Reverend James Flood in his usual hushed tone. "I have been looking forward to your visit, although not the circumstances of it. There is much unhappiness here, as you know."

"Thank you, Sir," she replied. "It is very comforting to be back in my favourite chapel."

"You do surprise me. I have always thought our modest chapel a poor cousin to the places of worship you are used to with your father's glorious Lichfield Cathedral and your grandfather's chapel at King's College."

"They are both magnificent but rather ornate, and too dark and baroque in the case of King's. One can find a moment of peace for contemplation in this simple place."

"Your father is well, I trust. And what of Sophie, is she still a source of irritation to you?"

"My father is well and now retired. As for my little sister, she is becoming more strident by the day in her views about women's place in society and whether gentlewomen should work. I fear we are set on different courses, and she is no comfort to me in my distress."

"I think you will find many families are increasingly riven around the same issue," he sighed. "The current difficulties here at Guy's will no doubt be used by both sides to bolster their arguments.

"Now, Miss Jones has asked me to give you the Coroner's Report in preparation for your meeting this afternoon. It's not too long but it is shocking in the details."

She took the report and as she opened it, the chaplain leaned closer to her and whispered, "Dr Pavy has been most insistent on the cause of his patient's death as neglect and cruelty inflicted by Nurse Ingle. He claims her actions can be laid at the door of Miss Burt and her reforms. It is most upsetting."

"I am truly distressed by Dr Pavy's accusations," she

replied, looking about her to make sure they were alone. "And as for Dr Habershon, I am appalled at his latest letter to the *Times* published last Saturday. Did you read it? It is offensive in the extreme. His behaviour has taken a turn for the worse. It is as if he has lost all sense of reason. I was so angry I had to write to the *Times* myself in defence of Miss Burt. Perhaps you saw my reply in Wednesday's paper?"

"Miss Lonsdale, may I offer some friendly advice?" he whispered. "Proceed with caution. Mr Lushington, on behalf of the President and Board of Governors, has placed an injunction on Guy's staff writing about the hospital's affairs in public, so you must hold your pen at least until after the trial has taken place."

"Well, his instruction has clearly been ignored by those physicians," came the sour reply. "Anyway, I am not on the hospital's staff... I am a private citizen, and my letter clearly shows my Lichfield address.

"Reverend Flood, do you think the case against Nurse Ingle has merit? I spoke with an old friend who is familiar with the law, and he thinks the case will be thrown out."

"I fear these are strange times and with the unceasing press campaign against Miss Burt and her reforms, and yourself, who knows what may happen? This is the culmination of a tragedy which has been long in the making. The physicians will have their day in court."

"And Miss Burt and the reforms will be the victim of this charade," sighed Miss Lonsdale.

He handed her the sheaf of papers bound in twine and, bowing, left her alone with her reading while he busied himself with preparations for the evening service.

The inquest, she read, had been held on Monday July 26 at Guy's Hospital by the borough of Southwark's coroner, Mr William Payne. The barristers, Mr Baggallay and Mr Chalmers, had appeared respectively for the hospital authorities and for the medical staff, and Mr Henry Taylor, a solicitor, had represented Miss Ingle, who was the nurse in attendance on the deceased patient.

How could Nurse Ingle afford a solicitor, Miss Lonsdale asked herself as she read the introductory paragraph. Miss Ingle must by now be quite destitute as she had been dismissed by Miss Burt and Mr Lushington on July 10 at Dr Pavy's insistence.

"Reverend Flood, I have a query concerning who is meeting the costs for the defence lawyers?" she asked the chaplain, who was laying out the prayer books.

He returned to her side to murmur, "Dr Steele is meeting all the costs. It is a great comfort to Miss Ingle in her hour of need. Blessed be his kind soul."

"Dr Steele," she echoed quietly to herself. She had long admired the man, who was nearly thirty years her senior; and she was charmed by his Scottish lilt and handsome looks.

"Dr Steele has been a staunch supporter of Miss Burt," Reverend Flood continued. "Did you see the papers on Tuesday when the details of the death were released… the *Daily News*, the *Times*, and the *Evening Standard*—"

"—I have seen the editorials and they are indeed cruel and misjudged. You surely cannot find fault in me rising up to defend the matron."

She turned away and read on. Mr Charles Morgan,

husband of the deceased and a local labourer, had explained that his wife had been ailing but was not seriously ill when she was admitted to Mary ward under Dr Pavy on June 9. She had complained of pains in the chest when he had visited her, but had said she was well enough a fortnight last Sunday to want to get out of bed and get dressed if a neighbouring patient could help her. She had had a fall, Mr Morgan explained, when she had tried by herself, but seemed to have suffered no harm.

On a following visit, Mrs Morgan had told her husband that she had been dragged along the ward and that the nurse had been cruel to her.

He testified that Nurse Ingle knew about the bruises that he had seen on his wife's arm and chest, and that she had wanted to explain them but he had declined to listen. Instead, he had warned her that if anything happened to his wife, she would have to account for it.

As Mrs Morgan deteriorated, her husband had been given permission by Sister Mary to visit morning and night until she died just after eleven at night on Wednesday July 21. On reading this, Miss Lonsdale closed her eyes in prayer for the dead woman. She could picture the ward and the deathbed, having served under Sister Mary on that ward during the spring.

She scanned the pages to see who else had given testimony to the Coroner. Dr Pavy's submission was followed by his houseman, Dr Howell, then Sister Mary had given evidence followed by the ward maid, Emma Costello.

Emma Costello?

She had to read it twice to take in what she was seeing.

Miss Costello was not well-regarded by the lady-nurses as her sly insolent behaviour had offended them greatly.

She tried to put her disgust to one side to concentrate on the report. Dr Pavy had confirmed that Mrs Morgan had been admitted for phthisis, or consumption, affecting the upper part of the left lung, and it was associated with hysterical tendencies. Her symptoms were not marked, he added, and she had had no fits, merely signs of hysteria and weakness.

Miss Lonsdale rolled her eyes at the lack of precision in this statement, and when she saw he had prescribed regular walking as the treatment, she thought it all guesswork.

Everything, Dr Pavy said, changed on Monday July 5 when he saw his patient during the afternoon ward round. He found Mrs Morgan was shivering. He testified that Mrs Morgan had told him that the nurse had taken her to the bathroom that morning and had placed her in a bath of cold water, and that she had been kept there for some time before the hot water was turned on. His patient had estimated that she had been in the bath for as much as an hour and a half.

He told the Coroner that he had found Mrs Morgan in a very distressed state and that she believed she had been punished by the nurse for soiling her bed and nightclothes. He related to the court that his patient, half crying, had told him how very cold and feeble she had felt.

She had spoken in such a low tone of voice, explained Dr Pavy, that he had had to sit on the bed to hear her speak while surrounded by his students. On hearing what had happened, Dr Pavy stated that he had sought out Sister Mary at once to make inquiries, and he instructed his house physician to get a fuller statement from Mrs Morgan and from the other patients on the ward who had witnessed the events of that morning.

Continuing his testimony, Dr Pavy stated that he had next visited the ward on July 7, when his houseman had reported finding bruises on the patient's body.

Dr Howell had reported his findings and concerns to Mr Lushington while Dr Pavy confirmed the bruises and opined that Mrs Morgan was under the influence of a powerful mental shock. As the symptoms got worse day by day, Dr Pavy said he had told Dr Steele that he thought the presence of Nurse Ingle was exerting a prejudicial influence upon his patient, and she was removed from the ward at his request.

Dr Pavy was under oath, Miss Lonsdale reflected, and his testimony certainly cast Miss Ingle in a very poor light. Had the nurse over-stepped the mark? Had she manhandled Mrs Morgan? Worst of all, had the nurse sought to punish the patient?

She picked up the report and read Dr Pavy's statement concerning the postmortem. He had confirmed there was some 'mischief' at the upper part of Mrs Morgan's left lung, which was indicative of consumption of old standing, but it was not in an active state. The condition of her brain, he had declared, with its tubercular and inflammatory disease, was the cause of death, and it was antecedent to July 5. To emphasise the point, Dr Pavy had confirmed to the coroner that in his opinion, the condition flared up after the bath.

In his view, the cold bath and the excitement of getting the patient to it, might in her state of health be a probable cause of the state of the brain. He had thought the patient's death had been hastened by the events on the morning of July 5.

The Coroner had asked whether the nurse would have had the authority, or be permitted under her own accord, to give a patient a bath without the consent of a superior. Dr Pavy had stated that he would not expect a nurse to take such authority upon herself but added that lately nurses at Guy's had undertaken to do this. He had informed the Coroner that the medical officers had strongly protested against this to the Governors and had explained to them that it was fraught with danger.

Miss Lonsdale sighed as she read Dr Pavy's houseman's testimony. It affirmed everything his boss had said without variation. It added nothing, and it seemed to her to be quite rehearsed.

Sister Mary's statement confirmed that Nurse Ingle had asked her for permission to give Mrs Morgan a bath, and that it had been given. She added that she had given no further directions concerning whether it was a cleansing or a medical bath. Asked about the time of the request, Sister Mary had estimated that it had been between half past eight and nine o'clock in the morning. Under questioning, she had confirmed that she had then gone about her other duties.

The Coroner's inquiries established that the distance from the patient's bed to the bathroom was about seventy feet, but it was in the other division of the ward, and to get there she would have had to walk past seven or eight patients lying in their beds.

Sister Mary confirmed that she did not hear any more about the bath until Dr Pavy had come to see her. Asked if she recognised the difference between a medical bath and a cleansing bath, she had replied that she did and that she would never have ordered a medical bath without his instruction and that a cleansing bath should take about twenty minutes.

Miss Lonsdale felt uneasy about this testimony as it seemed to her to be incomplete. It did not create an understanding of what it was like on the early shift when there was so much to do. She knew only too well how busy it was getting all the patients up and fed, and then washed and dressed. And with a ward of thirty or more patients to see to, nurses were always under pressure, working hard against the clock.

The Coroner, in her view, should have asked about the staffing levels for that shift as the hospital had been reducing the number of nurses on the wards. She questioned whether Mr Lushington's pursuit of efficiencies had placed an unreasonable demand on the nurses. She made a mental note of this point for Sir John to examine further in court.

Miss Lonsdale was shocked as she turned the page and read Emma Costello's testament. The ward maid had sworn that she had seen Nurse Ingle drag the patient to the bathroom at about nine o'clock. She had claimed the nurse had held the patient by the arm and that Mrs Morgan could not walk. Miss Costello, who had occasion to be in the bathroom, had stated that Nurse Ingle had said of the patient 'she has been very dirty,' as the maid left them there to go about her work.

On her return about an hour later, she had found Mrs Morgan at one end of the bath trying to raise herself to get out. She had found her shivering all over and her teeth were chattering. Miss Costello said that she had sought out Nurse Ingle after the patient had cried that she was cold, and she claimed that the nurse had told her that Mrs Morgan was very obstinate and unwilling to help herself.

Miss Lonsdale felt angry as she read the statement and was enraged when she read the claim that Nurse Ingle had said, 'I am determined I'll not have it.'

Miss Costello had claimed she had asked another patient to help her lift Mrs Morgan from the bath, and she had sworn she had witnessed more cruelty. Nurse Ingle, she said, had dragged the patient from the bathroom and she had pushed one of the patient's legs with her knee.

Asked about their different positions on the ward, Miss Costello explained to the jurors that 'Ingle was nurse, and I did the rough work.' She swore that they had not had any disagreements, but then admitted that she had never liked her.

Miss Lonsdale turned to the final page to read the transcript of Nurse Ingle's examination.

'Pleasance Louisa Ingle was called and asked by the coroner if she wished to give evidence. Mr Taylor said he advised her to answer every question fully and freely.

Witness then said she did not know for what complaint the deceased woman was in hospital. She was led to believe it was for hysteria.

Coroner – The physician has shown us a paper which was hanging at the patient's bed.

Witness was understood to say that she had not looked

at it until after the bath had been given. She did not notice anything about consumption.

Coroner – Or phthisis?

Witness said she had no idea the case was consumption until the Treasurer asked her if she had read the paper. She had given the bath because she had found the patient in a very dirty condition when she went to make the bed. Having obtained permission from the sister, witness took the patient out of bed, and, putting her arm around her, supported her to the bath. She did not remember seeing Costello the ward maid in going to the bath or saying to her that the patient was so dirty. She thought the patient's object was to get carried, and witness found she could walk. Witness then described minutely what she had done in putting the patient in the bath, in which there was then no water. She then turned on the water.

Coroner – Which? The hot water? While she was in the bath?

Witness – I believe I turned both on together. Altogether there was not more than six inches of water in the bath. Witness said she then left in order to make the patient's bed. She only complained of one leg being useless. Witness went back once or twice to see if she was alright. Once when witness went in the patient had slipped and was clinging to the side with one arm with her head hanging down. Witness turned the water off and turning it on again the patient exclaimed suddenly that it was too hot. Her foot was just where the water came in. Witness instantly turned it off.

Coroner – How long was she in the bath?

Witness – It might have been quarter past nine when I

first went for her, and I think certainly before ten o'clock that I brought her back. Witness said she had to lift the patient out, as she had lifted her into the bath. Costello, the ward maid, came to witness once and said the patient in the bath was so cold. Witness replied that she had been to her and felt her back, and that she was perfectly warm. She did not remember saying anything to Costello about the patient's obstinacy. She might have said something about it but without meaning to infer that she had to remain in the bath longer than necessary.

Directly witness found the patient had finished cleaning herself, she took her out. Witness had been matron and nurse at the Cottage Hospital. She was trained at Winchester. She considered that she had been very unjustly dismissed in this case. The Treasurer had told her he acquitted her of everything but want of judgement.

The coroner having summed up, the jury, after a short consultation, returned a verdict of manslaughter against Nurse Ingle.'

"Miss Lonsdale, are you watching the time?" whispered Reverend Flood. "I believe the matron is expecting you at five o'clock?"

Miss Lonsdale slipped on her boots. "Thank you, I was completely lost in the report. I will see you later for the end of month service... I am very much looking forward to it... and may we say a prayer for Miss Burt?"

Eighteen

Sunlight streamed through the west-facing windows, illuminating the neat stacks of papers and documents awaiting attention on the matron's desk. Amongst them, copies of recent editions of the *Times* and *Daily News* lay open with some of the columns ringed in heavy black ink.

"Miss Lonsdale, I am delighted to see you again. How have you been these past few months?" inquired Matron Burt of her protégée as she entered the room and curtseyed to her former superior. Miss Jones, who was seated at the desk readying her pens and ink pot to take the notes of the meeting, looked up and smiled at her old friend and colleague.

"I am well, thank you, Miss Burt, but very distressed at the current situation. I should like to assist in whatever way I can," replied Miss Lonsdale, taking off her bonnet and drawing a chair alongside Miss Jones, who shuffled along to make room for her. The pair, both devout High Church women, had a shared passion for the Anglican Sisterhood of Nursing and for Miss Burt's reforms.

"How were your room and supper last night?" inquired Miss Jones as she opened her writing portmanteau and placed a sheaf of fresh paper on its green leather slope. "I suspect our modest facilities were a disappointment compared to those at your home in Lichfield."

"They are as I remembered them," came the reply as Miss Lonsdale stood to pour the glasses of fresh lemonade that had been prepared by the kitchen for their afternoon refreshment.

"And your journey down to London yesterday?" inquired Miss Burt.

"Pleasant enough," came the reply. "The trains and Euston station are greatly improved since the London and North Western's investments, so long may they continue."

"That is most satisfactory," said the matron as she took her seat. "We have until half past six to prepare the brief for Sir John Holker and his assistant. We must consider the likely arguments and recommend where best they could examine the evidence in more detail. We need to prepare a list of potential witnesses to counter the prosecution's case. And we must consider Miss Ingle's welfare if she is found guilty."

A sombre silence followed at the prospect of a Guy's lady-nurse being found guilty of manslaughter at the Old Bailey. The thought of a former colleague being surrendered in court and manhandled by police officers as she was taken down to the cells below the courtroom was too horrifying to contemplate.

"The shame of it," cried Miss Lonsdale. "I am sure the case has no merit; it will be thrown out."

"No, Miss Lonsdale," responded the matron. "The court proceedings will follow their course and to some, the truth will be clouded by ingrained prejudices concerning the malign influence of our Sisterhood on the necessary reforms to nursing."

"I'm afraid I have to agree." Miss Jones gently nodded. "You only have to look at the hostile editorials in Tuesday's *Times* and *Daily News*. They clearly show great sympathy with the medical staff and seem to echo Dr Habershon's vitriolic letter printed in last Saturday's *Times*."

"There will be a reckoning after all this is done," assured Miss Burt. "We expect Guy's staff to be loyal and to refrain from airing their prejudices in public. That we have had to issue an injunction speaks for itself. Both Dr Habershon and Dr Pavy have gone too far this time.

"And despite your entreaties, Miss Lonsdale, no gentleman has come forward to defend my office," she complained, pointing to the letters page of Wednesday's edition of the *Times*.

Silence followed as Miss Jones concentrated on writing her notes while Miss Lonsdale thought about her letter and the forceful rebuttal she had made against Dr Habershon's wild accusations about popery being rife in Guy's.

"Miss Lonsdale, what advice have you to offer for Sir John's brief?" asked the matron.

"I have read the Coroner's Report and I have checked the lawyers' credentials, and I have identified some areas for your consideration, Ma'am. I believe the testimonies made to the Coroner by Dr Pavy, Sister Mary and Emma Costello can be roundly challenged—"

"—Dr Pavy is an eminent physician," interrupted Miss Burt. "His statement about Mrs Morgan's journey to the bath and the bath itself being the likely cause of death of his patient by stimulating her brain lesion will carry so much weight that it will be difficult to counter."

Miss Jones glanced up. "Added to this supposition, we have the sworn statements of Mr Morgan, the husband of the deceased, and Dr Howell, the houseman, which concur with Dr Pavy's views... and they cannot be challenged for decency's sake."

"I believe a second opinion on the pathology and progression of Mrs Morgan's lesion will call into question these assumptions," asserted Miss Lonsdale. "I also think Dr Pavy's vague diagnosis of 'hysteria' and his ideas about how it might be treated with exercise and a medical bath must be examined. We need to establish that Dr Pavy is woolly in his thinking and thereby erode the cornerstone of the Coroner's guilty verdict."

"That is a bold assertion, Miss Lonsdale," replied the matron. "And which physician of equal weight in London do you suggest might testify against a fellow physician in the current circumstances?"

"Sir William Gull is an expert in such issues, and he is superior to Dr Pavy. His testimony could introduce an element of doubt in the minds of the jurors."

"A bold assertion indeed, Matron," repeated Miss Jones. "It is well known that there is no regard between the two and Sir William was our Medical Superintendent and senior to Dr Pavy. He is still a Consulting Physician to Guy's and of course, he is the Queen's Physician. Miss Lonsdale's suggestion has merit and I think we should put it before Sir John, but may I offer a caution?"

Miss Burt nodded, and she continued, "It will probably bring the Royal College's Council down on our heads and in their wake, the medical press will follow. It will be most unpleasant."

"I agree," replied Miss Burt, as she contemplated the consequences of following this course. "But Miss Ingle's liberty is at stake here. Miss Jones, put this to Sir John. And please brief Dr Steele to engage the President and Registrar of the College with great diplomacy while calming the editors of the medical press and the *Times*. They won't support us but neutrality will do."

"Sister Mary's testimony is weak," continued Miss Lonsdale. "She has demonstrated a neglect of her duties. She left Miss Ingle with no clear instructions about the type of bath to be given to Mrs Morgan, and worst of all, she abandoned her nurses at the ward's busiest time of day. She must be challenged and shown to be negligent."

"Sister Mary's continuing indifference to the reforms has been nothing but trying. I agree with Miss Lonsdale's suggestion," added Miss Jones, consulting her notes. "I believe Mr Poland will call for the prosecution Miss Costello, the ward maid, and the nurses who were on duty, Miss Elizabeth Collins and Miss Kate Leak."

"Well, we know what Emma Costello will say... the question is, will the nurses support her lies and damn the reforms and Miss Ingle in the process?" scoffed Miss Lonsdale.

"That is too offensive," interjected the matron. "They are on Guy's staff."

"Forgive me, Matron," replied Miss Lonsdale. "I have had a long day and my tiredness has dulled my judgement."

"For the defence, may I recommend Nurse Blanche Topham and Nurse Sarah Johnson," said Miss Jones. "They were on duty at the time, and I believe they are honest. They will be supportive of Miss Ingle despite any pressure, however subtle, that might be exerted by Sister Mary, or threats, not so subtle, made by Miss Costello."

"May I also suggest the postulant Miss Charlotte Distin," added Miss Lonsdale. "I believe she was nursing on the ward that day and helped Miss Ingle to lift the patient to her bed after the bath. As a woman in holy orders, her testimony will be unimpeachable."

Miss Burt nodded to her secretary to add the names to the list for Sir John's perusal. "Miss Jones, please make inquiries concerning Mr Poland's intentions to call any patients who witnessed the incident that morning and whether he will call Mr Morgan and Dr Howell."

"Was there another physician on the ward?" asked Miss Lonsdale. "There must have been a medical registrar on duty in addition to Dr Howell, as he was only a houseman. Who was his senior? And wouldn't this physician have been present at the post-mortem? What has he to say?"

"I shall check," murmured Miss Jones. "From memory, it was probably Dr Mahomed."

"Thank you, ladies," said Miss Burt as she rose from her

chair. "I need to see Reverend Flood to check the details for this evening's service. It will be delicate as we must offer prayers for the trial... and not everyone in the congregation will be sympathetic. Miss Jones, please get the brief to Sir John this evening. I shall see you both in the chapel."

The ladies stood and curtseyed as the matron departed. Then the two friends sat down and relaxed into their chairs, helping themselves to more lemonade and spicy biscuits.

"Margaret, it is so lovely to see you again, and your suggestions have been very helpful. We have sorely missed you here at Guy's, especially since all this started a few weeks ago. Is life at home in Lichfield to your satisfaction?"

"Victoria, my life in Lichfield is different to my life in London... the peace and quiet has given me some much-needed rest after the spring's tumultuous months... the change has been very welcome." Miss Lonsdale sipped her lemonade.

"Your letter has caused a sensation," whispered Miss Jones as she picked up Wednesday's copy of the *Times* from Miss Burt's desk and pointed to the top right of the page. "Look, Matron has marked page 7 and ringed your letter to the editor."

"I had to write after Dr Habershon's diatribe in last Saturday's paper. He is such a self-satisfied tyrant. And all that nonsense about popery at Guy's and secret prayer meetings. Is the man altogether in control of his mind? He seems to me on the verge of madness.

"And then the hostile editorials in Tuesday's papers after the inquest made my blood boil. Those lazy editors have merely repeated the same old narratives and false accusations peddled by the medical staff... and you know I am not one to hold back when I am riled."

"Although she would never tell you herself, I think Miss Burt was grateful for the supportive voice in your letter," confided Miss Jones. "And your call for a chivalrous gentleman to stand up in her defence was masterful. Of course, none have come forward yet."

"I despair of them," sighed Miss Lonsdale, toying with her glass. "They are as thick as thieves, and will support each other even with the flames of hell licking at their door."

"After your letter, you are becoming an object of query. 'Who is Miss Lonsdale?' is the question on everyone's lips," said Miss Jones. "Well, Margaret, what should I say?"

"That I am a gentlewoman of good heart and that I will not stand by and see a decent woman as is our matron belittled and vilified by vicious men who should know better. Now pass me the *Times*, I want to remind myself of what I wrote."

"No need, I shall read it aloud for you," replied Miss Jones as she quoted parts of it:

'Sir, Since the affairs of Guy's Hospital are to be discussed in the public papers, it is scarcely fair that the medical staff should have it all their own way; therefore, I hope you will allow me to say a word in favour of the much-enduring matron, Miss Burt, upon whose conduct an implied attack has just been made in your columns...

On her arrival at Guy's in November last, she found neglect of duty and ignorance among the sisters – even drunkenness and immorality among the nurses, and consequently misery among the patients – prevailing in some of the wards. She began at once to cleanse out foul corners and to replace aged, inefficient, or hopelessly corrupt nurses with better women.

Although the single religious observance which she enforced was the regular attendance of nurses and sisters alike at morning and evening prayers, read by herself in the hospital, the foolish cry of religious fanaticism and intolerance was raised against her; and although it has been amply proved to the satisfaction of the Governors that such a cry was groundless, it is again raised publicly in a letter to the *Times* of the 24th inst.

The matron was subjected to every kind of indignity for the simple discharge of her duty. False reports were freely circulated in the hospital concerning her, libels were published about her in the *Guy's Gazette* (a students' paper), and printed papers containing abuse of her were given to the patients and distributed among their friends by the old sisters and nurses who remained. Caricatures and squibs of a gross character reached her by every post. Why this persecution? Because she discovered patients dying, neglected, and covered with sores; ill-treated children; and inefficient or worse than inefficient nurses in the hospital, and considered it inconsistent with her duty as matron to allow such a state of things to continue.

Miss Burt has borne her portion as a reformer quietly and patiently, and has carried on the organisation of the nursing of 700 patients by day and by night to the satisfaction of the medical superintendent, in the face of opposition and undeserved abuse which might well have daunted a less courageous woman. Those who have ventured to make public insinuations against her and to trump up false stories against her nurses would hardly have done so had they not felt secure that Miss Burt's position made it impossible for her to contradict publicly the insinuations and to prove the stories false.

Were she to do this she must resign her position, because it would be practically impossible for her to keep it. She dare not break the regulation of the Governors that no one from inside the walls of Guy's Hospital shall write publicly about its affairs, upon which the doctors openly trample, and therefore her hands are tied.

The committal for trial on the charge of manslaughter of a Guy's head nurse, which is just now causing great excitement, is a sad and serious matter, about which the public may hastily make up its mind on insufficient evidence. To every trained nurse it appears that the sister of the ward must be held gravely responsible in that, according to her own showing, she gave permission to a nurse to put a consumptive patient into a bath without first asking for medical orders, and no doubt at the trial evidence on this point will be asked and obtained. The sister in question is an old Guy's sister, but she is a well-trained and an efficient nurse. I worked under her for some time. I have reason to know that she is this. But surely even this very grave charge cannot in any fairness be laid to the matron's account? Nor can it be charged upon the "new system" since it happened in a ward under the care of an "old" sister. But without for a moment trying to hide the undoubted fact that the nurse who is now accused of manslaughter has been terribly to blame, and whether she be held responsible or not, is it not possible that patients of whom the public never heard at all may have died of neglect, if of nothing worse than neglect, under the old system of nursing?

Is there, then, I ask, no public-spirited and chivalrous man among those who know the true history of this quarrel who will defend a woman whose professional prospects, as well as her reputation, are being injured, and who yet cannot defend herself?

There must be gentlemen in the medical profession who are well aware of the terrible abuses which still prevail in some of our old hospitals. Will not one of them undertake Miss Burt's defence by telling the truth about the need of hospital reform?

I am, Sir, yours faithfully, L. Margaret Lonsdale

The Close, Lichfield, July 27.'

"Margaret, this letter sets out our case for reform and praises the goodness of Miss Burt but why did you say the accused 'has been terribly to blame'? Miss Ingle has not been to trial yet and you seem to have undermined Sir John's defence. Remember, Mr Lushington's inquiry into the death found she was innocent of the charge and only that she lacked judgement."

"Victoria, I am a passionate supporter of Miss Burt and her reforms. She is our guiding light, and it is our duty to support her in whatever way we can. When I read the report of the Coroner's Inquest in the *Times* on Tuesday, I was furious with Miss Ingle. The jury had found against her, and her actions have vindicated the doctor's fears about our reforms. I believed that she was not one of us. I composed the letter in a state of great anger."

"I think you have done some harm in this," chided her friend. "The Coroner's Court is not a criminal court; it merely establishes the cause of death and Miss Ingle was not represented in her defence. There is still much to be uncovered by our lawyers at the Old Bailey next week and they will be aiming at a higher standard of inquiry."

"Perhaps it was impulsive of me," conceded Miss Lonsdale. "I should not have commented so readily; I thought I was being helpful to our cause and Miss Burt... Mr Paul has advised me to lie low for a while and stop writing letters—"

"—he offers wise counsel. Margaret, please do as he asks while we try to repair the damage you have done."

"There they go, Mr Payne," observed Mr Bryers as they watched the lady-nurses and ward staff file into the chapel. "All of 'em very worthy and pious, and not one of them married."

"That's right... that's why they're a sisterhood," came the reply as Mr Payne shifted his weight from one shoulder to the other as he propped himself up on the plinth of Mr Guy's statue.

"Sad bunch of spinsters... never seen these new ones down the pub like the old days... wonder if they get to enjoy the evening light like us?"

"Nah... they have to pray in the chapel... it's orders

from above," informed Mr Payne. "Hello, is that the notorious Miss Lonsdale sneaking in at the end of the line?"

Mr Bryers craned his neck to get a glimpse of her. "What's 'er business 'ere? Must be something to do with the trial. I wonder if the doctors know she's about... they're at daggers drawn from what I hear."

"She's better bred than the lot of them, that's why they hate her. Come on Mr Bryers, let's go in for our tea and get ready for the night rounds," suggested Mr Payne as he led the way up to the colonnade to the kitchens in Hunt's House.

Miss Jones and Miss Lonsdale crept into the chapel and took their seats in the back row as Reverend Flood was introducing the service. They both caught a whiff of the freshly picked roses that were now giving off their musky fragrance in the warmth of the evening sun. Miss Lonsdale spotted Sister Mary sitting next to Mrs Keogh, the Night Sister, towards the front, no doubt whispering to each other about the trial and their testimonies.

Reverend Flood, having introduced the service, asked the nurses to stand and sing psalm 23 with all their hearts for Guy's Hospital.

The Lord is my shepherd; I shall not want.
He maketh me to lie down in green
pastures: he leadeth me beside the still
waters.
He restoreth my soul: he leadeth me in the

> *paths of righteousness for his name's*
> *sake.*
> *Yea, though I walk through the valley of the*
> *shadow of death, I will fear no evil: for*
> *thou art with me; thy rod and thy staff*
> *they comfort me.*
> *Thou preparest a table before me in the*
> *presence of mine enemies: thou anointest*
> *my head with oil; my cup runneth over.*
> *Surely goodness and mercy shall follow me*
> *all the days of my life: and I will dwell in*
> *the house of the Lord for ever.*

The evening's sunlight flooded into the chapel, shining a spotlight on the matron, who was now standing at the lectern to lead the prayers.

As Miss Burt spoke about the need for common cause in support of the reforms, Miss Lonsdale's conscience pricked about that sentence in her letter to the *Times*. She regretted her ill-tempered rush to judgement. She had thought she was doing good and serving the cause of the reforms, but now she was pained as she realised her actions may have played into the hands of her enemies.

Bruises on a patient's body were often caused when frail people who could not help themselves were moved. They were on Mrs Morgan's chest and arms, she recalled, and that would be consistent with the patient's recent fall and a nurse gripping her too tightly to support her. She turned to Miss Jones and whispered that this point had to be included in the note to Sir John.

As they stood on Reverend Flood's request to sing the closing hymn, unbeknown to all but the priest and Miss Burt, Miss Ingle had followed the service in concealment from the vestry behind the altar. The nurses' singing drowned the sound of her sobbing as she tried to follow the words in her hymnal.

> *Abide with me, fast falls the eventide*
> *The darkness deepens Lord, with me abide*
> *When other helpers fail and comforts flee*
> *Help of the helpless, oh, abide with me…*
> *Abide with me.*

PART V: THE TRIAL

NINETEEN

S he closed her eyes and sobbed. Reading Miss
Jones's account brought back the misery of feeling
so alone, hidden in the vestry of Guy's chapel. It
was too painful, she thought, as she put Miss Jones's papers
to one side and listened to the sound of falling, tumbling,
crashing water.

The sun got lower and her thin cotton dress offered little
warmth. She pulled the shawl around her shoulders and
covered her legs and feet with her blanket to keep out the
late afternoon chill. Lost in her memory of the betrayal she
had suffered, she toyed with the pink ribbon that held the
sheaf of papers together. She flicked through the pages she
had read and sighed at the sorry explanation of who did
what to whom and why. None of it mattered. The trial of
Nurse Ingle was just a footnote in the history of Guy's
Hospital.

Her fingers were painfully cold, so she cupped her
hands and blew warm breath over them for some relief. One

more sip of laudanum and then she would make her way back down to the bungalow before it got too dark. Having lost track of the amount she had taken, she felt too drowsy to stand and drifted into an opiate-induced stupor as the last of the sun's warmth dissipated.

She became that anxious wreck of old as long-buried memories crept into her befuddled thinking. She saw herself seated on a hard chair in the drab holding cell below Court Room 3 of the Old Bailey, where she had been taken down to await the jury's verdict after the trial. It was midday on Friday August 6, 1880, when Judge Hawkins had summed up the arguments for and against her, having heard the testimonies over the previous two days.

She struggled with her demons as the events came to life. The court's police officer had had to help her down the narrow stairs to the basement. He had grabbed her arms tightly so she would not fall. *Manslaughter by cruelty and neglect...* she repeated the charge over and over. Isolated and cold, she was back in that dingy cell where no sun shone as she waited to hear her fate.

"Louisa... Louisa... Louisa... where are you?" Mary and Dr Macpherson led the search party in the fading light, holding their lanterns aloft to shed some light on the path up to the waterfalls. The houseboy ran ahead with his lantern to show the way, yelling constantly for the grown-ups to keep up with him.

"Where is she?" asked Mary, puffing for breath and in

great distress at the thought of her friend lying cold and injured under the chilly cloudless sky.

"We'll find her, Miss, don't you worry... rest here while we go up to the falls," advised one of the soldiers Dr Macpherson had recruited to join his search party.

Ahya had given Mary a bottle of the astringent witch hazel, promising it would help to revive Louisa if it was washed across her face. It was preferable to the harshness of smelling salts with its pungent ammonium that blew ladies' heads off, she had explained.

Mary gave the corked bottle to the soldier and instructed him in what to do when they found Louisa. One of the servants stayed with her to keep her safe as she sat on a rock to rest.

"Louisa... Louisa... Louisa... where are you?" called the press pack and members of the public from the road outside the Old Bailey as she, and they, waited for the jury's decision. It was the not knowing that had caused her such distress. Her terrified imagination had made things worse.

Dr Steele had been given permission by Judge Hawkins to attend to Louisa in her cell. He had comforted her as she had sobbed in fear for her fate. They had discussed the jury members' expressions and speculated whether anything could be discerned that might indicate some sympathy with her case. It was a useless exercise, but it had been a great relief to have had Dr Steele's company while she waited.

She shuddered as she recalled Mr Morgan's testimony. She had thought well of him when he had visited his wife of nearly ten years on most days. Mrs Morgan was only twenty-six years old, but the poor young thing had had the look of an old worn-out woman, the result of years of too much hard work and self-neglect. That was what poverty did for you.

She remembered that she had got on with Mr Morgan and that he had offered her flowers and a shilling as a reward for looking after his wife so well. But when Mrs Morgan had fallen seriously ill, his mood had changed. There had been a rumour, according to her friend Charlotte, Nurse Distin, the postulant, that Mrs Morgan's niece had been befriended by Emma, and the pair had concocted false accusations about Louisa.

They had convinced the ailing Mrs Morgan that Nurse Ingle was a cruel person, so she had told her husband that she was afraid of the nurse. When his wife's condition had deteriorated, Mr Morgan had informed Dr Pavy that he thought the cause had been Miss Ingle's cruelty and neglect which had been inflicted as a punishment for his wife's inability to control her bowels.

Not true, Louisa sobbed to herself as she recalled the falsehoods and the sense of injustice. She had felt depressed about the accusation then as now. She had had no redress, no voice, no justice over the intervening years. This conspiracy of lies had not been brought out in court, and neither the niece nor Emma had been called to testify under oath about any collusion between them. Despite Miss Ingle's references for being of good character, and for her kindness and humanity, Mr Morgan's injurious views about her had persisted.

Louisa winced as she recalled Dr Pavy's request to have her removed from his ward on July 9, and Mr Lushington's inquiries of her concerning Mrs Morgan's bruises. Not fair... not fair... she cried out to the sky at the memory of her dismissal from Guy's the next day for her 'lack of judgement'. What was this prejudice? she asked as her heart raced. No Sir, please, she had begged, to no avail. His and the matron's decision to dismiss her was the only course which would satisfy the medical staff.

There had been no privacy in that dingy cell, with its dull green tiles and grubby cream walls. The police officer standing by the door had listened to everything she and Dr Steele had had to say. She had not dared show any admiration for the physician, nor he for her, but she remembered his warm regard despite the officer staring into the dead space between them as they had faced each other across a small bare table.

"They will see through her tissue of lies," he had said of Emma.

"Did you hear what she said... 'I never liked her from the first time I saw her... she is my superior... I do not like her... she ordered me about...' She said I did not do my share of the back-breaking work... it's ghastly... it's not true. I worked each day from eight in the morning until bed at ten o'clock. I did everything to look after the patients... we did not have enough staff to do everything for nearly sixty patients." The words played over and over in her mind.

"She was performing to the gallery, and very skilfully," Dr Steele had replied. "She enjoys the limelight too much.

But Nurse Distin's testimony will outrank hers, and given it was the exact opposite of what the maid had said, our postulant has in effect called the girl a liar."

"Charlotte is the sweetest person, and my hopes are resting on her testimony. Does it not help that Nurse Collins and Nurse Topham have both sworn on oath that they had seen no cruelty… and that Miss Collins saw Nurse Distin help me carry Mrs Morgan as we walked her together, arm in arm on either side?"

"Indeed it does," he had replied reassuringly. "I suspect Miss Costello was never in the bathroom. Nurse Johnson never mentioned her presence when she was asked about the state of Mrs Morgan as she had attended to her in the bath. She swore that the water and the patient were warm.

"I have no doubt that Mrs Morgan was feeling chilled to the bone and was indeed very weak," he had added. "She was dying from tuberculosis."

Louisa, now cold and flopping about in her fog of confusion, wept as she recalled how busy they had been that day, like every day, with so much to do before dinner. Even the patients had tried to help where they could. In her mind's eye, she saw Patient Number 6, Sarah Bailey, quite clearly. She had been on the ward for many weeks and had given testimony in support of Louisa's version of events that morning, even recalling her cry for Nurse Distin to help her lift Mrs Morgan.

She looked up at the cloudless night sky full of stars shining like diamonds sparkling against a black velvet cloth. She marvelled at the Milky Way and the glistening planets, and the many shooting stars. Oh to be there, away from this prison of memories, she thought, as her opium-befuddled mind darted about and played more tricks on her.

Shackled to her recollections, the nightmare of Sister Mary's indifference came into her thoughts. She had given me permission to give Mrs Morgan the bath, Louisa said to herself with indignation. She had told both me and Charlotte that it was a bad case of hysteria and she had not explained the diagnosis card saying 'phthisis', or whatever the doctors called it. Sister Mary should have guided us more, she groaned with anger. She let us down... and then she abandoned us... she betrayed me.

As a spiral of depressive and destructive thoughts took hold, she recalled the terror of her conversation with Dr Steele about her possible fate. Her mind had raced as fast then as it did now as she thought about being deported to Australia in a convict ship or being imprisoned on a hulk off the Kent coast, or in one of London's notorious prisons. Was hard labour for life in Brixton or Holloway really any better than being hanged at Newgate prison?

Dr Steele's earnest reassurance that none of these appalling prospects were even possibilities in this modern age had fallen on deaf ears. Louisa had been locked, then as now, in the darkest of cellars in terror of what was to come.

Back at the bungalow, Ahya and the servants were busy preparing the fires and hot water. The place was ablaze with light. Ahya had given instructions that the oil lamps around the front garden and the pitch torches lining the path up to the church and the start of the trail should be lit. The festive decorations now looked at odds with the circumstances of that evening, but it was too bad: the light would help guide the party home.

As the hours passed, Ahya waited anxiously with Lydia and Sarah, who fretted about their missing companion. Jeanie, fed up with the gloomy prognostications, looked for something to do.

In Louisa's bedroom, she had made a fresh bed of crisp linen for her friend's return. Tucked at the back of the old oak armoire linen cupboard, she found a couple of small dropper bottles nestled in a rectangular box that could hold three. She lifted one out, held the curious little brown glass container up to the gas light and read the neat white round label. 'Supplied by Mr Ho, Calcutta Pharmacy.' On the other side, she read 'Laudanum – 10% Opium.'

Had Louisa been taking this along with the valerian Dr Macpherson had given her? She pocketed the bottle and joined the worried ladies waiting in the sitting room.

Nothing had prepared Louisa for the shock of entering the Central Criminal Court on that Thursday, August 5. She shuddered as she recalled being led to stand in the dock by two of its officers. It had been just a month since Mrs Morgan had fallen and had deteriorated, and Louisa had been dismissed over her 'lack of judgment' concerning the bath. It had been just over a week since she was found to be responsible for Mrs Morgan's death at the Coroner's Court, and now she found herself under guard at the Old Bailey on charge of manslaughter.

Then, as now, she had felt truly alone in this whirlwind of events. In her despair, she had prayed hard and reached out for the Lord, but he too had abandoned her in her hour of need.

The dark wood furniture and high barrel ceiling of Court Room 3 had made for a gloomy place as she had looked around for a familiar face. From her raised platform in the dock, she had felt like a prize animal standing before a curious crowd of onlookers. Heart thumping, she could not hold back the tears at her public humiliation.

She felt lifted at the memory of Dr Steele rushing forward with a glass of water to comfort her, and of Sir John Holker's reassuring smile. As she looked up at the night sky's sparkling stars, she recalled looking up at the public gallery to see Miss Burt and Miss Jones staring down at her anxiously. To their side sat Mr Lushington in conversation with Sir William Gull. She remembered the panic she had felt on seeing the pair and asking herself whose side were they on. She had lost all faith in them.

She reached out in her reverie, as she had done in court when she had spotted Charlotte's friendly face. Nurse Distin was seated with a group of her old colleagues from Mary ward, and they had smiled down at Louisa encouraging her to be brave. She was brought up sharp when a nasty recollection jabbed her. It was of Emma scowling down at her mouthing the word 'GUILTY' with seething hatred. Next to her was Sister Mary, who had offered no warm smile nor any sense of sympathy.

Cold and drifting in and out of consciousness as her breathing shallowed, Louisa was back in that court room with the sea of lawyers and clerks busying themselves in front of her.

She could see them all quite clearly in her mind's eye from her perch in the dock. They had gathered at their large semicircular table set below the judge's bench as they sifted through their papers and prepared their pens and ink pots, taking care not to spill any on their sheafs of fresh paper. They looked like crows dressed in their black gowns, and their horsehair wigs and white stiff-winged collars and stocks gave them an air of absolute authority.

As they chatted amongst themselves, she had surmised that the men around Sir John were for her defence, so the others must be the prosecutors. They looked very scholarly with their wire-rimmed spectacles placed awkwardly about their faces as they opened their law books and marked places of note with ribbons. They appeared like actors in a play, with all their dressing up in strange costumes and wigs, and their theatrical attitudes and ways of speaking.

She shifted uncomfortably in her shawl and blanket as new demons invaded her mind. The twelve jurors – a motley crew of worthy men – had taken their seats to her right and were chatting amongst themselves. And on her left, Mr Morgan and his relatives had taken their places and were regaling the press pack with the horrors of Mrs Morgan's last days.

Then she had seen Dr Pavy arrive with Dr Habershon and Dr Wilks. They looked sombre as they took their seats in the public gallery some distance from the matron. They peered down at her, as if she were a specimen under their microscopes.

The medical staff did not trust Mr Lushington or Dr Steele, let alone Miss Burt, so had engaged their own barristers to represent their interests. No wonder the lawyers' pit was so crowded, Louisa had thought as she watched their representatives scramble up to them for a last-minute consultation. The noisy room was stuffy with so many people crammed in for the trial and it remained so despite the efforts of the clerks to ventilate the place by opening the lofty top windows.

Louisa was shaken out of her reverie as she felt the ground shake. Thud...Thud... Thud... What was that noise? she asked herself, trying to sit up. It was no good, she was too weak to bother and fell back to stare at the stars.

Thud... Thud... Thud... the clerk of the court announced the entry of Judge Hawkins. She had watched the small man in his red robes and full horse-hair wig draping over his shoulders ascend to his throne-like chair at the front of the court room. Seated high up, he had turned his angular face and bright blue eyes to fix a gaze on her which had frozen her to the spot. She was as helpless and as speechless now as she had been then in the face of this man's absolute authority.

She had tried to concentrate on the witnesses as they gave their testimonies, but fear had created great confusion in her mind, and she had lost the threads of the legal arguments. She had not understood the legal procedures that seemed to interrupt everything constantly as she tried to remember the examinations and cross-examinations of the medical staff by the many lawyers who seemed to jump up from their table with an annoying regularity.

There was a mystery man who sat on the steps by the jury box who stared at her endlessly during the two-day trial. Was he the foreman of the jury? He had a sketchpad in front of him on which he seemed to be scribbling while looking directly at her. Louisa was most disturbed by him, and the distraction meant she could not concentrate on what the medical staff had to say about Mrs Morgan's death.

The demons ran in and out of the chambers of her mind, sowing confusion and creating anxiety while she lay cold and semi-conscious by the water. Just as the nightmare of Emma mouthing 'GUILTY' at her from the gallery had faded, Mr Poland, the prosecutor, came into view. His benevolent bespectacled face soon changed into a fiend yelling at her, 'Dead. Dead. Mrs Morgan is Dead.' The animated imp was terrifyingly lifelike. She cringed in her covers to hide from it.

And then as suddenly as it had all begun, the trial was over. Judge Hawkins had heard the closing arguments and had dismissed the court as the jury considered their verdict. While the judge and the lawyers had gone upstairs for their dinner, Louisa had been in a daze as she was led down the stairs to the cells to await the jury's decision. It was left to Dr Steele to explain to her what she had missed in Sir William's explosive testimony.

"Miss Ingle, Sir William has demolished Dr Pavy's credibility. Not only did he question Dr Pavy's diagnosis of the presence of a benign tuberculosis, he also questioned his understanding of the condition and treatment of hysteria. It was a very damning critique."

"Sir, had not his houseman, Dr Howell, and his registrar,

Dr Mohamed, offered confirmation of Dr Pavy's testimony?"

"Of course they did, they are part of his 'firm', and their careers depend on him, so they are hardly going to disagree with their chief. That is the significance of Sir William's intervention. He has no dependency on Dr Pavy; indeed, it is quite the reverse. And he has inflicted a mortal wound by stating his poor opinion of Dr Pavy's supervision of his juniors and the accuracy of their clinical notes. Miss Ingle, there can be no more injurious statement to a teaching hospital man."

TWENTY

S
he'd had no time to think. Suddenly the cell was bustling with activity as the clerk of the court had yelled over a clanging bell for the prisoner to be brought up to the bar. She had not eaten since early morning and yet the knots in her stomach had made her nauseous. She felt ashamed at how unkempt she must have looked in her crumpled plain clothes with her hair falling out of its chignon.

"Come on Miss Ingle, let's get you up them steps." The officer pushed her up the narrow spiral stairs. She took her place in the dock and grabbed the brass rail to steady herself. She recoiled under her shawl as she saw Mr Morgan and his family staring at her with contempt. Her demons returned to terrorise her as she recalled looking up at the crowds in public gallery. Her eyes darted over to the twelve men who sat as the jury, to the excited press pack and then to the busy lawyers' den.

The court room had been packed and noisy on that first

Friday afternoon in August. A summer-fair atmosphere had pervaded as the weather was fine, sunny and warm. And people would have been looking forward to their payday on Saturday and to seeing their friends or going on an outing on the coming Sunday.

Thud… Thud… Thud… that sound of her nightmares returned. Thud… Thud… Thud… it pounded in her head as she saw the clerk hammering his gavel on the bench to call the assembly to order. He was pleading for all to rise as Judge Hawkins entered the court room.

As she had looked around, members of the jury had stared at the floor or the ceiling while the lawyers had studied their papers. She could not catch anyone's eye for a drop of sympathy. She had felt a sense of foreboding as the clerk asked the foreman of the jury for their verdict. Squirming on the cold earth, she saw him as clearly in her mind's eye as she had done twelve years earlier.

He rose, looked at the judge and shouted 'Guilty'.

Louisa saw herself collapsing in the dock as pandemonium broke out in Court Room 3.

In her delirium, Louisa floated above the scene and watched Judge Hawkins thank the jury and instruct the clerk of the court to take the prisoner down to be remanded into Newgate prison overnight to await sentencing in the morning. She winced as she recalled it was London's place of execution for felons. It housed those waiting for death as well as other hardened criminals, petty thieves, drunks, prostitutes and vagrants. The thought of joining them was beyond her comprehension. And she would have to wait another terror-filled day to discover her fate.

She remembered seeing Miss Burt in a state of shock up in the gallery, her mouth open in disbelief as she gripped the edge of the balcony. Miss Jones, in her distress, had cried out 'No' in an instinctive guttural voice. Behind them, a terrible alarm had afflicted Louisa's friends, who were on their feet with their arms raised in outrage and horror.

As she watched them in her befuddled mind, Louisa tried to comfort a crying Charlotte. She then darted over to the other nurses to calm their protests as they shouted at the judge. She tried to reach out to that poor disheveled woman crying in the dock. It will be alright, she whispered to her old self, reaching out to support the collapsed wretch.

"No... No... Please, Sir... It's not true... I did not harm Mrs Morgan," she heard the poor thing say. "Please listen to me... I can explain the bruises... Sir, she fell... She fell... I helped her..."

It was no use; nobody was listening to the convicted criminal in the dock. There had been so much noise that her pleas could not be heard anyway.

Louisa looked on the scene and wept for her old self. Mr Morgan had hugged his family while greeting members of the press who had gathered around him for quotes. She had watched those reporters who had dashed into the street and around to the Fleet to file their lurid stories ready for the Friday afternoon edition of the *Evening Standard*, London's favourite paper.

She gasped as she remembered that man, the sketcher. She had despised him ever since Dr Steele had shown her his drawing of her as a harridan dragging a frail Mrs Morgan to her death bed. The picture had been used for the front cover of the *Illustrated Police News*, a tabloid purporting to be an official notice from the police. But it was no such thing; it was a sensationalist rag, no more than a penny dreadful. The danger lay in its reach. It was popular with the masses for its gruesome drawings of murder victims, bloody crime scenes and police officers staring at heinous misdeeds.

'Nurse Guilty of Manslaughter,' cried the headline, enticing people to buy a copy. She wept at the memory.

More cruel scenes played out in her mind as she saw the medical staff shouting at each other up in the gallery. They were accusing Sir William of a slanderous outrage against Dr Pavy. The atmosphere had crackled with unbridled anger.

"I see your hand in this… your behaviour has been truly unforgivable… there will be consequences for this travesty," she had heard Dr Steele accuse Dr Habershon. "And Pavy, don't think you and Wilks are excused from blame. I know what you've been up to."

It was all moving so fast; Louisa could not keep up as her memories came to life. She saw Dr Pavy and Dr Habershon on their feet yelling back at Dr Steele.

"We've been vindicated. Burt's reforms have killed Mrs Morgan, you pompous old northern windbag," Dr Pavy had shouted.

"The reforms are dangerous. We say reverse them now before more of our patients are killed by her zealots. Burt must go. These cruel reforms must stop," Dr Habershon had bellowed.

"Your shameful plotting has gone too far. Mr

Lushington and the Governors will be discussing your futures with the President," Dr Steele had replied coolly.

Louisa saw Dr Wilks place himself between Dr Steele and his colleagues.

"Sir, we are, as you can see, in great anger. The court has found our reformed nursing practices to be in want. We are willing to discuss the terms for their reversal," he had offered.

"You are much reduced in our eyes. You are unworthy of Guy's," Miss Burt glowered at them before taking her leave as she and Miss Jones left the gallery to return to the hospital.

Louisa despaired as she recalled seeing the lawyers conducting earnest discussions between themselves about her fate. She watched them consider what might be an acceptable sentence. Judge Hawkins, she learnt, had agreed to entertain their petitions as he was anxious to show fairness to all in this difficult case. You are talking about my life, she thought.

The great bulk of Sir John dwarfed Mr Mead, his assistant barrister, as they formulated positions in their corner of the den. She covered her eyes as she watched them decide to plead for a suspended or at most a light sentence and inquire about an appeal based on further investigations into the testimonies of Sir William and the ward maid. The defence barristers declared themselves baffled by the verdict. It had been obvious to them that the maid had been dishonest and that Dr Pavy's actions had fallen short of what might be expected of a senior physician at Guy's Hospital.

She stared at Mr Poland and Mr Williams. Having won their case, they were sifting their mass of papers while agreeing the words for the court records with the clerks. She listened to their chatter. They were anxious to get off as it was a Friday afternoon, and they had their weekend pursuits to attend to once they had worked their way through the scrum of onlookers waiting outside.

She watched as Sir John invited the prosecutors to join him and Mr Mead – they were all Inn colleagues – to agree what sentence might be acceptable before he petitioned the judge. They mulled over the options and considered the implications before Sir John approached the clerk of the court to gain access to the judge, who was by now taking some refreshments in his chambers.

The Central Criminal Court kept careful records, so once the final wording had been agreed, the official records of the court had to be written up in copperplate writing and then the notes had to be copied several times by the clerks for copies to be deposited in different files.

She had learnt from the officer that the legal procedures were made more complicated by the presence of the medical staff's own counsel. Sir John thought they too had to be satisfied, but they were too busy to talk to him. They were taking new instructions from their clients concerning Sir William's testimony and the slur made on Dr Pavy's reputation.

And then there was the press, he had explained. They always hung around the court rooms hoping for a juicy quote from the lawyers. Sir John had been too busy with his task of persuading the judge to show leniency, so Mr Mead had been deputed to offer a few words.

"We believe there has been a gross injustice here... an over-reliance on the testimony of a foolish ward maid... we shall appeal," he stated.

Louisa wept into her shawl as she recalled Emma cavorting before the press, playing with the ribbons of her bonnet. She had been the star witness for the prosecution and found the attention pleasing until Sister Mary had pulled her away and scolded her for being indiscreet. They too left the court room to return to Guy's.

She saw Charlotte calling to her old self, but the crumpled wreck in the dock could not hear or see her as the police officer helped the pitiful soul to descend the steps to the cell.

"I'm coming down for you. I will pray with you. I have a Bible for you. God bless you, Louisa," shouted Charlotte above the mayhem as she made her way down to the court to ask permission to attend to Louisa. As a postulant, she was granted special permission to accompany the felon in prayer.

Charlotte had been a great comfort to her, Louisa recalled, as she flopped from side to side on her blanket feeling the cold rising from the earth to numb her pain.

"Sir, what happens now?" Charlotte had inquired of the police officer.

Louisa buried her face in her hands as she had done on that Friday afternoon and listened to their dealings. She had felt like a bystander in her fate as a prisoner awaiting sentence. She still suffered the loneliness of the isolation of that day. It was the not knowing that had so distressed her.

"I'm afraid it's Friday afternoon, Miss... the lady will 'ave to wait 'cos the clerk is very busy... it's all backed up by this time of day, you see... the courts are emptying out at the same time and Newgate gets the lot on a Friday. When the bell goes, I'll take 'er up the corridor to the prison. She'll get in before they finish serving the bread and soup at six o'clock... then she'll be in a remand cell for the night... they're not as bad as the real cells."

Charlotte and Louisa had sat in stunned silence. The thought of what the officer had said was horrifying.

"She can have a bit of a rest in there before she's up in front of Judge Hawkins in the morning for sentencing," the officer had added, finishing his well-rehearsed patter.

Louisa had put her head in her hands on the table and collapsed into gut-wrenching sobs. Charlotte had cradled the inconsolable woman and opened her Bible.

"Shall we recite psalm 23... I find this one of great solace, Louisa, don't you... then let's say the Lord's Prayer... Reverend Flood is coming with Miss Jones soon so we can pray together," Charlotte had suggested with her soft soothing voice.

Louisa didn't have the heart to tell her friend that she had lost her faith in prayer, so she had gone along with the postulant's suggestions. Charlotte was such a good soul, she thought, as the past devils pranced in front of her torturing her with terrible painful memories.

"Reverend Flood and Miss Jones for the prisoner," the clerk of the court had announced to the officer, who had showed them into the cramped cell. Charlotte had stood and curtseyed to her superiors and had offered Miss Jones the spare chair.

"Miss Ingle, this is not how it should be," Miss Jones had said to her. "Mr Lushington has instructed Sir John to prepare an appeal. You must keep faith while these procedures are completed. I know it will be grim for you tonight as our request for you to reside in our care until sentencing tomorrow has been denied."

Louisa tossed and turned in her blanket, trying to push the irritating roar of the waterfalls to the back of her mind. She thought about how the chaplain, Miss Jones and Charlotte had prayed and talked about her and the trial as if she was not there. She saw them addressing her, but she could not take in what they were saying. She was as befuddled now as she was then.

"Tonight, I am very sorry to say, will be hard for you my dear," Reverend Flood had said. "Miss Burt and I have visited many prisoners over the years and the first night is always the worst."

"Miss Burt has been granted permission by the court to let you have these linen squares to rest your head on tonight," Miss Jones had added. "Matron suggests you cover the straw pillow with them, and I have a pouch of rose petals for you to perfume, as best you can, your place of rest. It is a small gesture made in the hope that you can bear the conditions until we sort your release tomorrow."

"Dr Steele has arrived for the prisoner," the clerk had announced as the cell door opened.

While Reverend Flood and Miss Jones took their leave

of Louisa, Charlotte had hugged her as she left her Bible on the table next to the precious gifts of linen squares and fragrant petals. Dr Steele, his face creased in worry, had taken the chair, and had stared at Louisa across the table. Oblivious to the officer standing over him, he had reached out to touch her hands.

"Miss Ingle, this is a terrible situation, but we have work in hand to make amends. I have a small gift for you, too. Some biscuits… you must be hungry by now… and it will be a while before you get some sustenance tonight. The judge has kindly agreed."

"Thank you, Sir," whispered Louisa as she saw herself in that cell. "I fear I shall not sleep tonight for worry." Oh, how she wished it had been different. She shivered with the cold. I need more laudanum, another sip; where is that bottle? she asked herself, fumbling around for it.

Searching about her in the dark to no avail, she mulled over how her life had taken a very wrong turn that summer. As her mind played tricks, she asked herself the same question over and over. How did I go from being a busy head nurse on Mary ward to a convicted felon, guilty of the manslaughter of Mrs Morgan, facing a life of incarceration?

Dr Steele had told her about a row between Sir William and Dr Pavy. He had admitted that he had been taken aback at the ferocity of the exchange.

"How could you slur me and betray us… we are astonished at your conduct… you apologise at once… I insist upon no less." Dr Pavy had been so incandescent with rage that he had had to be calmed by the equally indignant Dr Habershon.

"I gave fair testimony to what I believed I saw in your bad practice. I think you must look to yourself before you accuse me of any wrongdoing," Sir William had retorted.

"I cannot put up with it… you are a disgrace to the Royal College… I shall write to the President to have you censured by the College's Council," Dr Pavy had countered.

"My lawyers will be ready for your petition. Good day." Sir William made his way down the stairs to the street.

"I am astonished. Wilks, he says my diagnosis was incorrect and that I know nothing about hysteria. I want him censured. And as for his comments on my supervision of Dr Howell and Dr Mohamed, it is a slander, nothing short of a slander," Dr Pavy had blustered.

"What was his charge about the quality of the clinical notes?" Dr Wilks had asked. "Lushington is bound to call for our comments. Is there anything that could jeopardise our case, Dr Pavy?"

"Of course not, how could you ask?" Dr Pavy had snapped. "He shall pay for this slur. I shall not tolerate it. I am senior member of the College, and they will back me. I want him censured."

Dr Steele had despaired at how ungentlemanly their conduct had been in the corridor of the Old Bailey. By now, he had added, they will have hissed and fumed their way through the heaving Friday afternoon traffic to return to the West End.

Her old self, Louisa recalled, had thought bitterly that they were probably already walking in Grosvenor Square, taking in the pleasures of an early evening summer while she was confined to that dingy basement cell awaiting entry into Newgate Prison.

In her delirium, Louisa watched the medical staff as they formed a huddle with their barristers in front of her at the waterfall. The lawyers were being instructed to draft a letter in the strongest of terms demanding Sir William withdraw his testimony and apologise to a fellow member of the College. She was disgusted with them, yelling at their ghosts in rage.

She saw Dr Steele standing over her taking her pulse. She was weeping for her fate as he tried to count her heartbeats. She recalled his kindness.

"I have had a word with the Governor, and he has allowed me to prescribe some valerian to ease your worry and help you sleep tonight. The prison matron will give you two drops. Miss Ingle, do you understand? Two drops will be of great help tonight."

With that, he had taken his leave as the police officer had ordered her to accompany him along the transfer corridor to the prison. Dr Steele had not been permitted to go with her; she was all alone then, as now.

"Will they cut off my hair tonight?" she had asked the officer as they had walked along the dingy damp basement corridor. "Will I have to wear prison clothes tonight?"

"No Miss, I don't think so, not tonight," the officer had replied.

Louisa had not been able to concentrate on his replies as she fretted about being beaten by the other prisoners for killing a poor, innocent woman. Her terrors were magnifying by the minute, just as they were now as she yearned for her laudanum and an extra blanket.

'Louisa... Louisa... where are you?' cried the opium devils, teasing her again in her stupor as she was plunged into the dank corridor of shame that connects the Bailey's holding cell with the grim reception and custody room at Newgate Prison.

'Louisa... Louisa... where are you?' yelled a rabble of oglers and the press pack from the streets.

'Louisa... Louisa... where are you?' cried Charlotte, searching for Louisa's lost faith.

It was all a muddle in her mind as she drifted in and out of consciousness, struggling against her shivering body's craving for more opium. I am done... I am so exhausted... I have had enough of these battles, she said to herself. Just let me die here in the cold earth where I belong.

"Did you hear that?" asked Dr Macpherson, holding up his torch to peer around him.

The searchers held their fire sticks and pitch torches aloft as they hurried up the path to the waterfalls.

TWENTY-ONE

Thud... Thud... Thud... The army scouts knew the terrain and its animals well. Elephants sometimes drank at the water. It was too dark to see ahead, but the searchers knew their smell as they approached the falls. The men crouched low and waited for the scouts to give the 'all clear' before proceeding.

"Sir, it is safe," one shouted to Dr Macpherson, who rose and directed the men to fan out along the paths that led up to the waters. Their fire sticks bobbed about in the dark as they ran along the trails calling for Miss Ingle. It was a chilly night and the falls could be treacherous to those not familiar with their slippery rocks and deep pools.

The searchers made a terrible commotion with their running about, holding their flaming torches in the air while shouting for her.

"Sir... Sir... over here," yelled one of the beaters. "Sir, we have found the lady... It's the lady... Sir, come quickly." The scouts ran to the place and held their torches high for others to see. They formed a circle of light around the ghostly form. Dr Macpherson pushed his way through and crouched over Louisa's motionless body.

"Give me those blankets and get my flask," he shouted at one of the soldiers. He felt her wrist for a pulse. He put his ear to her lips and listened for her breathing. He thought he detected a faint gasp. He rubbed her icy cold feet and hands as the men wrapped her in the blankets. He gently lifted her head up and poured a little water into her mouth. He got his mirror out in the torchlight and held it over her mouth to detect any breath. Come back to us, he whispered, as he observed hardly a puff on the glass.

"I think she has died… has she died, Sir?"

The men stood back in silence, staring at the limp body in the flickering light of their fire sticks.

"No… No… she is lingering between life and death. There is still time. We must get her back to the house immediately. We must rescue her while there is some life left," Dr Macpherson replied as he lifted her blanketed lifeless body. "Light the way," he commanded. "I must not stumble tonight."

The gaggle of torch bearers, scouts and beaters made their way down the hill, lighting the path for Dr Macpherson and his men. Mary and her escort saw them coming. She ran to meet them.

"Louisa, Louisa, where is Louisa?" she shouted as she saw the party.

"Dr Macpherson is coming with her, Miss… she is almost gone, Miss, but he is saving her."

Mary was filled with dread as she saw the doctor

coming down the path towards her holding a bundle in his arms. She cried out as she realised it was the limp body of her friend. Following close by was one of the soldiers, carrying Louisa's basket containing the sheaf of papers bound together with pink tape and the little empty bottle he had found by her body.

Mary instructed the houseboy to run ahead to alert Ahya, and to see the fires stoked and hot water readied for their return. The path from the church up to the falls was ablaze with the crocodile of lights as the party approached the estate.

"Louisa… Louisa… she is found… thank the Lord," cried Mary. "Does she still live?"

"There is a chance… but we must act quickly… her breathing is very shallow, and she is so cold," replied Dr Macpherson, who was sweating from the effort of hurrying along with his precious bundle.

"The lady has been found but she is close to death. She is cold. Ma'am wants hot water and the fires lit," yelled the houseboy, waving his torch to attract the housekeeper's attention. Ahya, who was standing at the front door, immediately roused the ladies, who were dozing in exhaustion as they waited for news.

They stirred and rose to take in what the boy was saying. As they comprehended the seriousness of the situation, they started rushing around to help keep the fires and hot water going. Jeanie ran out to meet the party.

"Dr Macpherson, has she died… tell me, has she died?"

"No, but we must act with all haste if she is to live," he

replied as they entered the house and felt its comforting warmth.

Mary, flushed from her exertions, led the way into Louisa's bedroom where Dr Macpherson gently laid her on the fresh linen and plumped pillows. He joined his men on the terrace, who were resting while waiting for their instructions, as the ladies undressed their friend and mopped her damp body.

Having rubbed Louisa's hair dry, and having dressed her in a fresh nightgown, Mary called for Dr Macpherson to attend to his patient. He was disturbed by her shallow breathing and cold goose-bumped body even though she had been wrapped in warm blankets.

"We need more coals on the fire," he cried, as Mary turned up the lamps and Ahya brought in a jug of hot water and fresh towels.

There was much activity in the household that night as they fought to save Louisa's life.

"Bring me some tepid water to bathe her face," Dr Macpherson instructed Ahya as he propped his patient up to gently give her a few drops of warm honey water.

"Shall we try reviving her with laudanum?" asked Mary, who showed him the empty bottle that one of the soldiers had found about Louisa's person up at the falls.

"There is mischief here," replied Dr Macpherson. "Where did you get this? Does Miss Ingle make a habit of taking draughts from this bottle?"

"I think it is her normal comforter," said Jeanie. "I found these in her linen store... that little bottle is part of this set." She showed him the rectangular box containing the two bottles.

Morphia, she is full of it, he sighed to himself. That explains her shallow breathing and pimply cold skin. He checked her breathing on his pocket mirror and took her pulse once again. He detected weak flickers of life. Oh Miss Ingle, he whispered to himself, what has caused you so much distress that you have swallowed the whole contents?

"She will need to see this out," he informed Mary and Jeanie, putting the laudanum to one side. "We will feed her warm honey water through the night, and we will keep the fires going. She needs to be kept warm and she needs fluids. We will take two-hourly turns to watch over her. She is going to have a very restless night as she craves more laudanum."

Mary and Dr Macpherson took the first watch while Jeanie explained all to Ahya, Lydia and Sarah, who were waiting anxiously in the adjacent sitting room. The search party had by now returned to their quarters, leaving the ladies alone in a lounge festooned with Christmas decorations. Those festive garlands and ornaments now seemed terribly out of season.

While Louisa lingered in a delirium between life and death, Mary and Dr Macpherson sat with her in the soft lamplight as it approached midnight. Mary dozed and stirred periodically; Dr Macpherson ate a little bread and cheese and drank some tea while he thought about the night's work.

He stared at the bottles of laudanum and thumbed Miss

Jones's report, puzzling as to what it could contain to cause such distress. He checked on his patient as she gasped and momentarily stirred. He looked at her pale face. "What ails you so?" he whispered. "You are a mystery to me." Taking his seat by the fire, he picked up the sheaf of papers and started to read.

"Follow me, Miss, and mind the walls... it's a little bit damp and cold along this passage," the police officer had explained as Louisa followed him to Newgate Prison's reception and custody room.

Louisa tossed and turned in her bed as she remembered being pushed from pillar to post that day. She could still smell that grim passage; it reeked of musty unwashed bodies and mildew. She twisted her head from side to side in her nightmare, lost and confused in this unknown world of the strange rituals of the Old Bailey and the trial, and now of Newgate Prison.

She had been warned about vermin by the officer, who had told her to look out for rats, saying they could do nothing about them as the Fleet River ran down under the Old Bailey to the Thames. She had inspected the corridor's floor intensely as they had crossed over to the prison, and she had clutched her precious gifts of linen squares, rose petals, Charlotte's Bible, and Dr Steele's shortbread for dear life.

Once in the custody room, the clerk had explained the rules to her. First, her hair would not be shorn unless she had nits. The matron would inspect her person shortly and she would be present if her hair was to be chopped. Second, she would have to undress and wash in the matron's presence in the washroom. She would be permitted to keep her clothes unless she had lice, when she would be given a prison dress to wear. Third, she would be given a pint of soup and some bread for her tea in her cell at half past five when she would be locked up for the night until six in the morning.

"No need to worry about the men," the clerk had told her, "they're in a different block... can't get at you unless they can jump a twenty-foot wall."

As she cried out in disgust, Mary and Dr Macpherson were at her side in an instant. While Mary held her hand, the doctor felt her forehead and checked her temperature.

Louisa sobbed into Mary's arms as she relived being inspected in the women's washroom.

"No nits or lice; she can keep her clothes and hair for now," yelled the matron to her assistant.

Outside, it was a fine summer evening. People were going to the parks or standing on the bridge to admire the river and enjoy the summer's warmth. At the Borough, the pubs were already full of raucous regulars while others strolled along the Thames to Southwalk's lively night fair.

She screamed in rage as Dr Pavy and Dr Habershon came into view and displaced the demonic matrons. Their features were distorted as she watched them take their evening walk together in Grosvenor Square. Mary dabbed Louisa's face to calm her; the splash of cold water reminded her of her first prison wash.

She could hear the people gathered outside the prison walls shouting for her. Then she saw rats. They crawled about and sniffed the air. Dr Macpherson and Mary stood by helplessly as they watched her grip the blanket and fight with someone or something in her confused state.

She fought with her demons all night to protect her packet of biscuits, but the rats kept coming back, followed by the faces of Sister Mary and Emma shouting at her. As they took their turns sitting next to her, the ladies watched helplessly as Louisa repeated her exhausting day and night. No evening walk in Grosvenor Square for her, she fretted in her delirium, only a long night waiting for the dawn and her return to Court Room 3 for sentencing.

Louisa, in her reverie, saw herself standing in the doorway of the 'first night' cell, staring at the spartan, rectangular room that had just enough space for a single bed and washstand. The far brick wall had a window high up which let in the evening's summer light.

She gently laid her gifts on the bed and felt the rough pillow of straw which had seen better days. It is only for one night, she had murmured to herself.

"You're lucky, Miss… you're not in the big room with the others… stinks in there, and the noise," said the keeper. "You got this one to yourself… I'll be along with your soup and bread soon."

Louisa had sat on her bed in a state of deep misery and thought of her mother and father. Thank the Lord they were both dead, she whispered to herself. The shame of all this would have killed them. She lifted her feet up, took off her boots and swung her legs round to lie on the bed. The stale pillow repulsed her.

She spread one of Miss Burt's linen napkins onto the

pillow. To mask the stink, she scattered a few of the velvety carmine petals about as she laid her head to rest. It had been a long, exhausting, and terrifying day, and she had dozed off despite the circumstances, clutching her Bible close to her chest.

"Soup, Miss, and some bread for your tea... better eat up as you won't get anything more until porridge at six," the lady keeper had yelled, shaking Louisa to wake her.

Louisa clenched her fists and turned restlessly in her reverie. She coughed and spluttered as Mary tried to administer a teaspoon of honey water. For Louisa, it was like the salty broth of her first night in prison. Dr Macpherson stayed Mary's hand in case she inadvertently choked her friend.

"Eat up; you will need the sustenance," the matron had barked as she marched into the cell, keys jangling. "Now, you've been clerked, washed and inspected. Before we lock the cell for the night, is there anything you need? Dr Steele has asked the medical officer to give you some drops to help you sleep. First nights are always the hardest."

"Yes please, Matron... I want to sleep," replied Louisa as the reality of this grim place and her miserable predicament sank in.

"Papa, I am so sorry," she had whispered to her long dead father. He had been a surgeon in his younger days when he had settled in Norfolk to raise a family with his wife, Pleasance, also now dead for the last two years. Louisa had thought about them, and her brothers and sisters. Life in rural Norfolk on the north coast had been happy enough, especially as they had been quite wealthy from her mother's family. Then she had thought about her training as a nurse in Winchester, where she had done well enough to gain a place at Guy's Hospital with her glowing references.

Her sleep was sporadic as the bells of St Paul's and the churches nearby rung to mark every quarter hour.

By nine or ten o'clock (she had lost track), the streets around the prison were alive with night revellers, prostitutes and vagrants yelling their drunken heads off.

She had thought of her dear brother Freddie, who had joined the merchant fleet as a midshipman only to die in the waters off the coast of South Africa when his cutter had foundered. He was only sixteen. She had shut her eyes and covered her ears to get some sleep. The valerian drops had been insufficient to knock her out, and while the linen square and rose petals were quite lovely, they had lacked the potency to cover the underlying musty stench and unpleasantness of the much-used straw pillow.

The prisoners in the women's wing, bored with their own company and that of the others in the communal dormitories, had started shouting and banging the doors for attention. They had been matched for noise levels by the men in the adjacent wing, who had started up in reply. It had been cacophonous.

Startled, Louisa awoke to get away from the nightmare. Dr Macpherson and Jeanie, as his new watchmate, tried to calm her as she thrashed around fighting the unseen demons.

"Laudanum… I need more drops."

"No," replied Dr Macpherson firmly, nodding to Jeanie

to bring the valerian from his bag. "No more laudanum. Let's try a little honey water and some valerian."

Louisa struggled with her demons as Jeanie carefully administered the doctor's order. She fell into a stupor as her friend smoothed the bedclothes and covered her once again in the blankets that had been tossed to the floor.

"Is there nothing more we can do to ease her discomfort?" asked Jeanie.

"No more laudanum. She must get through this craving. The valerian drops will help," replied Dr Macpherson, who was by now very tired as he returned to his chair by the fire.

While Louisa tossed and turned, he started to read Dr Steele's account of the day that the West End physicians decided to move against Miss Burt and her reforms. He found the report so incredible, he had to pause to think about each section while Jeanie sat with Louisa and held her hand to let her know she was not alone as her nightmares raged.

What a vipers' nest, Dr Macpherson thought as he read about the conspiracy to get Miss Burt and Miss Lonsdale gone. These physicians' world was very different to his as an army surgeon and he despised them for their arrogance and cruelty. These deeply religious women, he concluded, were sincere in trying to make things better for their patients. They were not being unreasonable in trying to improve the nurses' education. He could read no more; he needed a break, so he opened the bedroom's shutter doors and stepped into the garden to stretch his legs.

It was well before the dawn and the stars lit up the inky black sky. He loved this time of the night when the stars were at their brightest. He took a seat on the veranda and stared up at the light show of shooting stars. He caught a pleasant waft of musky perfume from the roses.

"Dr Macpherson, Louisa is awake," whispered Jeanie, come out to fetch him. "She is shielding her ears as if she can hear something terrible. Perhaps she has come down with hysteria on account of her being so chilled this evening?"

"No Jeanie, there is something else at work. I think her distress is much deeper than we can imagine. She has malevolent influences from her past in addition to those from the opium and they are torturing her. I am trying to piece it all together."

Lydia and Ahya came in with fresh tea as they changed the watch and Jeanie joined Mary in the sitting room for a rest. Lydia plumped up Louisa's pillow while Ahya changed the linen-square cover and scattered a few fresh rose petals on the bedside table. This the housekeeper did each night as it greatly comforted her mistress. Lydia took her place next to Louisa and held her hand while Dr Macpherson tried to make out what Louisa was saying in her moments of lucidity.

Suddenly, his face froze in shock as he realised what she had whispered to him.

"I am ready... let me go... I do not wish to live," she pleaded.

Lydia cradled her while Dr Macpherson checked Louisa's breathing.

"Is she going to die?" asked Lydia, her eyes brimming in tears in the soft light.

"It is close... her will to live has gone," he replied. "We must work to bring her back. Louisa... Louisa... wake up," he spoke softly, trying to rouse her.

"I am not worth saving," she whispered, her eyes flickering open.

In the privacy of her secret world, she drifted back to that filthy cell. She had not been able to sleep for the worry and the noise. She had remained awake all night watching for the dawn light through the high window. She had listened to heavy footsteps and keys jangling, doors slamming and violent yelling which reverberated around the corridors like an echo chamber.

"Six o'clock... time for porridge and bread... up you get," came the instruction from the night-shift's lady keeper.

As Louisa had stirred, the cell door had already been closed and the food tray deposited on the floor. Being awake at six for a breakfast of porridge and bread was like her routine at Guy's, although the circumstances at Newgate were so much more frightening. She could not face eating the grey lumpy porridge. Instead, she considered what changes Saturday August 7 would bring.

Twenty-Two

D r Macpherson settled himself into Louisa's plump fireside armchair and turned up the lamplight. He pushed his thick mat of steel-grey hair off his weatherworn face which had seen too much sun over the many years he had worked in India. Sitting in his crumpled clothes, he looked shabby, but at nearly sixty he was well past caring about his appearance.

The walls of Louisa's bedroom were a shade of soft sandstone. They were decorated with a collection of fine paintings in the local Mughal style bought from the Army and Navy Department Store in Calcutta on one of her annual trips down to the capital. The distressed white wooden shutter doors opened onto the veranda and the bungalow's richly planted garden, which came to life as the dawn crept in over the eastern horizon.

Discarded shawls and towels tossed on the floor made for an untidy room, worsened by the debris that accompanies an invalid's requirements. Lydia was asleep in her chair nearby, covered in a counterpane placed gently on her by Dr Macpherson, who did not want to wake her despite it being her watch. Sitting by the low fire and sipping a whisky and water, he kept an eye on Louisa, checking now and then her irregular breathing and disturbed eye movements.

As an army surgeon, Dr Macpherson had seen and dealt with much that was distressing. Caring for badly wounded and traumatised men had become all too often part of his daily work. He despaired as he read about the antics of the 'West End physicians'. In the army hospitals in India, there was simply no time or inclination to engage in the workings of medical politics that bedevilled many of the big teaching hospitals at home.

He was appalled at the account of the conspiracy by Dr Habershon, Dr Pavy and Dr Wilks, with their friends in the press, to run down Miss Burt and her followers. Well spoken, he said to himself as he read Dr Moxon's warning about the deleterious effect on medical morals from living and practising in the West End.

He warmed to Dr Steele, another Glaswegian, who, unlike the other senior physicians, had never taken up residence in the West End. He had chosen to live his whole life at Guy's and had managed his 'outsider' status, seemingly, with aplomb. Maybe Dr Steele's more scientific training had reduced the pain of being shunned, he mused, as he stared at the glowing embers in the fireplace.

Dr Taylor intrigued him. He seemed to have been secretary of the conspirators. He was younger than the other physicians, and his role as one of the new medical school administrators had made him an outsider too. Was he one of them or was he the informer who warned Dr Steele of the plot?

Louisa turned in her bed to face the partly open veranda doors. She watched the dawn creeping into her garden. Her eyes followed the walls around her room to see Lydia fast asleep in her chair and Dr Macpherson engrossed in his reading. She watched him twirl a familiar pink tape between his fingers.

She stared at the ceiling and pictured the lawyers squaring off over the details of her sentence. The tall and overweight Sir John dwarfed his assistant, Mr Mead, and Judge Hawkins, while the theatricality of Mr Poland and indeed his assistant, Mr Williams, would have been entertaining in other circumstances. She felt the hopelessness of it all again as she watched her old self waiting in that prison cell for what seemed like an age before she had to walk down the stinking corridor back to the court room.

Dr Macpherson knows about the death of Mrs Morgan, she thought, as she watched him study the papers. Once he has pieced the story together, he will despise me; and once my friends know, how will they forgive me?

She turned to look at the sunrise and to listen to the waking birds, as she remembered the sound of jangling keys.

"You haven't eaten your breakfast," the matron had observed.

"No ma'am, I couldn't eat this morning," she had replied meekly. "I am too afraid."

"You may keep the biscuits that the doctor gave you for later. They will have to sustain you until teatime, by which point you should know where you are going."

Although well meant, the matron's words had given Louisa little comfort.

"You can keep your linen squares and petals, and your Bible too. We will pack them up for you as your court time is fast approaching," the matron had offered as Louisa ruminated on her fate.

There was a growing noise from outside her cell as the other prisoners stirred.

She squeezed her eyes shut, but the opium cravings called for another dose. She recalled the slam of the heavy prison gates as she had left Newgate to walk back to the courts along the stinking corridor. The smell of carbolic rising from the freshly doused floor was not strong enough to cover the lingering fetid odour that permeated the passage.

Her spirits lifted as she remembered Dr Steele waiting for her inside the holding cell. He had reassured her that Sir John and Mr Mead had worked tirelessly through the night to get a suspended or light sentence for her. He had been very optimistic. Louisa had thanked him for the sustaining shortbread which had cheered her with their lovely rich sweet taste.

She felt for her reassuring linen square and the petals scattered around her pillow. Ahya had been most attentive to her need to have these things about her, especially at night. With her eyes half open, Louisa looked at Charlotte's

Bible lying on the side table. She had been such a good friend.

Louisa closed her eyes and heard a clanging, after which the clerk of the court had yelled for her to be brought up. She remembered standing, but her legs had given way and she had to be helped to climb the narrow stairs up into the dock. Only forty-eight hours earlier she had had no idea about this place and the way it worked, and here she was, familiar with all the sights and sounds, and its peculiar routines.

Standing in the dock, she had stared at the busy lawyers' den and watched the clerks of the court fidgeting as they waited for Judge Hawkins's entry. Thud... thud... thud; the sound had resonated around the court room as the clerk hammered his gavel on the bench.

"Be upstanding for His Honour, Judge Hawkins," the clerk had intoned.

Louisa froze as she recalled the judge's eyes piercing hers as he climbed the steps to his bench. He had called the lawyers to approach him for a consultation. The clerks had readied themselves for the sentence after shuffling their papers as the lawyers returned to their seats.

Judge Hawkins had peered at his papers and then he had looked directly at her.

"Pleasance Louisa Ingle, I sentence you for the manslaughter of Mrs Morgan by cruelty and neglect to twelve weeks in detention with no hard labour."

Louisa saw herself collapsed in the dock as the jury was thanked and dismissed, and the court sent into recess for lunch. She had not taken in anything else, and it was left to

Sir John and Dr Steele to explain that she was to serve her sentence in the Westminster Correctional Centre for Women and Children in Tothill Fields, just northwest of the Houses of Parliament.

"No Hard Labour is a mercy of the Court, Miss Ingle," Sir John had explained with a kindly tone, but its meaning was lost on her. She remembered a haze of disbelief and confusion as the clerks went about their routine business of closing her case and packing up their papers.

Back in the holding cell, Dr Steele had explained that the prison used to be for men, women and children, but under the penal reforms, it had been designated for women and children only.

"Sir John is correct; it is a blessing that there is no hard labour. It means you will spend your time working in the prison's infirmary or in the school. As it is summer, you may be allowed a little time to work in the kitchen garden. Sir John and I will have a word with the Governor, and the Medical Superintendent is an old friend of mine. I am sure he and the Matron would welcome a pair of helping hands in the hospital."

Sir John had added, "Miss Ingle, hard labour would have meant hours and hours of sitting in silence while picking oakum or working in the back-breaking laundry or the heat of the kitchen, but you have no hard labour."

Tears fell from Louisa's closed eyes as she recalled learning about her fate as a convicted felon. Dr Macpherson opened the veranda doors a little wider and Louisa's bedroom became flooded with the early morning's light. He tried to administer some honey water to no avail as Louisa turned her face away. As he gently opened her eyelids to see if her pinpoint pupils had relaxed, he watched a flood of tears roll down her cheeks onto the linen napkin covering her pillow.

"Miss Ingle, what is the cause of your distress?" he whispered.

"Sir, I have a terrible past and I can pretend no longer… my burden is great… I am exhausted by my nightmares… the demons come for me most every night… I can't go on," she murmured, and closed her eyes in relief that she had spoken her secret.

"I know, Miss Ingle… I have been reading Miss Jones's account," he replied softly. "Rest now and we will talk of it when you are stronger. Your secret is quite safe with me."

Dr Macpherson returned to his chair by the fire to continue reading while she and Lydia slept on. What injustice has been done here? he asked himself as he turned the pages. The events reported in these papers took place over twelve years ago, yet it is as if they were only yesterday judging by their impact on Miss Ingle.

Lydia awoke and asked Dr Macpherson if it was time to change the watch. She had been particularly useless, as she had been asleep for most of the time, but no matter.

"Help me to sit Miss Ingle up so she can eat something," he requested of her. "And ask Ahya to bring some soft eggs and maybe a little sweet custard, and some peppermint tea. Our patient needs a light breakfast after her terrible night."

Lydia stretched herself as she stood and left the room to organise the repast. Alone with Louisa as she slowly opened her eyes, Dr Macpherson whispered, "I have read the circumstances of Mrs Morgan's death at Guy's and the accusations that were made against you in 1880. It was a travesty... I'm afraid, Miss Ingle, you were fitted up, as we say in the army."

"Sir, I am in such distress... I need my laudanum... it is in my linen cupboard... please Sir, would you get it for me?" She motioned him to the cupboard.

"No... no more opium... let's talk this out. I am going to help you. You don't need laudanum. Miss Ingle, I have cared for soldiers after battle, and some have been so deeply traumatised by what they have seen and done, and the fear they have experienced, that the memory of it is vivid and lives within them, gnawing away at their soul until they yearn for death."

"Sir, I am not worthy... these demons haunt me so much, I need my laudanum," she begged.

"No more laudanum," he insisted. "Eat some breakfast and rest. I will return this afternoon when we can talk about your nightmares. You can tell me about what happened and how you came to live in Ranchi. You have a life here now with us, your friends, and we are worth living for."

Ahya brought in the beautifully laid out breakfast tray and the ladies joined her to encourage and support her. They spoke of their worries for Louisa as the previous night's dangers had become apparent. Louisa nibbled at the food. Little do they know of my shame, she thought, dreading the moment when she would tell them.

· · ·

Mid-afternoon was a glorious time to take in the joys of a garden, thought Louisa, now dressed and refreshed after her terrible brush with death. In need of a drop of laudanum, she was on edge as she could not find her secret store.

"How are you feeling, Miss Ingle?" inquired Dr Macpherson as he checked her pulse and pupils. "Let's walk in your lovely garden while you tell me about Mrs Morgan's death and the trial you had to endure. Please tell me what still haunts you about this injustice after all these years."

They strolled to the far end of the garden where they could not be overheard.

He spoke softly. "You have done well, Miss Ingle, to keep this secret, but I think it has been at a cost? Tell me about the nightmares and the awful memories that so disturb you."

"Any one of several tormentors come for me when I close my eyes. The laudanum helps me to push them to the back of my mind. It helps me to live each day," she said, pleading for the return of her comforter. "Mr Morgan points at me accusingly; his wife reaches out to me pleading and crying that she is so cold; the physicians point at me in condemnation; and the ward sister and maid, my colleagues, hiss and spit at me."

"As I read the account, I felt there had been a great injustice and that they had been most cruel to you. I suspect the vengeful process was too much to bear?"

"Sir, it felt like I was tied to the front of a train that was careering out of control." She shed a tear at the thought of it.

"I can see the pain this is causing you, Miss Ingle."

Louisa paused and took his arm. She had never spoken of these events to anyone. She found herself willing to let Dr Macpherson in on her secret world. And she felt some relief at being able to unburden herself as she told him of the horrors of her first night as a convict.

"It was the disgusting personal inspection for nits and lice and the prospect of having my hair cut off that confirmed to my incredulous mind that I was now a prisoner for twelve long weeks," she recalled. "I entered Newgate on August 6, so I would spend the late summer and autumn incarcerated. And then what? Released from jail in late October to face the winter with no hope of getting employment as a convicted woman. Sir, it was the prospect of the workhouse or the streets."

"You paid a heavy price for the wounded pride and vanity of the physicians, and the tragic thing is that I suspect they gave no more thought to your plight once the trial was over. Your life was to them expendable. It is an awful truth. Shall we have an early supper together and while Ahya is preparing it, perhaps you might tell me about your time in the women's prison?"

Having put the household to work, Dr Macpherson and Louisa sat at the far end of the garden in the warm sunshine as she told him of her transfer to Tothill Fields to serve her time.

"I stayed in Newgate for seven nights before I was transferred to Westminster prison. On Saturday August 13, I was led in handcuffs to join a miserable group of convicted women waiting in the street outside the prison. We were bundled into the waiting Black Maria."

She fell silent and closed her eyes as she remembered Dr Steele at her side to protect her from the jostling crowd while advising her to ignore them and the press, to merely concentrate on surviving.

"Sir, have you seen the inside of a Black Maria police van? It is an intricate design for the transport of prisoners, who are not permitted to speak to each other despite their proximity. To separate and isolate them, their bodies are confined to narrow cubicles arranged along a central passage. And all this is contained in a van.

"I obeyed the instructions and took my place in a coffin-like box, and I ignored the cries of the other women around me as we progressed slowly from the Old Bailey along Fleet Street to Trafalgar Square. I pictured a map in my head which I followed as the horses pulled us along the crowded streets down Whitehall to the Houses of Parliament, where we turned north and west to Tothill Fields."

They talked about the smells and the noises of the journey as Dr Macpherson chipped in about his similar experiences travelling to unknown places across India in crowded troop trains which stunk to high heaven of unwashed bodies.

"You haven't lived until you've been on such a journey," he ventured, to make her smile. "And our journeys took days, Miss Ingle, not hours."

"Sir, there was kindness on that dreadful day. I was allowed to keep my gifts of linen napkins, rose petals and my friend's Bible. But fear of the unknown was ever present, and I was gripped by its terror as I entered Westminster Prison on that Saturday afternoon.

"It was a place of impoverished women who were caught thieving or selling themselves to live another day. Many were regulars, habitual drunks and vagrants who had fallen from grace. And the children... it was shocking to see future adult convicts in these unfortunates who had had the bad luck to be born poor. I taught some to read and write in my time there and I cared for some of them and their mothers in the infirmary. It was a place of respite from the tedious hard grind of everyday life in prison."

"Enough for now," said Dr Macpherson. "Hungry? Let's go in for some of Ahya's finest."

TWENTY-THREE

L ouisa took Dr Macpherson's arm as they strolled through the garden back to the house. They stopped to admire the bank of camellias with their bright lime green leaves and fat buds bursting into colour. Her bungalow had been part of an earlier plantation estate where the British had tried to grow enough tea to rival the plantations further north in Assam and Darjeeling. But in Ranchi, the climate was not as good for the camellia species that made for tea leaves, so the estate had been turned over for bungalows for British settlers who wanted lovely flower gardens.

"When was the last time you saw Miss Jones?" asked Dr Macpherson.

"When I went back to the holding cell after sentencing, Miss Jones was there, and she had brought extra pins for my hair. I must have looked a sight in court. She brushed my hair and tidied me up, and she brought me a fresh blouse and a slip.

"Dr Steele joined us and said I would be allowed books, and some paper and writing materials. He was so kind.

"Miss Jones promised to send more linen squares and rose petals after I had told her that they had given me such comfort." Louisa cupped a rose to admire as they walked back to the house. "And she gave me a prayer card from Miss Burt for my daily office."

"Miss Ingle, were you as devout as the other ladies?"

"I like to think I was, but I fear I have lost my faith... I go along with the rituals so as not to offend and I read Charlotte's Bible to be close to her in spirit, but I have no enthusiasm for the Lord anymore."

"We are kindred spirits are we not, Miss Ingle? I think you may be forgiven for your pretence. From what I have read, you have suffered a great injustice, a terrible travesty. This Mrs Morgan had tuberculosis, no doubt arising from her poverty, and she died of it. The bruises can be explained by her frailty... such holding marks are common."

"Would that you had been there twelve years ago," sighed Louisa.

"And this nonsense about hysteria... even in 1880, I believe Dr Gull's observations were correct and his criticisms of Dr Pavy quite reasonable. The medical staff were unpleasant to Miss Burt because her reforms threatened them and their established order. Miss Ingle, I must say that they were selfish and cruel in what they did to you."

"Thank you, Sir, your words offer comfort."

"As for Sister Mary and Emma, they too were cruel in what they said and did. And from what I have read in Miss

Jones's account, I believe Miss Lonsdale had helped to create the sour conditions on the ward that led to your tragedy. I am afraid, Miss Ingle, although it is of little comfort to you now, you were in the wrong place at the wrong time."

It was time to go in.

"Ahya, you have done us proud," praised Dr Macpherson when he saw the delicate morsels laid out on Louisa's best porcelain dishes spread across the dining table. "You will surely have something to eat with me, Miss Ingle? Let us celebrate the goodness of Dr Steele and Miss Jones." He raised his glass.

"And Charlotte too, she was most kind to me." Louisa smiled and felt her spirits lifted.

Over supper, they chatted about her garden and his life in the army, and about the pleasures of living in India. Neither missed their original homes, not even at this festive time. Afterwards, they sat by the fire in the sitting room. Having served them tea, Ahya withdrew to the kitchen and sent the other servants to their quarters.

"Miss Ingle, I should like to know more about prison life. Were they cruel to you?" asked Dr Macpherson.

"Sir, to be frank, it was a relief to leave the nightmare of Newgate Prison where I was left to idle in filth and reflect on my sins for a week after the trial. The noise never stopped, and the food and conditions in the open dormitory were so terrible my prison clothes hung from me like I was a scarecrow. Being cooped up in a coffin, side by side with the other prisoners, in that Black Maria was bearable even with the shouting and protesting, and the smell of the horses, as we trotted along London's streets to Westminster.

"It was a hot summer's day and the journey through the crowded streets seemed to take forever," she recalled, her eyes closed. "When we arrived at the prison gates, we were dismounted one by one from our cubicles. Standing there in the street in handcuffs, I stared at the walls... it was one huge expanse of brick wall... must have been at least twenty feet high.

"Well, we were marched through the stone arch and lined up in the outer yard to be signed in. Sir, I was in fear as the Black Maria disappeared and the grinding hinges of the gates groaned shut. All I could think of was how to survive my incarceration for twelve weeks, less one, in that wretched place."

"Out by the end of October by my reckoning?"

"Counting time off for good behaviour, I was discharged on Thursday October 14," she replied, before resuming her story.

"As I stood in the outer yard, I took in every detail of my arrival on that summer day. There was an imposing Governor's House with a pair of wide steps going up to the grand front door. It dominated the formal garden to its front. To the left, overlooking the garden, was the lesser Matron's House; to the right, stood the Principal Warder's House."

"It sounds almost as if you had arrived at the front quad of Guy's, Miss Ingle."

"I waited my turn in the custody hall as the women were processed by the matron and her turnkeys, by then quite familiar with the clerking process. I had already been given my prison number by which I would be known for the rest of my sentence. I was taken to the washroom and inspected by the matron, and as I had no lice or nits, I was given my prison uniform and my clothes were sent to the storeroom for when I was discharged."

"Same again as when you entered Guy's, I think?" asked Dr Macpherson as he poked the fire.

"Correct," she replied, sipping her tea. "We wore heavy cotton serge prison dresses and white caps. They were indeed like our uniform at Guy's, only the twill had been dyed brown rather than the blue of our nurse's dress."

"Miss Ingle, that fabric was probably weaved from cotton grown near us here in Ranchi. We use the same for our army uniforms, with a bit of wool blended in for the cold days."

"I was allocated a single cell rather than the communal dormitory with the other women. It was a mercy given what I had endured in my week at Newgate. At Tothill, I think about four hundred of the prisoners were in cells and the other two hundred or so slept in communal quarters. I learnt the prison routines quickly and I cultivated becoming a nobody, being invisible."

Louisa's mind drifted to the concerns of her friends. They had been so worried about her, and their relief when she had recovered enough to smile at them during their breakfast chatter was genuine. She felt touched by their naïve worry.

"A little more tea, Miss Ingle?"

She thanked him and continued her story. "My cell was very confined. It was six by eight, and the ceiling was nine feet I think, which made the cell a bit airy, and I had a small window high up. I got a little light from six in the evening until late. The iron bed and straw mattress covered in ticking was sufficient for a small person like me and we were all allocated a footstool and a zinc pan for our bodily needs."

"Sounds like Jankers! That's what we in the army call being so confined," exclaimed Dr Macpherson cheerfully. "Miss Ingle, we have another shared experience, I think."

"We were permitted a wash once a week and if the stench was too bad or infection was rife, especially in the communal dormitories where typhus lurked, the matron would come along with her sulphur puffer. I do not know which smell was the harder to bear," she regaled him. "At six in the morning, the bells clanged to signal our porridge was ready. After eating the grey slop, and sometimes a little bread, it was time for our work."

"I know you had no hard labour, so what was your work?"

"I was allocated to help the teacher in the girls' school room, or to nurse the sick in the infirmary. Sometimes, if they were short of staff, I was allowed to work in the nursery. August and September see many newborns in prison on account of their mothers selling themselves for shelter in the winter months. November and December can be brutally cold in London's backstreets and doorways."

"Sounds like it could have been the local workhouse!"

"Sir, it was. I was shocked to find that none of the children and few of the women could either read or write. Over half the women were habitual offenders, most had been in Westminster at least four or five times, and a third were defaulters on fines who were serving a few days, sometimes a week. It was a system of circularity, a system of madness for the poor."

"I always suspected thus, but at least those wretched unfortunates got some food and shelter for a few days or weeks," groaned Dr Macpherson.

"I did like caring for the babies. We had about thirty, maybe thirty-five, at any one time to look after so there was always much to do and the time passed quickly," she said, with a glint of pride. "It was the same when I was sent to help the girls in the school room learn to read and write. I was surprised to see they wore smart blue-and-white spotted cotton frocks and white caps with deep frilled borders, just like the uniform I wore to school when I was their age."

"A teacher as well as a nurse... Miss Ingle, I do admire your many talents. So, this is what 'no hard labour' means? The work sounds onerous to me."

"Sir, you have no idea. The women I saw on our twice daily walking circuits around the exercise yard looked so exhausted, they could hardly stand and maintain their walking pace for the required hour. Working in the laundry, or the kitchen, or the dreaded oakum-picking room, took its toll."

"How did the older or frailer women, or new mothers, fare in such conditions?"

"There were jobs that were less severe, like working in the knitting room or the straw plaiting room. But sitting on benches for eight to ten hours finger-working needles and yarn or weaving tools resulted in exhaustion, too. We used to receive the knitters and plaiters regularly in the infirmary. We took them in as they needed the rest."

"Straw plaiters?" queried Dr Macpherson. "What on earth do you want with plaited straw?"

"Sir, it is used extensively to make straw hats and boaters. Our bundles were used to make the hats for the inmates at Hanwell Lunatic Asylum over in west London."

"Well, you learn something new every day! Miss Ingle, I shall ask Ahya to watch over you as I shall have to return to my quarters shortly. I will give you a couple of drops of valerian but no laudanum. I shall return tomorrow to check on your recovery. You have had a terrible shock to your system, so rest now."

As he departed, Louisa felt her spirits lifted. Perhaps it would be better from now on to think of her time in prison as time spent serving poor women and children in a workhouse. That certainly felt more worthy and less painful.

Ahya turned the lights down low, shut the doors and put the fireguards in place as she closed the house for the night. All was calm as Ahya dozed in the chair outside Louisa's bedroom. It had been a terrible twenty-four hours, but her mistress seemed in better spirits now.

That evening, the first since her unburdening, Louisa had a fitful night's sleep as the memories of prison life flooded her mind. She had not told Dr Macpherson about the punishment where women and children were placed in handcuffs in darkened cells and left in solitary confinement. Sometimes, their meagre rations were stopped.

She saw the prisoners after their time in 'the locker', as

they called it, when they were brought to the infirmary to recover.

She looked around her room in the soft gaslight and tried to think about some of the simple pleasures that had kept her going during her sentence. Walking around the exercise yard every day, no matter what the weather, became a time to take the air and think about her childhood in Norfolk. As the prisoners walked around and around in single file, two to three feet apart, she had looked at the sky and had thought of her parents.

The old melancholia crept in as she remembered the monotony of that dull prison food: porridge, soup with potatoes and bread every day, morning, noon and teatime. Everyone lost weight, so much so that the Medical Superintendent kept his eye on the particularly starved-looking individuals and those with symptoms of scurvy.

Starvation, typhus and scurvy were all hazards of prison life and Louisa was alive to their existence, as she had been given the job of filling in the returns that quantified their presence to the Home Office. When she had seen the figures rising, she had always volunteered to work in the kitchen garden, despite the backache it caused, as the Governor had allowed the workers an apple allocation from the harvest. She could also listen to the birdsong as they worked on lifting the vegetables.

Finishing work at half past four and being locked up from six was bearable in high summer when she had arrived; the light faded between nine and ten at night, so she could read and write letters and notes in her journal. But as August gave way to September, the dark nights came earlier and earlier so that by October, it was too dark by teatime to do anything. That had been the most miserable period of her imprisonment, just sitting in the dark until bedtime with nothing to do.

Louisa shut her eyes to draw a curtain over the unpleasant memory and turned in her bed, rolling her face in the fresh linen square laid on her pillow by Ahya. She thought of Dr Steele. He had visited her once a week by special permission of the Governor and the Medical Superintendent, and he always brought a gift of something good to eat, and more linen squares and rose petals from Miss Jones. They became a source of much joy, especially on those long autumnal nights when she had had nothing to do.

Wide awake, she looked up at the ceiling and thought about her childhood home in King's Lynn, the small market town in Norfolk on the Great Ouse river. She and her brothers and sisters used to follow the river down to its mouth at The Wash and one summer, they had travelled over to Holkham Hall on the north coast where they had family connections on her mother's side. It was a lifetime ago, and she knew with sadness that she would never see the place again.

She felt the need for a drop of laudanum to calm her nerves, but Dr Macpherson's caution rang in her ears. Fretting, she asked herself how she would cope. She stared at the ceiling waiting impatiently for the minutes to pass, just like she had done on those long nights in her prison cell.

As she pulled her soft cashmere cover around her, she

thought about the rough scratchy blanket she had been issued while in prison. It was like an old worn-out rug, but it had been useful as the long summer days of August became shorter and chillier by mid-September.

Prison work had been relentless, and with the daily and weekly routines, the calendar soon turned to October. She still remembered the lift she had felt when she was given her discharge date. *Thursday October 14.*

She thought about her excitement on being told she would make a trip to the prison's clothes store the day before she was released. Accompanied by the matron's deputy, she had walked over to the capacious room where the women's belongings were stored. She had been so happy to sign for her bundle of clothes and pair of boots.

She smiled as she recalled that reek of sulphur that had filled her cell as she opened her parcel. The smell had lingered all night as she had waited for the dawn and her Freedom Day. She had put her worries about her future to one side for the duration of her sentence but, as she had prepared to re-join society, they came back to terrify her.

Wrapped in her cashmere cover, Louisa closed her eyes, and the tears came as she felt once again the utter loneliness and isolation on that morning of her release. Who would give her a decent job now as a convicted felon? What respectable man would ever look at her as a forty-year-old who had served jail time? She had had the mark of Cain placed upon her, and from that day to this she could not erase it.

PART VI: A BEGINNING

Twenty-Four

L ouisa watched as Ahya crept into her room at first
light to put in a new fire. She felt the morning's
chill as she sat up and pulled her dressing gown
around her shoulders. As the light grew, Ahya served a pot
of tea and a plate of fresh fruit cut into small pieces which
Louisa picked at as she admired her garden. She saw Mary's
flower list for the church's decorations on the table and
sighed at its banality.

"What day is it, Ahya?"

"It's Friday, and Christmas Day will be on Sunday. Will
you be strong enough to attend the church's Christmas
dinner, and maybe even the Officers' New Year's party?"

Louisa frowned at the idea of making merry, even
falsely for the sake of her friends.

With Ahya's help, Louisa returned to her bedroom and
prepared herself for a new day. She dozed by the fire as she
waited for Dr Macpherson. She felt irritated and in need of
some laudanum to calm her nerves. Napping gave her some

relief, but her mind had been excited by the memories of her time in prison and recollections of her discharge.

She smiled as she recalled how her clothes on entry to prison had been fine for a summer's day in early August, but quite inadequate for her re-entry into an autumnal London. The matron had given Louisa a shawl to warm her and, along with their good wishes, a gift of some money from the staff who Louisa had worked with in the infirmary. She had felt humbled by their generosity as she stepped into the street outside the prison walls.

On behalf of Guy's, Miss Jones had arranged for a two-wheeled hansom cab to take her to Eltham in southeast London, where a room had been booked for her in a respectable boarding house for women in need of after-prison care. Louisa had known Eltham in happier times. She had lived there with her mother, an annuitant, and a brother when they had moved to London from Brighton, where they had settled after her father's death.

Dr Ingle, her father, had been a Director of the Ely and Huntington Railway Company, which became the Anglian Railway Company as the county's rail network had expanded.

Louisa's mother was from Norfolk's well-to-do Partridge family. She had relations who had married into a local prominent banking family, the Gurneys, who had lived in Norwich's Gurney Court and at Earlham Hall, to the west of the city. One of the Gurneys' daughters, Elizabeth, was Mrs Fry, the prominent prison and social reformer. Had she been alive, Louisa thought she might have written to her about the success of her policies to segregate and educate women and children prisoners.

Dr Macpherson appeared in the doorway. "Delighted to see you have recovered, Miss Ingle. Do you feel strong enough to take a midday stroll with me up to the church? It has been dressed delightfully for the Christmas service on Sunday."

"Sir, I would like that very much," Louisa replied as she wrapped a shawl around her shoulders and Ahya helped her to stand.

They walked slowly up the lane and into the churchyard, where they sat on a bench to enjoy the bright sunny day.

"Did you sleep well?" he inquired. "Did the nightmares come again?"

"Sir, they did, and I sorely felt the need for a drop of laudanum to calm my nerves. Please help me. I need you to replenish my supplies."

"There is no life there, Miss Ingle. You must learn to do without it. It is the devil's brew, and it will bring you nothing but misery."

Crestfallen, she stared into the middle distance and wished for a life without her struggles.

"May I ask where you went after leaving prison?" he inquired.

"I went back to my old haunts in Eltham. I had lived there previously so had the comfort of being familiar with my surroundings. And Miss Jones was very kind in arranging for my passage to a safe house. The journey took an age, but it was so lovely to be free, I just sat back in the carriage and enjoyed the ride across south London before it got dark.

"I can still recall the details as we trotted over the river at Vauxhall Bridge with its incline so steep we had to slow to a walking pace. It gave me a chance to see the Thames for the first time since my trial. I loved the river with its bustle. And we rode past the infamous Vauxhall Pleasure Gardens... I would have been pleased to have stopped for tea, but not in October."

"You must have crossed through Peckham and joined the Old Dover Road at Blackheath... I did that journey many years ago when it was like travelling in the lawless wild west as I made my way to the coast." Dr Macpherson leaned back on the bench to enjoy the midday sun.

"It must have taken over two hours, not that I minded as I was free to enjoy the journey."

"What were your quarters in Eltham like?"

"Modest... the boarding house was in Well Hall Road... it is the main road and rather noisy. The landlady, Miss Edlon, was an elderly spinster who left me alone after she had shown me to my room... I just sat there most days staring out of the window. There was another boarder, a Miss Dawson, but I hardly saw her, and I took my meals on my own."

"It sounds like you had moved from one confinement to another."

"I walked most days, but as the winter rolled on and the weather closed in, it brought me little joy," she confessed. "It was then I realised the full horror of my predicament. You see, Dr Macpherson, as a convicted felon, I could not get a job for a decent woman, and as my family's legacy would run out one day, my future was destitution... it would be the workhouse or death on the streets for me."

"It is too dreadful to contemplate... shall we walk around the churchyard and enjoy this lovely day," suggested Dr Macpherson.

They strolled in silence as she remembered those icy winter days walking by the pond in the park, hidden in the swirling freezing fog that clung to her like cobwebs.

"Did you ever see or hear from Miss Lonsdale again?"

"I never met her again, but she did send me a book to pass the long winter nights. The parcel was waiting for me when I returned from one of my walks. It had been posted from mid-Wales, so I had no idea it was from her until I opened it. The book had been written by her and published by Charles Keegan Paul of London and it was a biography of her mentor, Sister Dora."

"Was it interesting?" he asked, as he guided her around the churchyard.

"Not really... I tried to concentrate on the details of this good woman's life, but it all seemed meaningless after life in prison."

"Miss Ingle, how did you come to Calcutta from Eltham... it is quite a change?"

"I saw a poster on the side of a building advertising for women to travel to India to serve the Empire. They wanted nurses, teachers and governesses, and it offered women like me a chance of anonymity to start over again."

"I remember when I first came to India how much we missed the company of women," he reminisced. "I think there was an effort to populate the place with more ladies from home and some who came in the early days were very forlorn. They were looking for husbands and most of them got one. And it meant the lonely wives of the officers had some company too, so everyone was happy."

"I had nothing to stay for and nothing to lose. And my father had died in Calcutta when I was only thirteen, so I felt a strange affinity for this faraway place. Perhaps it was a chance to be near him again. He is buried in Calcutta.

"Although he was originally a surgeon, he came here as an adviser, and as an investor, in the new Bengal Railway Company."

"Early fifties... a bit before my time. I arrived after the Uprising when the East India Company got kicked out. By the early sixties, we had a fine railway across all Bengal."

"Dr Steele visited me a few times when I lived in Eltham. He commiserated with my situation. When I discussed my plans with him, he was very worried for my safety. But in the end, he helped me buy a passage on one of the steamers and he saw me off at the dock. I never saw him again although I have often thought of him, especially recently.

"He was from Brechin... perhaps you know the place? He spoke with the same accent as yourself. He was so kind to me. On my last day in Eltham, he came for me in a fancy carriage... I think he borrowed it from a rich friend... he lifted my case down the stairs... I had so little I was embarrassed at its lightness... I said farewell to Miss Edlon, and we rode to the docks in east London."

"I know Brechin... it's a bit to the south of my home in

Braemar," replied Dr Macpherson. "My hometown is the home of the Highland Regiment, and I am proud to be one of its surgeons in the Bengal Army."

"My cabin was not the best, but at least I was not billeted in steerage class... the facilities were extremely limited down in the bowels of the ship. The berths were separated by only a sheet of canvas, and the smell was rotten, like in prison. I was allowed on deck each day and after we had faced the rough seas in the Channel and the Bay of Biscay, it was very pleasant when we sailed past Cape Trafalgar into the Mediterranean."

"I've done that trip a few times and know that feeling of calmer seas and balmier weather," he commented as they took another turn around the churchyard. "In the early days, when I first came to India, it took several months to sail around the Cape of Good Hope... Africa is such a big country, and the seas can be very rough indeed as you sail eastwards into the Indian Ocean. It is much easier now with the Suez Canal. How long was your trip?"

"I was fortunate to go by the Canal route and it took less than a month." She shielded her eyes from the midday sun. "That was over ten years ago... I believe the modern steamers, especially the mail packets, can now sail it in two weeks!"

"And to think, all those investments were in the name of China Tea. The Empire needs its tea from China promptly, and we are now the beneficiaries."

"Dr Steele settled me into my cabin and gave me a fresh packet of biscuits for the trip... I loved that shortbread; it's still of great comfort to me and I have a tin of it sent from

Fortnum's in London every few months. It is such a treat, and it reminds me of him." She wiped away a tear.

"As the ship's horn blasted, he waved me off from the dock until I could not see him anymore... I thought he might come to India one day, but that day never came. May he rest in everlasting peace."

They stood together in contemplation. Only when they set off again did Dr Macpherson remark, "My sailings on the troop ships were always so busy looking after the men and trying to stave off scurvy and typhus. I suppose you had *Sister Dora* to pass the time?"

"Sir, I left it on the table in Eltham... it was part of my old life. Anyway, I was terribly seasick despite the calmer waters off Libya and Egypt... and when we had passed through the Canal and sailed into the Arabian Sea and Indian Ocean, it got worse by the day.

"After my misery in London, despite being so ill, I found it exciting to discover new foods and treats. The Canal is narrow, so the boats must sail so slowly we were able to haggle with the local hawkers who came alongside to sell all manner of exotic fruits and dates... they were so fat and tasty," she recalled with a sense of joy.

"To help pass the time, I was able to assist in the infirmary and the ship's doctor gave me a reference. It helped me to settle when we disembarked in Calcutta."

"When did you start using laudanum?" he asked.

Louisa was startled out of step with her companion. "Sir, I knew of it when I was nursing as we used it to relieve pain and to help our patients to sleep. I tried it when I was very seasick on the suggestion of the ship's doctor. It calmed me. It was helpful, and I use it now and then when I am having a bad night.

"Sir, I need my comforter... please return my bottles... I know you have them," she pleaded.

"Miss Ingle, you must learn to do without this prop. It will do you no good... believe me, I have seen the terrible effects of opium dependency. Shall we look in on the church... it has been dressed splendidly for Christmas."

They strolled through the bright churchyard, glancing at the headstones of those who would never return home, and came to the church.

"Ah, lovely and cool in here," murmured Dr Macpherson. "The ladies have done us proud with the floral displays."

"Mary is such a dear... she loves nothing better than organising us, and those are from my garden." Louisa pointed to the sprays of camellias and roses with pride.

"Will you be joining the ladies and the Regiment at the parish's Christmas dinner on Sunday after the service? I am told it is quite a feast."

"No, Sir, I am happy to spend the day alone after the service. I find it a melancholic time and fear making a fool of myself."

"I shall call to escort you to the dinner... how about that?" he persisted as they admired the figures of the nativity crib. "Tell me about your arrival in Calcutta."

"Very well. After passing the Canal and the Red Sea in extreme heat, we were escorted by flying fish and dolphins as we sailed through the Gulf of Aden into the Arabian Sea. It was very choppy as we crossed over to Colombo in

Ceylon, where several of the ladies I had got to know disembarked."

"Ah yes, they will have been returning to the Empire's great tea plantations up at Nuwara Eliya, south of Kandy, bartered off the Dutch. It is not a bad life being a gaffer on the tea plantations. Cool in the summer and like being in the Lake District."

They stood looking at the altar festooned with Christmas decorations and candles of many sizes standing to attention waiting to be lit.

"I learnt all about life in the hills from the ladies I met on the ship. We sailed from there to Madras... that last part of the journey we hugged the east coast all the way... Pondicherry, I think they called the region... and then we set sail for our last stop, the great capital of India, Calcutta."

"The beating heart of the East India Company. At least they left some of the country's riches behind to invest in the city before they were sent into oblivion."

"I was awestruck when I arrived in Calcutta. The sight of so many magnificent municipal buildings and hotels around the central square reminded me of Trafalgar Square and the great institutions surrounding it. And the Army and Navy Department Store was a short walk from my boarding house. I loved walking around the store and once a year, I still go down to the city with my friends for our annual shop for things from London."

"How did it compare to Eltham?" he asked wryly.

"I fell in love with the place. I visit Calcutta as often as I can. They are the agent for Fortnum's, and stock the best linens and cottons, and silks, and all the latest fashions from

London and Paris. Anything that appears in one of my journals, they will have in stock within months."

"Did you go down to Hooghly River… it's a bit different down on those docks," he replied. "When I first arrived here, the remnants of the East India Company had their splendid opium store and many other palaces for their loot everywhere you looked. Miss Ingle, they were responsible for much of the opium problem we see across the east, and at home. It's a ghastly business keeping our men away from the stuff."

"Sir, my need for laudanum does not make me an opium addict. I do not visit the opium dens and I have never had anything to do with those ruffians. Mr Ho, the pharmacist and herbalist, makes up my potions and he is always careful to advise me to only take a few sips when I need it to calm my nerves and dampen my nightmares."

"Miss Ingle, I despair. Have you chosen a hymn for the Christmas service?"

"I have not. I have lost my faith, and while I join in the singing so as not to offend anyone, I find no solace there."

"Abide with me… Abide with me…" hummed Dr Macpherson. "That is the soldiers' anthem, we always sing it when we are in church. Nothing to do with whether we believe in any of it. It is a nice tune. I think one of the ladies has chosen it for the service."

"It brings so much sadness to me," she sighed.

He led her back to the churchyard and down the lane to the bungalows. "I fear it is time for me to return to my duties, but I am very pleased with your recovery. I shall see you at the Christmas service on Sunday and I will press you to stay for some dinner. You can eat as little as you like. And you will not stand out… you can be invisible if you want, but you need to be part of the festive throng."

He bade her farewell as she joined the ladies who were assembled in her garden for their usual afternoon game of cribbage and lolling about with their journals while taking tea and eating cakes. They were feverishly excited about the coming Christmas celebrations and the party at the Officers' Mess. The men of the Scottish regiments, wearing their full dress uniforms, always had pipers to see in the new year and the ladies wanted to dance the Gay Gordons and Military Two Step, and every one of the jigs and reels.

"Louisa, I insist you join us for Christmas dinner after the service. I have already instructed Ahya in what to make as your contribution to the feast, and we are going to support you at the party," said Mary in her bossy manner. "I know you like being shy, but we are going to make sure you enjoy this year's Christmas party. It will mark your recovery from that terrible collapse on Wednesday."

"Oh Mary, it is too soon," pleaded Louisa. "Anyway, I do not wish to attend the party. I am a fifty-year-old spinster and parties are for those younger than I… my time has passed."

"Nonsense," came the enthusiastic reply. "Have you chosen your Christmas hymn yet?"

Twenty-Five

Christmas morning was so balmy that after breakfast Louisa strolled around her garden, cutting a few more fresh flowers for the dinner table. Mary had already taken the best of the blooms for the church's decorations the day before. Of the three seasons, Louisa loved these pleasantly warm dry days best.

Ahya had been busy in the kitchen preparing Louisa's contribution to the table. She had already laid out Louisa's best pale blue cotton skirt and cashmere shawl which, in consultation with Mary, complemented the outfits that the other ladies would be wearing. Ahya had chosen a white silk chemise and a daring traditional dark blue silk cummerbund to complete Louisa's outfit.

"Ma'am, watch the time… the ladies will be here for ten o'clock and the service starts at eleven. Your outfit is ready for you… we just need to pin a corsage at your shoulder."

Louisa continued ambling along the garden path enjoying the fine morning. The hill stations around Ranchi were so verdant, and, even though it was a day's train journey down to Calcutta for her annual shopping trip, she had never regretted her choice to settle on the estate and work for a few days a week in the local hospital. Her training and experiences in one of south London's poorest districts had stood her in good stead for treating the ailments of the local women and children.

Mary and Jeanie were first to arrive, dressed in their best clothes and fancy hats. They handed their baskets of food to Ahya and took their usual places on Louisa's veranda.

"That's a bold sash, Louisa, and it sets off your waist very nicely," observed Jeanie. "Where did you find that quality of silk?"

"Ahya knows the local agent and is always checking for offcuts before the bales are sent down to Calcutta," Louisa replied. "They are the same bales that appear in Liberty's in London."

"What are you two taking for the table?" Mary asked. "I'm taking a selection of vegetables and fruits grown by my own fair hand, and some refreshing lemon sherbet."

"Well, I've got a cake and a tray of biscuits to remind us of home, and I see Lydia and Sarah have shared their enterprise in preparing a couple of chickens which are now in Ahya's safe hands," Jeanie added, beckoning her friends to join them on the terrace.

"I love khichuri so I'm taking rice, smoked fish and eggs, and some spices and herbs to add when the ingredients are mixed," Louisa replied. "I know it's a breakfast dish but it's what I like."

The assembled ladies wished each other a merry Christmas and chortled on about their plans for the rest of the day and who was going to sit where to avoid being next to whoever at the table.

"Goodness, look at the time… we had better get off to church," cried Lydia as she led the way to the front door where Ahya had readied the food baskets and serving dishes for the servants to take up to the church hall.

"It's pulling… it's too heavy for the delicate material… try pinning it onto your sash," Mary instructed Louisa as she tried to fix the corsage of camellias onto her chemise. "There, now that looks very nice against the dark blue," she commented as the flowers were moved to Louisa's waist.

The ladies adjusted their hats in the hall mirror and made their way into the front garden, and then strolled up the lane to the church chatting about everything and nothing as they enjoyed the fine weather. They joined their fellow worshippers who were gathering in the churchyard. The place was bustling with seasonal attenders, who nodded to each other politely while offering Christmas greetings. When the priest appeared, the gentlemen doffed their hats and the ladies curtseyed, and they all followed him into the church and took their places in the neat rows of pews.

Nearby, Ahya and the servants from other households, having made their way up the lane with the baskets of food and the serving dishes, took over the hall to lay out the Christmas buffet. It was quite a spread with the polished silver platters, cutlery and glassware sparkling in the festive candlelight and bright sunshine.

The church was full of whispers as the congregation

settled and the entourage of altar servers and candle bearers formed a procession at the back. Louisa admired the floral displays and their musky perfume as she waited for the service to begin. Looking at the hymn board, she picked up her hymnal to check which carols had been selected. The usual, she observed, with the addition of one she had not sung since her childhood days in King's Lynn, 'I'm Going Home', the old Quaker anthem. Who chose that one? she wondered.

The organist struck the opening chords for 'Oh Come All Ye Faithful'. Everyone stood to attention in the time-honoured way and sung their hearts out as the procession escorted the priest down the aisle to the brilliantly lit and flower-festooned altar and, to its side, the shrine to the nativity. As members of the congregation turned to watch the procession, the priest nodded and smiled to all on this, the most joyous occasion of the Christian year.

It was a very traditional English service with prayers of thanksgiving for the great Queen and her subjects across the Empire; for Lord Lansdowne, the Viceroy of India, and his administrators; and for the nurses and doctors from the local hospital who had looked after the sick so diligently.

"Praise be to God for all their souls," they cried in unison as the organist played the opening bar of 'Silent Night'. The congregation sang the familiar words from childhood days with great passion, especially its chorus each time it came round: 'Sleep in heavenly peace... Sleep in heavenly peace', and 'Christ the Saviour is born... Christ the Saviour is born.'

The Highland Regiment was out in force and the men's

voices boomed out from the back of the church, prompting the vicar to offer prayers for them too.

"Let us also thank the Lord for Her Majesty's army, especially our own Colonel Charles Grant, 'VC'," said with great emphasis, "who led the successful campaign against the Manipur insurgents in the spring of last year up on the Burmese border, in Assam Province."

"Praise be to God for all their souls," came the congregation's fervent reply.

For the first time in years, Louisa felt blessed with festive cheer, despite thinking of her last Christmas in England, in Eltham. It had been a miserable day with freezing weather, leaden grey skies and fetid yellow fog that choked the lungs. She had been in despair sitting alone in her room, contemplating her fate over the coming decade. She could never have imagined her present circumstances in those grim far-off times.

The altar bell tinkled to signal a moment for silent prayer. She closed her eyes and whispered a petition for the soul of Dr Steele. He would have been pleased with how things had turned out for her, despite his misgivings. The organist played the opening notes of 'Abide with Me' to restart the singing. The easy refrain was on everyone's lips, except Louisa's.

"Why aren't you singing?" asked Mary of her silent companion. "I chose this one."

"Mary dear, I need to tell you about my past."

"Louisa, we all have a past, and you will find most do not wish to remember or hear of such things. That is why we are here. We have a chance to start again. The present is sufficient. Now, let sleeping dogs lie and sing along."

As the congregation's voices were drowned out by the rousing singing of the men at the back, Louisa's thoughts drifted back to her trial and incarceration. It is time to put these memories to one side, she reflected, as she wrestled her thoughts to childhood days.

The Ingle family's Christmases began with a service at St Margaret's church in King's Lynn followed by a brisk walk out on the mysterious Fens. It was bitterly cold out on those flats as the north-easterly winds blew in straight from the Russian steppes, so the children quickened their pace to get home sooner. There, the Christmas dinner and their presents were waiting for them. It was the happiest time of Louisa's life in the company of her six brothers and sisters and their devoted parents.

"We come to the final part of our service this Christmas morning," announced the priest, aware that many would by now be yearning for the feast laid out next door. "Let us pray for many more healthy years for our sovereign Queen who, despite her many sorrows, still watches over us with a mother's tender love.

"And let us pray for the coming year. May 1893 bring you all peace and great success, and to those of you going home, we wish you a safe journey... and to those who have just arrived, welcome to our family of compatriots. Our last hymn is taken from the old Quaker hymnal... 'I'm Going Home', chosen by one of the Regiment's surgeons, Dr Macpherson."

As the congregation thumbed their hymnals looking for

the correct page, Louisa turned her head discreetly to see him from under the wide brim of her hat smiling at her from his vantage point at the back. The organist struck up the opening note and the choristers roared:

> *Farewell vain world! I'm going home!*
> *My Saviour smiles and bids me come*
> *And I don't care to stay too long...*
> *I am glad that I am born to die*
> *From grief and woe my soul shall fly*
> *And I don't care to stay too long...*

The service over, the congregants stowed their hymnals and filed out in good order, row by row, into the pretty churchyard filled with bright sunshine. Amongst the seasonal greetings, there was much excitement in the conversations about the sermon and the singing, and considerable speculation about what was on the buffet table that awaited them.

"Now wasn't that last hymn uplifting," cried Jeanie as she adjusted her hat to shield her eyes from the bright sunlight. "I remembered all the words from my younger days. Dr Macpherson chose well, and he did a bit of research in the library before selecting it."

"I too remember the words from my childhood days in Norfolk," replied Louisa, humming the chorus as Dr Macpherson milled about in his Medical Officer's dress uniform. He had spruced himself up for the service, thought Louisa, who was more familiar with his usual unkempt appearance. He sought out the ladies as the hungry congregants started to make their way into the church hall, forming a neat line behind the vicar.

"From grief and woe thy soul shall fly," he whispered to Louisa. "That is my wish for you this Christmas. Live your life here with us amongst your friends and put your past behind you."

Spicy aromas enticed people to view the spread before taking their seats. As they jostled each other for the best position to make their preliminary choices, the servants, standing to attention behind the buffet table, watched as the diners pointed at the dishes and made enquiries and comments about the delicious looking food.

"Nothing too spicy for me," cried Lydia to Sarah, who was heaping a selection from the serving dishes onto two fine bone china plates for her companion and herself while Lydia saved their seats. Mary and Jeanie picked their way through the buffet, selecting their favourite breads and spiced meats while suggesting choices to those around them.

Ahya caught Louisa's eye and pointed to her smoked fish, egg and rice dish and the glass goblet of cooling yoghurt to complement the ginger and turmeric spices. Louisa helped herself to a modest portion of both and sat with the ladies as the punch and lemon water were served. It was such a warm afternoon that Lydia and Sarah quaffed their drinks with unseemly haste, calling for seconds while Mary and Jeanie sipped from their glasses with more delicacy.

"No punch for me, thank you." Louisa stayed the hand of the server.

"What did I hear, no punch for me?" asked Dr Macpherson. "Miss Ingle, it is Christmas and I think you might join the rest of us when we toast the Queen. Come now, let me fill your glass... I shall not hear of any protest.

"It is a great feast which I have been looking forward to all morning," declared Dr Macpherson as he squeezed himself into place next to Jeanie, facing Mary and Louisa, and a couple of schoolteacher colleagues of Sarah and Lydia.

"I would like one of your best hoppy India Pale Ales if you have one," he called to one of the servants as he laid out his spread of breads, lentils and rice, and a selection of spicy meats and fish.

"Wasn't it a wonderful service?" asked Jeanie of Dr Macpherson. "Why did you pick that old Quaker hymn? It is many years since I have sung that one."

"It is from the Norfolk Country Parish Churches Collection, and I chose it for Miss Ingle to make her smile and to help her in her recovery," he replied, beaming at her.

"What a kindness," commented Mary, who prodded Louisa to acknowledge his gesture.

"Sir, I am very grateful for your choice, and I enjoyed singing it," she offered.

As the afternoon progressed, the diners' plates and glasses were topped up constantly by the attentive servants. By teatime, the savouries were followed by a broad selection of sweets and biscuits, jellies, sherbets and fruits, and plenty of port and sherry.

While the diners, by now sated with Christmas pudding and too much drink, lolled about in a state of semiconsciousness, the army's bandsmen had assembled on the stage and started to tune up. It was a chaotic, merry and boisterous scene. Ahya and the other servants watched in silent wonder at how such normally well-mannered ladies and gentlemen fell into such disarray on this big celebration day every year.

"Who would like to practise the Gay Gordons with me?" inquired a jovial Dr Macpherson.

"I should be delighted to have the first dance," replied Mary. She loved dancing and had had little opportunity since her husband, a railway engineer, had died of typhus many years ago, like so many of the settlers from home.

The accordion gave the first note and the band struck up as the awkward partners took to the floor for the opening traditional Scottish dance. It was a toe-tapping familiar tune and those watching laughed and clapped their hands as some of the turns went the wrong way and couples crashed into each other. Others swayed their heads and nodded along to the band, egging the dancers on. And on the afternoon and evening went, hour after hour of merrymaking.

"Some need to practise their steps before the Officers' New Year party," commented Lydia to her friends as she rubbed her sore feet which had been stepped on too many times by inebriated and careless partners. "Louisa, are you attending? I didn't see your name on the list."

"I am no dancer, and I am well past all that at my age, so I shall not be attending," she replied. "These parties are for younger women like you and Sarah."

"I shall teach you a couple of jigs and reels and we will

have a fine time," offered Lydia. "We have a week to practise, and we will have a lot of fun in doing it on your terrace. How about that as an offer? Louisa, you cannot spend New Year's Eve on your own."

"It will be a lovely party at the Mess... couldn't be a better place to celebrate," added Jeanie. "I know the Military Two Step as well."

Drinking her lemon water, Louisa contemplated the thought as Ahya and the servants cleared away the plates and debris from the dinner. Most of the revellers were now too fatigued to notice the bustling going on and some of the men had retired to the makeshift bar set up at the back of the hall, where they could drink a bottle of pale ale shipped all the way to India from home.

Late into the evening, after several cups of tea and plates of confectioneries, the tired and tipsy ladies prepared to depart. They found their long-discarded hats and stoles, squashed their aching feet into their shoes, and formed a queue along with the other partygoers to give their thanks and good wishes to the priest, who was standing at the door ready to receive their offerings.

"Another successful Christmas," remarked Jeanie on behalf of the ladies as she handed over an envelope of notes. "And this is our contribution for the poor and the orphans."

The ladies nodded and smiled as they bade the priest farewell and strolled down the lane to Louisa's bungalow, where Ahya and the servants were busy sorting the clean dishes into neat stacks ready for stowing. There had been a new moon at the beginning of the week, so it was very dark in the lanes except for the dim light shed by the oil lamps.

The ladies stepped carefully along the path, concentrating on keeping their balance.

Groups of ladies on foot were always accompanied to their doors by members of the Regiment and Dr Macpherson joined Louisa's party, still singing and dancing his jigs with an imaginary partner, much to the ladies' delight. Talk returned to the New Year's celebrations.

"Miss Ingle, you must come to our party… there is nothing like spending the New Year with a Scottish Regiment, and Highlanders at that," Dr Macpherson implored. "There will be Scottish folk songs, and reels and jigs to see in the New Year… and whisky galore."

"Louisa, you are sufficiently recovered from your collapse to join us," added Jeanie. "I so look forward to the Regiment's party, it is the highlight of the year. I know we are not young anymore, but we seem to manage to have fun."

Settling into the garden chairs on the veranda, the tipsy ladies stared at Louisa, willing her to decide in favour. Feeling under pressure, Louisa asked for lemon sherbets, whisky and pale ale to be served.

"We need more dancing practice, and I am ready for another reel. Gentlemen, will you oblige?" asked Mary of the escort party.

The men were delighted to help as everyone got to their feet and a space was cleared on the terrace, where Mary organised two columns ready to dance a reel.

"We have no band, so, gentlemen, please make the music for us," she commanded.

They did their best with cries of 'Dah de dah de dahs' as

they played their invisible squeeze boxes and the dancers had fun crashing into each other while Dr Macpherson called the steps. Louisa was delighted they felt so at home on her veranda, as if it was a home from home, and she joined in with the hearty clapping and foot stomping as the revellers tried to keep in step.

"That was such fun, but I am jiggered," puffed Jeanie in a state of collapse. "The curse of age."

"One more reel," pleaded Lydia.

"It is too much," replied Mary. "Tiredness has caught up with us. Time to depart."

As the late evening's chill started to bite, the men collected the oil lamps Ahya had prepared to light the way, and the ladies gathered in the hallway for a final round of festive greetings before they set off down the lane. It had been a most enjoyable Christmas, Louisa felt as she waved them on their way.

Thoughts of her childhood days in Norfolk and running across the Fens filled her mind as she lay in bed waiting for sleep to come. She thought of how kind Mary and Jeanie, and Lydia and Sarah, had been to her. She was not alone, and Dr Macpherson had been a real friend too. She resolved to start her life anew and put her unhappy past behind her.

Could she now be content to be a footnote in the history of Guy's Hospital?

TWENTY-SIX

The bandsmen had gathered in the hall for their final practice as they tuned their violins and accordions, and the servants laid out the linens to dress the tables. The drummers and pipers had been banished to the garden by the Chairman of the Mess's Party Committee to rehearse.

Down in the barracks, the soldiers pressed their dress uniforms and polished their buttons and shoes while the servants checked there were enough lengths of Black Watch tartan and shoulder clasps to dress the officers. Others picked over the garden to remove all but the best blooms and then dressed the trees and shrubs with red Chinese lanterns that had been brought up from the brigade's headquarters in Calcutta.

The kitchen was a hive of activity as the cooks cut the vegetables and prepared their dishes and the scullery boys rubbed off the tarnish that blemished the silver salvers and cutlery. In the hall and on the terraces, the punkawallahs checked the fans under the supervision of the Chairman, who also directed the polishing of the mirrors and the hanging of the Queen's and General Rollo's portraits. Everything was to look its best for Her Majesty and the Regimental Colonel.

Across the estate, the younger ladies like Lydia and Sarah fretted about their dresses and hairstyles, and their gloves and dancing slippers. The Officers' New Year's Eve party was one of the social highlights of the calendar and, for many, it was a chance to find a husband. The older ladies like Mary and Jeanie worried about the same things but made less of a fuss about it.

Louisa had her trusted companion Ahya to confide in about such matters. Most of all, she wanted to look presentable for a woman in her early fifties. They settled on a fashionably not too fitted dress of pale blue silk with a hint of white stripes running the length of the gown. There were to be no ornate lacings or bows but Louisa did agree that a wisp of chiffon draped around her shoulders might draw attention to her swan-like neck and flatter her neat French pleat of dark hair.

After a final fitting, Louisa was relaxing on her veranda with the latest magazines and journals arrived from London when a shout from the front gate broke her concentration. Ahya walked over to the post boy, who was waving an urgent letter from Ranchi's post office.

"You need to sign for this one," he said. "It has come by express all the way from London."

Ahya checked the postmark and studied the handwriting as she recorded its receipt. Alarmed, she sent the houseboy to Dr Macpherson with a hastily written message informing him of the unwelcome arrival before handing the package to Louisa.

"Please open it," sighed Louisa as she too recognised the writing. What further woe does this bring, she wondered, as Ahya picked up the garden scissors and sliced open the envelope.

They stared at another long letter, before Louisa unfolded the papers and carefully smoothed them out on the table.

'Louisa, may the Lord's joyous blessings be with you this Christmas. I hope that this, my final letter, reaches you in your far-away home before the great day.

I have news for you. After much sadness concerning the death of our dear Dr Steele, I find myself unable to continue as matron of this great hospital and have decided to resign my position. I have been here at Guy's for many years and the last eleven as its matron. I think Guy's has had the best of me and I now need to care for my sisters.

I shall leave in the new year when my successor, Miss Florence Nott-Bower, will take charge. She is familiar with our routines as she trained at Guy's from 1882, just after your time.

She was matron of Huddersfield Infirmary for a while before returning to Guy's to be our Lady Superintendent of the Nurses' Training Institute. She is most capable, and she has vowed to look after the interests of our nurses.

Miss Burt has suffered for many years from rheumatoid arthritis and her end is near. After her three strenuous years at Guy's, she returned to the Midlands upon her marriage to a Mr Field of Leamington. I am thankful that she had two happy years with him before his premature death. I understand he had made generous provision for his wife so that she has been able to live in comfort in her old age.'

Louisa put the letter down on the table as she shuffled about in her old deck steamer chaise and thought about Miss Burt and what she had endured while at Guy's. At least she had known what it was to be loved. Louisa picked up the letter and turned the page to study more of Miss Jones's neatly written composition.

'Louisa, it fills me with sadness to think of your lack of regard for our medical staff. They are not bad people, only obsessive in matters close to their hearts. Some came to a sorry end while others just faded from memory. Since you left, there has been a complete changing of the guard and those involved in your tragedy are long gone.

You knew that both Dr Habershon and Mr Cooper Forster resigned from their posts at about the same time that you were released from prison? They were due to retire anyway but their relations with the President and the Governors, and Mr Lushington and Dr Steele, had been so greatly injured by the dispute and your trial as to be irrecoverable. Sadly for them, the body of the medical staff did not rise up in protest at their leaving, although each received a fine salver for his service.

Dr Habershon became Vice-President of the Royal College of Physicians about five years ago, but his tenure was short as he died from a gastric ulcer just over three years ago. Ironically, this was his specialty. His devoted wife, Grace, had died a few months earlier, but they were blessed to see their beloved son, young Dr Habershon of St Bartholomew's, appointed as Mr Gladstone's physician.

As for Mr Cooper Forster, the statuesque rower who was our head surgeon? After leaving Guy's, he went on to be the President of the Royal College of Surgeons. He died about six years ago, only two years into the job. Besides being remembered for being very tall and very wealthy, his fantastic collection of ferns now stands in his honour at Kew Gardens.

Dr Pavy's disdain for Sir William Gull intensified into an ugly dispute following your trial. Dr Pavy objected in the strongest terms to Sir William's testimony. The argument rumbled on for many months and involved the president of the Royal College of Physicians. It became very unpleasant but Sir William stood his ground and was having none of it.'

Louisa closed her eyes and imagined what the atmosphere on the wards must have been like. She did not care for either physician, but held Dr Pavy in particular contempt because of his accusations against her. She had felt bitter for all these years about his and Dr Habershon's actions that saw her sacked, tried and jailed. She sighed in despair and wished them ill as she thumbed the remaining pages and wondered whether it was worth reading on.

Ahya placed a fresh pot of tea on the table and gently reminded her that she would need to get ready for the party soon.

"Ahya, I am afraid I cannot go... my spirits are too low," she sighed.

"Ma'am, these things that trouble you from your past are in the past," came Ahya's reply.

Louisa slumped into her chaise and stared into the mid-ground as her mind wandered back to those terrible people. She was curious to know what had happened to them in the intervening years. Had they suffered as she had done? Curiosity got the better of her and she picked up Miss Jones's letter and carried on reading.

'Louisa, I admired Sir William. He gave Dr Pavy as good as he got. Despite his humble origins, he rose to be the Queen's Physician and a Fellow of the Royal Society. He died three years ago, and we still mourn him. He was buried by his own wish in the churchyard of his native village in Essex. He is worthy of your forgiveness and respect.

His son, Sir Cameron Gull, after remarkable success in his law studies at Oxford, has inherited his father's baronetcy and has qualified as a barrister at Lincoln's Inn. He is a credit to his father, and we are all hopeful that his aspirations to enter politics will be successful.

As for Dr Pavy, he retired from Guy's ten years ago, but is still active in his Societies, although he is now hard of hearing. His continued devotion to the Medical School has resulted in generous endowments. He too deserves your forgiveness and respect.

He was never happier than when his charming daughter, Florence, married Sir William Scovell Savory's son, Borradaile, in the summer after you left for India. He is now Rector of St Bartholomew-the-Great, the hospital's church, where his father was the senior surgeon. Florence will become Lady Savory when Sir William dies, and her husband inherits his father's title, and they have a son who is now ten years old.'

Oh Miss Jones, how can you ask me to forgive and respect them? They ruined my life and then sailed on into the sunset without a second thought for me. I detest these people who have no regard for the likes of me, or Miss Jones herself for that matter. We are invisible to them.

Louisa checked her unkind thoughts and read on.

'Louisa, both Dr Moxon and Dr Fagge died before their time. They had shown such promise but becoming senior physicians at Guy's was not to be.

Dr Fagge was only forty-five when he died after a long, painful and debilitating illness. We have just had a memorial service to mark the ninth year since his death, and his textbook of medicine is still the course text at Guy's Medical School. He was a good man and a wonderful physician, and we mourn him to this day.

As for Dr Moxon, he was always an unhappy soul despite his brilliance and popularity with the medical students. He died by his own hand three years ago. We were all so shocked at the manner of his death. He drunk prussic acid and died in agony of cyanide poisoning. I had understood from Dr Wilks at the time that Dr Moxon had failed to cope after his mother's death. At least his death was quick.

Since his retirement, Dr Wilks has been more forthcoming with me in private. He had warned Dr Moxon about his overuse of narcotics for some years before his death but to no avail. Dr Moxon needed his opium and when this addiction failed to quench his cravings, he used chloral as a sedative and hypnotic in addition. It is truly ghastly to think of the poor man in such a state of paralysis of the mind and want.'

Louisa dropped the letter in fright. She thought about her own need for laudanum and Dr Macpherson's recent warnings.

"Ma'am, why are you distressing yourself with this letter?" inquired Ahya.

"Ahya, such news was important to me once, but it is mostly meaningless now," she reflected, looking at the sheaf of papers. "Miss Jones wishes me no ill, she is trying to close an unhappy chapter in my life so that I can live anew. She is well-meaning in her wish for me to forgive those who caused me great distress in my old life in London."

Sitting before the dressing table mirror, Louisa watched as Ahya carefully brushed and folded her long dark hair into a neat French pleat that sat in the crook of Louisa's neck. They admired the stylish look together.

"How very elegant," commented Louisa, staring at herself in the mirror.

"Tonight, you must launch yourself into the rest of your life with your friends. Put the past aside for it is done, and do not let it cause you further harm."

"Thank you, Ahya. I promise I will try. I must just do one thing before I go." Louisa strolled out onto the warm terrace bathed in the late afternoon's sunlight. "Please bring my writing portmanteau, pen and ink."

Sitting upright at the table, Louisa finished reading Miss Jones's letter.

'Louisa, I find myself weeping for Dr Steele frequently.

Mr Lushington has been most sympathetic, and has informed me that Dr Cooper Perry, one of our senior physicians who took charge of the Medical School when Dr Taylor retired, will be taking on the Medical Superintendent's role in addition.

He is so capable and respected that Mr Lushington is confident he will fulfil both roles without detriment to either. Personally, I think this new joint arrangement will have the desirable effect of putting a stop to the Medical School asserting its independence and working against the hospital authorities. I believe he has ambitious plans for a Dental School.

Mr Lushington continues as our administrator, ever generous with his time, although he is now talking of his retreat from public life. He will probably retire to the country in the next year or two after a long life lived here and in India. The Bengal region was his home for many years as you know, and it is a pity that you will never share your reminisces about Ranchi and Calcutta with him.

After the trial, he ordered all the papers, including the medical staff's correspondence and minute books which recorded the details of their conspiracy, to be placed in the hospital's vault. He shut down the house magazine to stop any discussion about the events of that summer and an embarrassed silence has pervaded the place to this day about Miss Burt and the dispute. I believe he, like many others, is ashamed about the course of events that gave rise to your ordeal.

Louisa, I have news of Miss Lonsdale and then I will finish. She has had mixed fortunes. After her dismissal from

Guy's, she returned to her home in Lichfield. Although headstrong, she is a born nurse, and after your trial, she took charge of the hospital in Llandrindod Wells in mid-Wales before returning to Walsall about eight years ago to become matron of Sister Dora's hospital. She has acquitted herself well, but controversy was never far behind.

After much effort and many rebuttals, including from Mr Gladstone who declined her request for support, she raised sufficient funds for a statue in honour of Sister Dora which was erected in Walsall. But she fell out with the local gentlemen of the town in the process and relations have soured.

Her writing career looked very promising when Mr Keegan Paul published her biography of George Eliot six years ago, and a year later, Miss Lonsdale was considered for the Principal's post of the newly-opened Royal Holloway College. Despite much support, she was rejected on account of being too controversial. It was a blow from which she has yet to recover. I am afraid the world is not yet ready for the likes of women such as Miss Lonsdale.'

Louisa had had strong reasons for hating Miss Lonsdale, but felt sympathetic to her plight. The loneliness that comes with rejection was very familiar to her. She picked up her pen and dipped it in the ink pot, looked at the garden bathed in the late afternoon light, and composed her reply.

Afterwards, Ahya helped Louisa into her gown. Louisa trembled as Ahya crushed a few rose petals and stained her lips and cheeks with a tinge of pink. Then she picked up her cashmere shawl and ambled up the lane to join the excited guests who were milling about on the Mess's terraces overlooking the Estate's extensive gardens.

The band played one of the Regiment's favourite tunes, 'The Skye Boat Song', as old friends sought each other out and the servants filled the buffet table with the evening's feast.

Louisa, Jeanie and Mary strolled about the garden admiring the Chinese lanterns which bobbed about in the light breeze as they enjoyed their sherbets. Lydia and Sarah worked out the dance order and their desired partners as the band got ready for the first of the reels.

"I wish I could live my life again," spoke Louisa. "I should have gone to more parties when I was younger. I would have married and had a different life."

"As I did, Louisa," came Mary's reply. "But we have ended up in the same place... husbands die, and we are left alone... it is our plight."

They stepped into the hall to join the throng as the band struck up a reel. The crowded floor was full of young ladies and their partners who formed the lines and squares and displayed an air of confidence in what they were doing. They had rehearsed their steps well, thought Louisa, as she looked on from the side seats.

She glanced around discreetly for Dr Macpherson while her friends smiled and clapped in time with the music, wishing someone would come by and ask them to dance the next reel. The men of the Regiment were dressed in their finest. A cluster of officers drinking ale at the bar caught her attention with their guffaws at the jokes being told. She blushed when she saw Dr Macpherson smiling at her and holding up his glass in salutation.

"Dance with me, Miss Ingle, I want you to be my partner, dance with me," he asked on approaching her. "You look very fine this evening and I know you know the steps, so no excuses."

Mary and Jeanie applauded as Louisa got up and took Dr Macpherson's hand and joined the dancers. Reel after reel, on they danced and clapped until the Chairman called a halt for the toasts.

"Ladies and Gentlemen, please be upstanding and charge your glasses," he cried. "A toast to Her Majesty, Queen Victoria. May God bless Her this New Year's Eve."

Everyone chorused their reply and held their glasses up enthusiastically to the Queen's portrait. They then turned to the painting of General Sir Robert Rollo and toasted him before sitting down to eat. The servants, ready with their full platters, served the feast.

The officers, resplendent in their dress uniforms with their tartan lengths and polished buttons and clasps, helped to serve the drinks and the food as was the tradition, while a piper played old Scottish folk songs. They were interrupted several times by calls for more toasts to the men of the Regiment, to the padre, to the surgeons and nurses of Ranchi hospital, and on and on to whoever they could think of that was deserving of their goodwill.

The meal over, the band struck up another round of reels and everyone joined in, partner or no partner. A display of Scottish dancing followed, to great delight and cries for more. Tipsy, the partygoers jigged about in squares and eights and crashed into each other as they were determined to dance all the way to the midnight hour.

Louisa and Dr Macpherson took an interval out on the terrace.

"I hear Miss Jones has written another letter?"

"She is leaving Guy's to look after her ailing sisters in Balham, and as it is her last letter to me she has informed me of the fates of those I knew."

"Are you upset?" he asked. "Your recovery is still fragile. I fear for you."

"Sir, do not be concerned for me. Those of my past hold no more terrors for me. They have mostly died but all have forgotten me. It is as if I never existed, and I am learning to put my terrible past behind me and live life as I find it here in my home in Ranchi."

He smiled as he heard the chimes of the big hall clock strike and the band getting ready for a chorus of the traditional New Year's Eve lament, 'Auld Lang Syne'.

"I hate that ritual," said Dr Macpherson drolly. "And nobody knows the words."

"I do not wish to remember any of them," replied Louisa, so they stayed out on the terrace as the clock chimed in the New Year and the partygoers sang the familiar tune.

"May 1893 be a good year for you, Miss Ingle," he said as he looked up at the bright full moon.

"And you too, kind Sir," she replied as the guests crowded around them to watch the fireworks brought all the way from the Chinese Store in Calcutta.

Off they fired into the night sky to the delight of everyone, who continued toasting the Queen, the General, the cooks and whoever else came to mind.

As the night wore on, the band eventually gave up and packed their instruments, and the servants cleared the debris of the feast. The ladies, in a state of exhaustion and dishevelment, collected their oil lamps and joined the escort party for the walk home. Off they sauntered along the path into the first dawn of 1893, humming 'Speed Bonnie Boat...'

"Sir, I have enjoyed this evening," said Louisa, holding on to Dr Macpherson's arm.

"Miss Ingle, I would like it very much if you were to call me Mac."

"Sir, I shall try," she replied, as they strolled arm in arm down the lane.

CODA

Louisa Ingle lived for another thirty years in Ranchi where she died of old age, in her eighties, in 1920. She lived long enough to see three monarchies rule India: Queen Victoria's, which ended with her death in January 1901; her son's, King Edward VII, which ended when he died in May 1910; and her grandson's, King George V.

She saw the horrors of the Great War in Europe (July 1914–November 1918) and the Flu Pandemic which followed in 1918. The virus spread rapidly across India from Bombay in June 1918 when a troop carrier bringing men home from the war in Europe infected the local population. It reached Calcutta by August. 'Bombay Flu', as it was called, is estimated to have killed up to fourteen million people in the British-ruled districts.

Miss Ingle died a wealthy woman, leaving the equivalent of over £130,000 in today's money to her sole beneficiary, a distant relative, Miss Annie Isabel Fry.

Guy's Hospital went on to build its reputation as a great

Medical and Dental Training Institute, and Miss Burt's Nursing Training Institute is now one of the finest in the world. The medical staff and Mr Lushington are commemorated in the hospital's chapel and there are a few plaques for senior nurses, including for Miss Jones and the Night Sister, Mrs Keogh. There is also an obscure name plate to a Mrs Margaret Field. It is the married name of Matron Burt. And Miss Lonsdale? She was an early victim of the flu virus; she died of it in London in 1917.

The *British Medical Journal* published an anonymous poem on November 26, 1892, dedicated to Dr John Charles Steele, Guy's long-serving Medical Superintendent. He was loved by all, and especially by one. And the author? Was it Miss Ingle, Miss Jones, or Miss Lonsdale?

And he is gone! The man of honest heart,
Whose voice for truth and right was never
*   heard,*
The man who ever chose the better part,
Nor spoke an unkind word.
How we shall miss the dear benignant face
We knew so well within the grey old square.
Guy's will appear to all another place,
If he may not be there.
Calmly he sees the evening shadows fall,
The labourer rests at setting of the sun.
He hears – we cannot hear – the Master's
*   call*
"Servant of God, well done."
Around thy grave the weeping mourners
*   stand*
In grief bowed down. Ah! What shall break
*   the spell?*
Accept this heartfelt tribute from the hand
Of one who loved thee well.

SELECTED READING LIST

Having read *Louisa's Lament*, you may be interested in learning more about life in London in the late 19th century.

Jerry White's *London in the 19th Century*, published by Vintage Books in 2008, is a good starting point. You can thumb through Peter Ackroyd's *Thames: Sacred River*, published by Chatto & Windus in 2007, and George Bradshaw's *Illustrated Handbook to London and its Environs*, published by Bloomsbury in 1862, to add depth.

For more on the history of Guy's Hospital, you will find Hector Cameron's *Mr Guy's Hospital 1726–1948*, published by Longmans in 1954, and Samuel Wilks' and George Bettany's *A Biographical History of Guy's Hospital*, published by Ward, Lock and Bowden in 1892, give comprehensive monographs on the early development of the hospital and its medical staff appointments.

If you are interested in the burgeoning print industry and reading public at this time, Richard Altick's *Victorian*

People and Ideas, published by Norton in 1973, and his *The English Common Reader: A Social History of the Mass Reading Public, 1800–1900*, published by the University of Chicago Press in 1957, offer a good introduction.

Prison life is grim at any time, but real reforms took place, especially for women and children, during the mid-late Victorian period. To understand the scale of the problems faced by 19th-century governments, peruse Henry Mayhew's (with John Binny's additions) *The Criminal Prisons of London, and Scenes of Prison Life*, published by Griffin and Bohn in 1862. Michelle Higgs's *Prison Life in Victorian England*, published by Tempus in 2007, gives details of the daily routines of prisoners and prison staff.

Religious tensions were at the heart of Miss Ingle's story. If you want a reference text to dip into as you read about the Nonconformists, the High Church Anglo-Catholics, the Oxford Movement, and the problem of 'Rome' in English Society, one of the best is Owen Chadwick's *The Victorian Church, Parts I & II*, published by SCM Press in 1987.

Life for women underwent great change in the 19th century. I found Martha Vicinus's *Independent Women*, published by Virago in 1985, and Margaret Macmillan's *Women of the Raj*, published by Thames and Hudson in 1988, very helpful when writing about Miss Ingle's life as a professional woman in London and as an expatriate living in India. Susan Mumm's *Stolen Daughters, Virgin Mothers*, published by Leicester University Press in 1999, and Carmen Mangion's *Contested Identities*, published by

Manchester University Press in 2008, introduce the Anglican Sisterhoods.

There is much more. If you'd like further selected readings, or to share your thoughts on the issues raised in *Louisa's Lament* or any of the above, send a note to annie@patoakleypublishing.london and start a discussion.

CREATING THE
PICTURES TO
ILLUMINATE THE STORY

Working with artist June Schneider, much research went into creating the illustrations for the book and its cover. After years of reading and researching, I had built up vivid pictures in my mind of what it was like to live and work in London in the late 19th century. We spent many hours studying archive pictures and discussing how to convey key scenes from the story to give a feeling of the places in Louisa's time.

I know Guy's campus well as my teaching rooms for many years were in Hunt's House. Every week in term time, I crossed the front quad of Guy's, through the colonnade to the park at the rear, taking the same steps as the story's key players must have done. June visited Guy's and took photographs to get the necessary perspectives and we added further details from our research in image libraries.

Hector Cameron's book, *Mr Guy's Hospital 1726–1948*, was a rich source of pictures in developing the cover illustration and the frontispieces for Parts I and II which are set in Guy's. Similar efforts went into site visits to Brook and Grosvenor Streets, where the senior medical staff lived, which informed the illustration for the frontispiece to Part III. And walks around the City to St Paul's and its churchyard, which was Paternoster Row at the time of Louisa's story, and the Old Bailey, informed the illustrations for the frontispieces to Parts IV and V.

Part VI is set in northeast India in one of the hill stations popular with the British at the time around Ranchi. I travelled to Sri Lanka many years ago and stayed in such a station at Nuwara Eliya and the memory of it, and the pictures from Margaret Macmillan's *Women of the Raj*, informed the illustration for the frontispiece for Part VI.

We referred to Wikipedia's catalogue of images, especially for costume and carriage details. There are other comprehensive sources which must be acknowledged: the archives of King's College, London University and Guy's Hospital; the catalogues and archives of the British Library, the National Gallery, the Wellcome Collection and Sir John Soane's Museum; and Alamy's and Getty's picture libraries.

Finally, Charles Booth's *London's Poverty Maps* gives one of the best collection of maps, observation notes and photographs of the time. I drew on this publication constantly when thinking about the nurses' lives in Southwalk and its slums, which kept Guy's busy every hour of every day, and, in contrast, the West End, with its delightful gardens and rich mercantile districts, where the medical staff lived very different lives.

The illustrations are for sale as colour or black-and-white reprints and postcards.

About the Author

Annie Graham has consulted and taught on inter-professional conflict for over thirty years, with a PhD in Organisational Psychology, and a special interest in medical power structures and behaviours.

She has a Diploma in the Social History of Medicine and an MA in Nineteenth Century Studies which she uses to write fact-based novels to illuminate the ways in which organisations succeed and fail.

If you've enjoyed this book, please help to spread the word and consider leaving a review online. These are a huge help to authors.

Visit www.patoakleypublishing.london for more about the author, to sign up for news of future publications, or to purchase prints or postcards of the illustrations from this book.

 twitter.com/agbythesea

ACKNOWLEDGEMENTS

I would like to thank all those who have helped me to bring this story alive: Delia Caple, who is a master at turning my drafts into working files; June Schneider, who is a very talented artist giving my words such life in the book's illustrations; and Claire Wingfield, who edited my drafts so diligently and offered much wise counsel to improve my writing and manage the book's production.

Thanks are due to Jonathan for being the best history and writing tutor over the last forty years you could wish for, and to all my friends who were so generous with their time in reading and commenting on draft after draft.

I am grateful to my teachers at Birkbeck College, London University, who have taught and supported me when I studied for my PhD in Organisational Psychology and a Masters in Victorian Studies.

The proceeds from this book will be given to Birkbeck College to support the students' hardship fund in celebration of the College's 200th anniversary since its founding in 1823. Long may it continue.

Ingram Content Group UK Ltd.
Milton Keynes UK
UKHW040030140423
420099UK00002B/24

9 781916 472303